A REAPPRAISAL OF ECONOMIC DEVELOPMENT

A
REAPPRAISAL
OF
ECONOMIC
DEVELOPMENT

Perspectives for Cooperative Research

edited by
ANDREW H. WHITEFORD
BELOIT COLLEGE

ALDINE PUBLISHING COMPANY / CHICAGO

This publication was made possible by a grant to the Library of International Relations from the Johnson Foundation, Wingspread, Racine, Wisconsin.

First published in 1967 by
ALDINE Publishing Company
320 West Adams Street
Chicago, Illinois 60606

Library of Congress Catalog Card Number 66-17844

Printed in the United States of America

THE THIRD BIENNIAL MIDWEST RESEARCH CONFERENCE
ON UNDERDEVELOPED AREAS / 1964

Sponsored by The Library of International Relations, Chicago
and Rosary College *in cooperation with*
The United States Office of Education

ADVISORY COMMITTEE

CHAIRMAN
Philip M. Hauser
Department of Sociology
University of Chicago

Leonard Binder
Department of Political Science
University of Chicago

George I. Blanksten
Department of Political Science
Northwestern University

Wesley R. Fishel
Department of Political Science
Michigan State University

Norton S. Ginsburg
Department of Geography
University of Chicago

Bert F. Hoselitz
Research Center on Economic
    Development and Cultural Change
University of Chicago

George J. Stolnitz
Department of Economics
Indiana University

Sister Thomasine
Department of Economics
Rosary College

Andrew H. Whiteford
Department of Anthropology
Beloit College

SECRETARY
Eloise ReQua, Director
Library of International Relations

CONFERENCE PARTICIPANTS

C. Arnold Anderson	University of Chicago	Comparative Education Center and Department of Sociology
Robert Armstrong	Lake Forest College	Department of Economics
John Augelli	University of Kansas	Department of Geography
Jack Baranson	Indiana University	International Development Research Center
Leonard Binder	University of Chicago	Department of Political Science
George I. Blanksten	Northwestern University	Department of Political Science
Karl de Schweinitz, Jr.	Northwestern University	Department of Economics
A. A. Fatouros	Indiana University	School of Law
Wesley R. Fishel	Michigan State University	Department of Political Science
Norton S. Ginsburg	University of Chicago	Department of Geography
Philip Haring	Knox College	Department of Political Science
Philip M. Hauser	University of Chicago	Department of Sociology
James B. Hendry	Michigan State University	Department of Economics
H. Murray Herlihy	Lake Forest College	Department of Economics
Robert T. Holt	University of Minnesota	Department of Political Science
Bert F. Hoselitz	University of Chicago	Department of Economics
Scott D. Johnston	Hamline University	Department of Political Science
Frank H. H. King	University of Kansas	Department of Economics
Mordechai Kreinin	Michigan State University	Department of Economics
W. Arthur Lewis	Princeton University	Economics and International Affairs
Marvin Miracle	University of Wisconsin	Department of Agricultural Economics
Theodore Morgan	University of Wisconsin	Department of Economics
Manning Nash	University of Chicago	Department of Anthropology
Raymond L. Randall	Indiana University	Department of Government
Hugh Schwartz	University of Kansas	Department of Economics
Hal Serrie	Beloit College	Department of Anthropology
George Stolnitz	Indiana University	Department of Economics
Sister Thomasine	Rosary College	Department of Economics
Charles P. Warren	University of Illinois, Chicago	Department of Sociology and Anthropology
Edward Werner	University of Wisconsin	School of Commerce
Andrew H. Whiteford	Beloit College	Department of Anthropology
T. David Williams	Northwestern University	School of Education and Department of Economics
Daniel Wit	Northern Illinois University	Department of Political Science

U.S. Office of Education	Peter S. Mousolite, Acting Regional Representative (OC)
Library of International Relations	Eloise ReQua, Director
Library of International Relations	Jane Statham, Associate Director

TABLE OF CONTENTS

ANALYTICAL TABLE OF CONTENTS

FOREWORD

The central business of the Third Biennial Midwest
Research Conference on Underdeveloped Areas, as is made
clear by its theme, "A Reappraisal of the Process of
Economic Development," involved a species of theoretical stocktaking. Many of the social sciences have now
been concerned for more than a decade with problems of
the underdeveloped areas. After these years of intensive effort in theory-building and empirical research,
what have we learned and what are we now able to say
about the developing areas? In short, what do the social sciences have to show for a decade of systematic
attention devoted to this category of research problems?

As the following pages indicate, the verdict of
the Third Conference is that the answer to this question must be mixed. On the one hand, substantial progress can be reported in some areas, and social scientists may feel that, on the basis of some types of research results, the decade has been well spent. On the
other hand, fundamental lacunae remain, pointing to
still unresolved problems which, even at this late date,
lie ahead of the social scientist in the underdeveloped
areas.

On the positive side, the Conference makes it
plain that important strides have been taken in matters
of identification and definition. The process of economic development has now been substantially isolated
and operationally defined, and it is not necessary today, as it was a decade ago, to assign concerted effort
to the examination of the properties of that process.
This indicates, I think that that effort of an earlier
time was well directed, and that today the social sciences are, to an appreciable extent, profiting from the
results of that work.

Again, enough progress has been made in the 1950's
and the early 1960's to permit us to cope today with
new problems and different concepts than occupied the
attention of the social sciences a decade or so ago.
The Third Conference devoted its attention to such

questions as unemployment in the developing areas and
international issues such as the role of underdeveloped
countries in a world economy, the international politics of development, and the comparative study of newly
and old settled areas. As recently as the First Biennial Midwest Research Conference on Underdeveloped Areas, it would not have been possible to cope with such
problems.

Yet, impressive as these strides may be, we should
not overlook the problems we have not yet solved and
the issues still before us. One of these has to do
with the interrelationships among various forms of
change in the underdeveloped areas. On one of the
forms of change, economic development, much has been
done. A substantial amount of research has also been
devoted to the processes of social and cultural change,
and in the last few years political scientists have begun to grapple with the problems of political development. The varying degrees of progress made in the study
of these change processes reflect, among other things,
the differential in research results produced within
the relevant social science disciplines. Work has
hardly begun in interrelating the various forms of
change in the developing areas. Significant statements
of the relationships among economic development, social
change, cultural change, and political development remain to be formulated. Such work merits a high place
among research priorities, as was indeed pointed out at
the Third Conference in the closing session on perspectives for cooperative research.

Then, too, the disturbing question of whether the
current interest in development in underdeveloped areas
represents a revival of evolutionary theory in the social sciences is still with us. Although some work has
been done on this question,[1] much remains to be explored. Is economic development inevitable in the underdeveloped areas? Is there a fixed sequence of iden-
tifiable steps or stages in development? Is the developmental process unilinear? Evolutionary thinking is
implicit in a remarkably large proportion of what has

1. See, for example, Herbert R. Barringer, George I.
Blanksten, and Raymond W. Mack (eds.), Social Change in
Developing Areas: A Reinterpretation of Evolutionary
Theory (Cambridge: Schenkman Publishing Co., 1965).

been said about change in the developing areas. A high
priority should also be assigned to making these propositions as explicit as possible and subjecting them to
rigorous testing and evaluation.

Stocktaking is perhaps inevitably awkward. The
Third Conference, in causing us to look back on a decade of activity, impresses us with the major problems
awaiting attack at least as much as with the not incon-
siderable research payoffs achieved thus far.

George I. Blanksten

PREFACE

Interdisciplinary research in the social sciences is one of the most effective techniques developed to deal with the complex study of nations, societies, communities, and people: their fascinating and puzzling joinings and separations, their growths and their declines, their progress and their apathies, their plans and their expectations. Interdisciplinary research has brought a multifaceted approach to the examination of millefaceted phenomena.

The increased interest of social scientists in their sister disciplines has not been stimulated solely by intellectual exploration into the problems which they share and the particular insights which each provides. Much of the interest stems from the groping and searching concern of field workers who find themselves investigating problems and systems which cannot be understood adequately in terms of a single kind of analysis, be it political, social, cultural, historical, or psychological. Field work thrusts upon them the realization that their professional areas of concern overlap and converge upon aspects of life which traditionally (or academically) lie in the domains of other disciplines.[1]

In attempting to understand the "emerging" societies of the world, economists are constantly reminded that such phenomena as the growth of markets and the distribution and development of a labor force are clearly related to political policy, and the political scientists are constantly reminded that governmental decision alone is not sufficient to bring about the development of regional markets or effective land reforms.

1. We "knew," of course, about the relationships between our fields and others before leaving graduate school, but often it is only in the confrontations of research that we truly learn that data from these related fields are absolutely necessary for a full understanding of our own.

With the new concern of economists with problems
of underdeveloped countries it becomes increasingly difficult to say where economics ends and
sociology, social psychology, anthropology and
political science begin. The importance for
economic development of the political and cultural framework is apparent; development economists find themselves writing about such matters
as the relationship between literacy and "develop-
ment-mindedness" or "technology-mindedness," the
impact of village organization on economic motivation, relationship of childhood training to
personality traits and creativity, and the like.
What then is meant by "social aspects" of economic
development, as distinct from purely economic
aspects?[2]

Away from textbooks and deep in the problems of a developing country, both economists and political scientists often find themselves dealing with vast territories of villages and tribes which they once regarded
as the exclusive concern of geographers and anthro-
pologists--or missionaries. And they recognize that
these rural-peasant-tribal sectors cannot be ignored.
The complex and necessary relationship between these
sectors of the country and the urban society in which
the government is centered, and from which it deals
with the outside world, must be resolved before the
nation can move toward either political stability or
economic development. And it must be studied and analyzed before the social sciences can achieve any order-
ing of the elements involved and the processes at work.
Even this one problem--it is really many--is too broad
to be encompassed by any single disciplinary approach.
Every particle of knowledge any of us possesses must
be brought into common focus even to begin upon an
understanding.
      But not everyone who accepts the value of inter-
disciplinary research has the opportunity to participate in such a program; and almost no program is fully
interdisciplinary. The best substitute for the actual

      2. Benjamin Higgins, "An Economist's View," in
Social Aspects of Economic Development in Latin America
(Paris: UNESCO, 1963), vol. 2, p. 145.

experience of working in field collaboration with members of other disciplines is to meet with such colleagues in free and open discussion--to pick their
brains and allow them to criticize each other's interpretations. Simply living on the same campus does not
always serve the purpose; the daily duties have an
overwhelming tendency to interfere with such discussions. Many times the colleagues one would like to
consult, those who have dealt with problems, topics,
or approaches of special interest, are far away or
engaged. Getting together is more difficult than it
should be, and some catalyst is necessary to facilitate
meetings and exchanges.

It is here that such conferences as those sponsored by the Library of International Relations serve
an important and appreciated function. From throughout the Middle West--and often beyond--the conferences
bring together people from several disciplines who have
worked in various developing areas of the world for
three days of discussion (and argument). The group is
small enough to enable everyone to talk with everyone
else, but it is large enough to provide diversity of
experience, of training, and of convictions. The program is simple; the emphasis is upon the discussions
during which examples or ideas may be presented to
support or to criticize the argument, new proposals or
topics may be introduced for comment, or the introductory speaker may be grilled--or roasted. The only
major consideration of the program is to allow all
participants an opportunity to talk; this they do
throughout the conference, throughout the meals, and
often far into the night.

Discussion is not only desirable, it is necessary.
Professional journals carry space for reader response
to articles which appeared several months previously
and their book reviews often reflect at least one reader's disagreement with an author. This is far from
being a discussion, however. Some journals publish
symposia and books appear with the papers presented at
conferences. But those who did not attend almost never
know what reactions the papers inspired in the members
of the audience. Most conferences and practically all
professional meetings are so dedicated to formal programs that discussion is confined to the groups which
gather later in the local "lounge." Any paper serves

only a small part of its purpose if there is no opportunity to discuss it.

Those of us who have had the good fortune to
participate in the conferences of the Library of International Relations know what insights, what stimula-
tion, what a variety of questions and interpretations
can emerge from an untrammeled discussion following a
short but provocative paper. It is in the belief that
our colleagues, and perhaps others, will find considerable interest in the agreements and disagreements of
these discussions that we agreed to have them published
That the discussion sometimes ran far afield from the
original topic is obvious, and this was inevitable
where interest was high and the topic had many facets.
The chairmen of the sessions encouraged exploration of
any subject in which the members of the conference indicated interest by waving or shouting for his attention. Only the clock finally closed the sessions.

In editing the discussions, I have tried to bring
together all the comments on a particular topic; during the arguments, they were not always in this sequence. The introductory papers have been edited by
their authors and I have not tampered with them. Only
those few comments which elicited no response or which
appeared to be unrelated to the progress of the discussion were deleted, but I have retained many side-
comments or irrelevant remarks in order to preserve
the informal quality of the meetings. In each session
various issues and topics were introduced. I have
attempted to separate them and have given each a sub-
title which I hope will be of help to the reader.

All participants had the opportunity to edit their
own contributions, but they have not seen what I have
done with them. For any distortions I may have introduced, or for any unacceptable statements or words I
may have put in my colleagues' mouths, I hope they will
forgive me. It was a good and stimulating conference
and I am certain they will join me in expressing again
our appreciation to Eloise ReQua and the Library of
International Relations for inviting us.

                                    Andrew Hunter Whiteford

A REAPPRAISAL OF ECONOMIC DEVELOPMENT

UNEMPLOYMENT IN DEVELOPING AREAS

Chairman BLANKSTEN: As Chairman, my primary responsibility is to open this first session of the Conference.

I am very honored and pleased to be able to present Mr. W. Arthur Lewis. He is, as you all know, a
pioneering writer in the field of economic development,
one of the first to start a train of largely productive
thinking in the economic growth field.

I have always admired him as a man who, when it
seems wise to do so, does not hesitate to change his
mind and to admit that he does so.

Mr. W. Arthur Lewis will talk tonight on the problem of unemployment in the developing areas.

Mr. LEWIS: Underdeveloped countries did relatively well in the 1950's, with respect to the growth of
output. According to the United Nations,[1] real output
grew over the decade at an annual rate of 4.1 per cent
in Africa, 4.2 in the Far East, 5.2 in West Asia, and
4.6 in Latin America. All these rates exceed what most
experts would have prophesied in 1950. The subject of
this paper is the curious phenomenon that unemployment
seems to be growing as fast as output. I refer not to
disguised unemployment on family farms, but to actual
unemployment among people who work for wages. The phenomenon, if true, is curious because, after much discussion of this possibility in the early part of the
nineteenth century, economists have grown to believe
that unemployment must diminish in an economy growing
as rapidly as at 4 per cent per annum. We have special
explanations for cyclical unemployment, such as all developed economies experience regularly, and for struc-

1. United Nations. Department of Economic and Social Affairs. World Economic Survey, 1963 (New York,
1964), p. 19.

tural unemployment in depressed industries or areas, such as Great Britain experienced in the 1920's. Both result from declining investment. Unemployment associated with rapidly increasing investment is an unfamiliar animal.

I.

We must begin with problems of measurement. We are dealing only with people who work for wages, and are not therefore concerned with the surplus, if any, on family farms. Unfortunately there are no reliable measures of unemployment in underdeveloped countries. None has comprehensive social insurance, from which the numbers in receipt of unemployment compensation might be derived. Many have registers, to which the unemployed are invited to add their names. For example, the registered unemployed in India[2] increased from 254,000 in 1948 to 1,754,000 in 1961. However, since in most cases registration brings neither a job nor relief pay, many unemployed do not register, and doubtless some keep their names on the register even after they have found employment; also registration is usually confined to the larger cities.

A census can provide useful information if it includes questions about employment; and some countries have also made special surveys of unemployment from time to time. However, one of the problems is then to define the labor force. For example, 48,000 persons told the census takers in Jamaica in 1960 that they wanted a job and had never had one.[3] Should they be included in the labor force, of which they would then be 7 per cent? If so, the average rate of unemployment in the census week was 21 per cent, including persons who worked for part of the week. However, a substantial proportion of those who wanted a job but had never had one were over 30 years old, and must be presumed to be able to get along without finding employment.

Experience in Western Europe in the 1950's has emphasized that the size of the labor force depends on the amount of work offering. Thus in Great Britain the

2. United Nations. Statistical Office. <u>Statistical Year Book, 1962</u> (New York, 1963), p. 58.
    3. Jamaica. Department of Statistics. <u>Census of Jamaica, 1960</u>, vol. II, part H.

number of people aged 15 to 64 increased only by
400,000 in the 1950's, but the number of working people
in that age group increased by 1,400,000. Women seek
work where work is available, but not otherwise. Thus
in Lancashire, a cotton area, the proportion of women
in the labor force is much higher than in South Wales,
a mining area. If the number of persons in the labor
force is flexible even in a highly developed economy
like Britain, it is even more flexible in underdeveloped countries, which contain enormous reservoirs of
people outside the labor market who will enter that
market gladly if work becomes available. And if you
cannot define the labor force, you cannot say how many
persons are unemployed.

Another problem is that, alas, not all the unemployed are employable. Many young people who leave
school are unable to find continuous employment. They
then commence a disastrous pattern of living. A young
man gets one day's work here; gets no work tomorrow;
cadges a meal the next day from his aunt; finds another
job for a few hours; steals some small thing while the
owner is not looking; shares a meal with a friend;
borrows a few cents from a patron; and so on. After
one has lived this life for two or three years, one becomes unemployable, and could not do eight hours work
a day for five days a week even if it were offered--for
psychological no less than physical reasons. Thus
governments which set up public works programs to relieve the unemployed are sometimes puzzled by the dis-
crepancy between the numbers known to be unemployed and
the number who turn up for work. The unemployables
want only a few hours work per week, and cannot do
more.

It is unsatisfactory to talk about unemployment
without being able to define the unemployed precisely.
It is also unsatisfactory to assert that unemployment
has increased during the 1950's without being able to
document the statement. Nevertheless one must report
that this opinion is widely held. Throughout the underdeveloped world a few already large towns are ex-
ploding in size, with the number of people increasing
faster than the number of jobs. Unemployment, juvenile
delinquency and crime are becoming major concerns in
towns where it used to be safe to go out and leave
your door open. One knows cities where, in the absence

of unemployment pay, burglary has become the largest
industry.   One cannot offer statistics, but can only
report the surprise and despair of seasoned observers
who notice that in spite of rapid rates of growth of
output, and high rates of capital formation, unemployment nevertheless seems to increase.   Jamaica's may be
an extreme case.   There, as far as we can see, net investment during the Fifties averaged 18 per cent of
national income, and real output increased at an annual
rate of 6 per cent.   Eleven per cent of the labor force
emigrated, yet unemployment seems to have been as great
in 1960 as in 1950.

II.

Population pressure is not a primary cause of unemployment.   Countries with high population pressure
learn over the centuries how to provide some work for
everybody.   If farming is on a small-scale basis (in
contrast to wage labor), the farms get smaller and
smaller, and surplus labor stays on the farms, so
everybody has a claim to income, even though he may not
be fully occupied.   This is not possible if agriculture
is operated by large-scale capitalists who hire only as
many laborers as it pays to hire at the current wage.
The surplus is then driven into other sectors.   Social
custom imposes on the middle and upper classes the
obligation to burden themselves with hordes of useless
servants; having many servants becomes a status symbol
which extends even deep down into the lower middle and
upper working classes, if population pressure is severe;
it becomes almost immoral for any man of status to do
for himself what a servant could do for him, or to soil
his hands with manual operations.   Even entrepreneurs
get caught up in this spirit, if they accept the social
mores, and burden their businesses with large numbers
of useless clerks, messengers, and other hangers-on.
Wages are low, barely adequate to keep body and soul
together, not adequate for serious hard manual work,
and more of the nature of charity than of payment for
hard, serious labor, which is neither given nor expected.   The rest of the surplus swarms into casual trades;
markets are crowded with peddlers and stallholders making occasional sales; and there is a vast reservoir of
casual laborers, gardeners, dock workers, construction

workers, and porters. Thus everybody has some sort of job, however great the pressure of population.

Unemployment is due to the breakdown of this social system before it is fully replaced by another. When wages cease to be a form of charity, and start to rise sharply, jobs begin to be confined to those whose productivity meets the test of high wages. The economy divides into two sectors; a highly productive sector using capital and modern technology and paying high wages; and the rest of the economy. If these two sectors could be insulated from each other, there need still not be unemployment, but this insulation is not possible. If wages in the modern sector diverge sharply from earnings in the traditional sector, the latter can no longer hold the surplus labor, and disguised unemployment is converted to open unemployment.

We have usually expected wage rates in the modern sector to be about 50 per cent above the income of subsistence farmers. This brings the modern sector as much labor as it wants, without at the same time attracting much more than it can handle. It means, however, that wage rates in the modern sector must not rise with productivity in that sector: the increase in productivity must go to profits, or taxes, or to the subsistence sector via improved terms of trade.

It seems that during the nineteenth century modern sectors expanded very considerably at constant real wage rates. Historians dispute what happened in England. Some say that real wages were constant; others say that consumption increased.[4] These two are consistent with each other, since a transfer of persons from a low-income to a high-income sector will increase consumption even though real wage rates are constant. Students of the Japanese situation also conclude that real wage rates were constant there in the crucial first 40 years after the Restoration.[5]

This seems not to be possible in developing countries in the second half of the twentieth century.

4. For a recent survey, see the articles by E. J. Hobsbawm and R. M. Hartwell in the Economic History Review, April 1964.

5. Kazushi Ohkawa, The Growth Rate of the Japanese Economy Since 1878 (Tokyo: Kinokuniya Bookstore Co., Ltd., 1957).

Some discrepancies are fantastic. The bauxite mining industry in Jamaica pays unskilled labor a wage which is five times the normal. This is typical of mining countries--say of oil in Venezuela and Trinidad, or copper in Northern Rhodesia. Manufacturing and plantation industries cannot afford such wages, but they also tend to pay substantially more than is current elsewhere. Three factors operate to have this effect, which were not so powerful in the nineteenth century. First, trade unions. Secondly, a more powerful social conscience among capitalists, which causes them to wish to share the fruits of progress with their workers, and to limit profit ratios. Thirdly, strongly nationalist governments which support the claims of workers as against foreign capitalists.

A sharp increase of wages in a profitable sector has drastic effects. First, it reduces employment opportunities in that sector, and encourages instead highly capital-intensive production. Bauxite is merely scraped off the surface and carted away. At £5 a week this would offer employment to tens of thousands. At £15 a week the Jamaican companies invested instead £80 million, employing only 3,000 people. Half of 1 per cent of the labor force produces 9 per cent of gross domestic product. Secondly, these high wages act as a magnet, which causes towns to explode. When the urban wage is only 50 per cent higher than the rural, part of which is absorbed in higher living costs, demand and supply can be in equilibrium. But when the urban wage is three times the rural, there is a great influx into the towns, seeking nonexistent jobs. Having come in to town, men do not necessarily go back, for they are held by what the town has to offer--bustle, anonymity, water out of a nearby tap, freedom from obligations to relatives and chiefs, schools, cinemas, hospitals, buses, the chance of occasional employment, even in a few cases the chance of assistance from welfare agencies. Thirdly, and most of all, the high wages in the modern sector pull up wages in all other industries and occupations, helped perhaps by other trade unions as well as by normal human envy. If your cousin in the factory or mine is getting six pounds a week for unskilled labor, you are not so willing to be a garden boy for one pound a week, and so emerges the common phenomenon of employers complaining of shortage of labor, while workers complain of shortage of work. The clerk's wife kept a servant when all this cost was ten shillings a week; but a maid demanding three pounds a week is more likely to be replaced by an electric cooker, a refrigerator, a vacuum cleaner and a washing machine. The housewives get rid of their servants, and the businesses purge themselves of useless clerks and messengers. So the employment created by the modern sector can be more than offset by the effect the modern sector has on wages throughout the economy.

Adverse effects are not confined to the traditional sector. Other industries in the modern sectors are subjected to pressure. Wages in sugar, bananas, and factory industries have chased the bauxite wages. These industries are subject to international competition. They are therefore mechanizing as fast as they can, and dismissing labor. The rise of a new export industry can destroy existing exports, and existing industries compete with imports, not by taking away their labor, but simply by raising wage costs out of line with international competition.

Another new factor in the labor market is decasualization. It is normal in an underdeveloped economy for certain sectors to live by employing casual labor, attaching to themselves many more persons than they could employ continuously: most notably the docks, the building industry, plantation agriculture, and to a lesser extent the mines and the factories. Modern personnel theory is against casual labor. Men on the permanent staff feed better, work more effectively, have a higher morale, and cause less trouble. Unions also object to casual labor, because it is more difficult to organize. Decasualization does not increase the average level of unemployment, but it makes unemployment less supportable. If 100 men each work three days a week, they can all live. When 60 work five days a week and 40 become continuously unemployed, one faces a major social problem. High wages stimulate decasualization, since the employer seeks to get best value from those he employs; and also because high wages make him put in machines, which require him to train a staff and keep it.

In sum, high wages in modern industries cause the traditional sector to stop shielding the labor surplus and throw it openly on to the labor market; while at

the same time the modern sector expands by importing
machines rather than by taking on a lot more men. This
is probably the largest factor in growing unemployment,
but there are other factors to be probed.

III.

Another factor which differentiates the twentieth
century is permanent balance-of-payments crisis. In
the nineteenth century, countries developed in response
to growing demand for their exports. *Ceteris* *paribus*,
this results in a persistent tendency to run a balance-
of-payments surplus. In the second half of the twentieth century, several countries are trying to develop by
investing to meet home demands. Except insofar as the
goods produced are substitutes for imports, this results, *ceteris* *paribus*, in a persistent balance-of-payments deficit, since the increase in income is bound to
increase the demand for some imports, and neither a cut
in other imports nor an increase in exports is guaran-
teed.

Our interest is in the effect of the balance-of-
payments crisis on the prospects of industries which
have to meet international competition, whether export-
ing industries or industries producing for home consumption in competition with imports. As we have seen,
an increase in one export may destroy others by raising wages out of line with world prices; this, however,
is not a necessary result; it derives only from errors
of incomes policy, to which we refer later.

On the other hand, developing new industries with
an eye on the home market only is bound to cause what
the Latin Americans now call structural inflation. Un-
balanced growth produces the persistent tendency to a
balance-of-payments deficit; this makes necessary import controls and tariff protection; these raise the
cost of living, and therefore wages. Exports are dis-
couraged. Devaluation is forced. The cost of living
rises more, and so on. In such economies, investment
for the home market can be maintained by stricter and
stricter control of imports. Exports, however, tend to
be overlooked. Such countries have a chronic tendency
to price themselves out of the world market. The failure of export industries to expand is one of the causes
of growing unemployment in Latin America and in Asia.

IV.

An important factor in Africa is the recent explosion of the primary school population. In 1950 hardly
any African country south of the Sahara had more than
20 per cent of children in school. But one by one, as
new nationalist leaders came into power, universal
primary education was made an immediate goal, and some
areas were by 1960 taking as much as 80 per cent of the
seven-year-olds into school. The outpouring of these
young people into the towns has become a serious cause
of unemployment.

In a community where only 20 per cent of children
enter primary school, and only 10 per cent finish the
course, the demand for primary school graduates is such
that they command considerable salaries in white-collar
jobs. If the number entering primary school is pushed
up from 20 to 80 per cent of the age group within ten
years, as has happened in some West African countries,
the result is frustration. The children pouring out of
the primary schools look to the town for clerical jobs,
and are disappointed when they do not find employment.
The towns fill up with discontented youths, faster than
houses, jobs, water supplies, or other amenities can be
provided, and urban slums and delinquents multiply
while the countryside is starved of young talent.

The situation is sometimes blamed on the failure
of rural schools to adapt their curricula in such a way
as to orientate rural children to rural life. This,
however, is only part of the problem. The primary-
school leaver's expectations derive not from the curriculum but from the status which his immediate predeces-
sors have enjoyed. In a developed economy the wage of
an unskilled laborer (which is all that primary education produces) is about one-third of the average income per occupied person; but a primary-school leaver
in Africa expects about twice the average income per
occupied person. Obviously, if literacy became universal, it would be impossible to pay every literate person twice the average income. If the primary-school
leaver is to get twice the average income, he can fit
only into those parts of the economy which yield twice
the average income, and the rate of absorption of
primary-school leavers then depends on the rate at

which these modernized sectors of the economy are expanding. He will fit into a revolutionized agriculture,
with modern practices and equipment, but it is useless
to expect him to fit into the three-acres-and-a-hoe
farming of his father. Any good primary school will
widen a child's horizon and create expectations which
primitive farming cannot fulfill. So even if rural
schools concentrate on rural life, their products are
bound to suffer frustration unless the whole social
fabric of agriculture is being modernized at the same
time.

This is a temporary phenomenon. The young people
will discover that the towns cannot employ them, and
that work at twice the average wage is not to be had
anywhere. They will lower their sights, and learn to
make do with the opportunities in rural areas. But the
learning will be painful, psychologically and politically, and in the meantime, the towns will be in
trouble.

V.

I have mentioned at several points the excessive
rate of growth of towns, as one of the phenomena of
unemployment. People who should remain on the farms
where they have some income, and in Africa or Latin
America certainly add something to output (India and
Pakistan are more doubtful cases), turn up instead in
the towns, living by small opportunities for casual
employment.

Current reactions to excessive urbanization make
things worse. The best way to keep people in the
countryside is to spend public funds on providing
amenities in country towns--secondary schools, water
supplies, hospitals, electric power, and so on. Instead, public expenditure tends to be concentrated in
a small number of large cities, thus adding to their
drawing power. For this there are many reasons. The
tendency for political talent to concentrate in the
larger cities, depriving the countryside and country
towns of leadership and influence. Erroneous theories
that only large cities can carry the overhead of industrialization. The fact that the larger cities,
because they are growing fastest, seem to have the
greatest needs--which is really a circular argument,

since the more you concentrate public facilities there, at the expense of the rest of the country, the faster they grow, and the more they need.

European cities did not explode in the first half of the nineteenth century. Some tendency towards excessive urbanization existed, and caused concern: British poor-law authorities were trying to control it administratively at the end of the eighteenth and beginning of the nineteenth centuries. But when Europe was beginning its industrial revolution the logistic problems of large cities had not yet been solved, so industry had to develop in many small towns instead of a few large ones. The first suburban bus service started in Paris in 1855. Twentieth-century advances in transportation, sewage disposal, water supplies, preservation of milk and meat, and house-to-house communication by telephone make it possible for even the poorest nations today to struggle with heaps of four or five million people, while much richer countries in say 1870 would have found four or five hundred thousand barely manageable.

VI.

So far I have mainly been explaining why the labor surplus is no longer held in the traditional sectors, but is instead throwing itself or being thrown into open unemployment on the labor market. The other blade of the scissors is that economic expansion now seems to be more capital-intensive and less labor-intensive than in the nineteenth century. In country after country where the rate of investment was unusually high in the 1950's, there is astonishment at how little employment so much investment has created.

The proposition under consideration can be stated as follows. Let us suppose that in the nineteenth century x per cent of national income had to be invested, net, to provide additional employment for 1 per cent of population. It appears that in the second half of the twentieth century underdeveloped nations are getting less than 1 per cent addition to employment for x per cent of national income invested. I put this forward not as a proven fact, but as part of our agenda for research.

Let us first begin by analyzing the effect of

invention on the ratio of capital to labor. Suppose an
economy in which capital is stored-up labor, so that an
increase in wages increases the price of machines in
the same proportion. Suppose further that there are
two farms, one keeping the weeds down with machines,
and the other keeping the weeds down at the same cost
by hand. An invention may be of three kinds; it may
change the relative efficiency of weeding by hand or by
machine, without changing the relative cost of the machine; it may introduce a new technique which alters
the ratio of machines to labor; or it may reduce the
cost of making the machine, while leaving both its efficiency and the machine-labor ratio the same.

An invention which eliminated weeds easily by hand
would cause the first farm to abandon its machines, and
so reduce the ratio of capital to labor; an invention
which improved the efficiency of machines in eliminating weeds would cause the second farm to turn to machinery, and so increase the economy-wide ratio of capital
to labor. In general the trend of the past century has
favored ways of making things with machines rather than
other ways, so tending to increase the ratio of needed
investment per unit of employment.

Next, an invention which increases the efficiency
of a machine may increase, reduce or leave unchanged
the ratio of machines per man. If the ratio is unchanged, fewer men and fewer machines eliminate the
same quantity of weeds. Some inventions have reduced
the quantity of capital per unit of labor, for example
the substitution of the tape recorder for earlier re-
cording processes. But the general trend has favored
increasing the amount of capital per man.

On the other hand, statisticians tell us that in
Britain and the United States over the past 80 years,
the ratio of investment to labor in our terms has
varied very little. Capital per man measured at constant prices has enormously increased, but our interest
is not in this, but in the proportion of national income invested required to employ a man, which we can
identify roughly as the ratio of the number of men it
takes to make a machine to the number of men it takes
to use it, or the ratio of capital to the wages bill.
We are told that for several decades prior to the
Second World War there had been very little change in
the ratio of labor income or capital income to output,

or of net investment to output, both of which imply
that the percentage of net investment required to employ 1 per cent more people had remained roughly the
same. The explanation of this is the third type of invention, which reduces the cost of machines. This
works both ways. On the one hand it encourages the
displacement of labor-intensive processes, so increasing the economy-wide capital-output ratio. On the
other hand it reduces the labor-cost of capital, and
this has been powerful enough to offset all the other
factors making for an increase in the capital-employ-
ment ratio.

The countries developing today differ from those
which started during the nineteenth century in several
respects, which raise the investment-employment ratio.

First, we have already seen that for various reasons there is a persistent tendency for wages to rise
sharply. This would not alter the ratio of capital to
employment in a closed economy, since the price of capital and the price of labor would rise together. But
it is very important in an open economy importing machinery from countries where costs are not subject to
the same degree of inflation. This persistent increase
in wages has caused excessive mechanization in many
countries. But there are also other factors.

A second factor--minor but spectacular--is the
high ratio of public to private investment in the newly
developing countries. Nineteenth-century entrepreneurs
were willing to start factories in barns; private
schools or hospitals sprouted in the most unlikely
places. But public factories, schools, hospitals or
other structures are nearly always colossal, striking
and expensive, built to the glory of their architects
and their supporting politicians. So public capital
investment provides less continuing employment than
private investment of the same amount.

A third factor is that much of the capital invested in these countries is under-utilized. Capital is
going into many industries where the demand is insuffi-
cient for production on an economic scale; plants are
built ahead of demand, and run below capacity. Double
and treble shifts are not as popular as they were a
hundred years ago. Superhighways carrying a handful of
vehicles are a common sight. Strict economic calcluus
in investing capital is not practiced as it was a

hundred years ago. This is related to the greater influence of governments on investment, though it is not
confined to public investment; tariffs, subsidies, and
licensing are used to protect private investments which
would otherwise be made more modestly.

A fourth factor in comparisons with developed
countries is that the difference in per-capita outputs
is greater in the capital-producing industries than in
other industries. Hence, insofar as the underdeveloped
make their own capital goods, it takes more investment
to support a unit of employment. They can import machinery, and this reduces the ratio, but the terms of
trade will lie between the developed countries' ratios
and theirs, so the ratio of capital to wages should
still be higher in the less-developed countries. In
equilibrium, therefore, an underdeveloped country would
have a higher capital-wages ratio in those industries
which were capitalized, but would have fewer industries
capitalized than a developed economy because of the
greater cost of capital.

Fifthly, the product-mix is different. Developed
countries achieve 4 per cent overall growth by having
5 per cent industrial growth and 3 per cent for the
rest of the economy; while underdeveloped countries get
the same overall result by having 8 per cent industrial
growth and 3 per cent for the rest of the economy.
Since the modern industrial sector is the most highly
capitalized part of the underdeveloped economies, its
high growth rate increases capital formation sharply
while doing little for employment.

Finally, high capital intensity is probably a natural consequence of technological lag. Approaching
these countries from the angle of the Ohlin version of
the Law of Comparative Costs, economists have argued
that they should avoid capital-intensive investments.
The Ohlin version assumes that technologies are everywhere the same. The Ricardian version focuses instead
on differences in relative efficiencies. Capital should
be used where it adds most to income. This is more
likely to be in those parts of the economy where capital
brings much more productive technology than in those
parts where efficiency depends rather on skill. When
one orders industries in terms of the comparative efficiency of resources, Ricardian style, underdeveloped
countries will be nearly as efficient as developed

countries in industries where capital is the crucial factor, and will be least efficient in those where advanced skills are the crucial factor. So, even after the relative scarcity of capital is brought into the account, some highly capital-intensive industries will still prove to be the most productive investments.[6]

When the effects of technological change are considered, there is no a priori reason why economic development must increase rather than reduce employment. This is an old story. You will remember that Ricardo demonstrated to Malthus that investment must increase employment. Their model has an unlimited supply of labor at a subsistence wage. Hence extra capital is met by extra labor in the same proportion; the rate of profit is constant; and unlimited expansion is possible--except for a shortage of land.

Later Ricardo thought again, and added to the third edition of his Principles a chapter on Machinery, admitting that an invention which reduced the cost of machinery could destroy more employment than it created. However, he argued, this would increase profits, savings, investment and therefore employment. Here we have the distinction between the sort of investment which merely produces more of the same--two factories in place of one--and therefore increases the use of labor, and the sort of investment which embodies new invention, which may reduce the cost or increase the effiency of capital, and so cause it to be substituted for labor.

Marx added nothing useful to the distinctions. He simply asserted flatly that the course of history would be that the amount of unemployment created by the flow of labor-saving inventions would exceed the amount of employment created by more investment of a duplicating kind, so that the number of unemployed must grow continuously. Marx was clearly wrong for developing economies in the nineteenth century. But we cannot deduce that he must be wrong for developing economies in the twentieth century. There is now such an accumulation of labor-saving processes which have not yet been introduced into underdeveloped countries that the

6. For an arithmetical example, see my paper, "A Review of Economic Development," American Economic Review, May 1965.

potential for destroying employment by new investment
is very considerable. It is not at all inconceivable
that a stream of new investment in transport, distribution, and agriculture would create much more unemployment than a similar stream directed to industry and
services would absorb. Output and investment could
thus increase while employment declined.

VII.

I began by saying that unemployment is not created by population pressure, since a well-ordered society
absorbs a population surplus in its traditional sectors.
This is no longer true when the social mechanism breaks
down. We have seen how high wages cause the traditional sector to throw the surplus onto the labor market,
and cause the modern sector, by becoming highly capital
intensive, to leave most of the surplus on the market.
The bigger the surplus, the bigger the unemployment; so
population growth, absorbable when the society is in
equilibrium, causes growing unemployment when the society is in disequilibrium. Putting all these factors together, it is no surprise that unemployment is growing
despite high levels of investment.

VIII.

If there are remedies for this situation, the most
important would be to prevent wages in the modern sector from moving out of line with incomes in the traditional sector.
The fact that the mining industry is profitable is
no justification for paying miners five times as much
as other workers can earn. The higher productivity of
mining is a rent element which should accrue neither to
the workers nor to the capitalists, but to the owners
of the natural resource, which should be the state.
The proper answer to abnormal profits in a particular
industry is not higher wages in that industry, but a
system of royalties or taxes which draws the rent element into the public treasury, where it can finance the
public services, and capital formation. In general,
wages in the modern sector should be kept at about 50
per cent above the farmer's income, and excess profits
should go not to the workers but to the general public.

Worker's incomes should be raised partly by aggressive
measures increasing farm productivity, and partly by
the steady transfer of men from agriculture to higher-
paid jobs in other sectors.

This policy is anathema to unions, but several governments of new states have already adopted it--espe-
cially new states in which the government is the largest employer of wage labor, but also by some which want
the profits to spend on schools or roads, and do not
therefore support union demands. This is producing a
crisis between union leaders and political leaders, for
example in Nigeria and in Northern Rhodesia. It is also producing a new philosophy of the role of trade unions in developing countries, for example in Ghana and
in India. The problem of unemployment can be solved
only at this political level.

GENERAL DISCUSSION

Chairman BLANKSTEN: We do not have any specially
appointed discussants for tonight's session and we will
therefore be able to move more directly into the general discussion.

The Rural Sector

Mr. NASH: I cannot quarrel with Mr. Lewis's analysis of the modern sector, but when he takes the other
part of his dual society, I think he errs badly.

The developing countries have not been, since colonial impact, at least in Asia and Africa, in any empirical state of equilibrium. They have been accommo-
dating to their surplus population by in fact decreas-
ing the per capita income of everybody in it. They do
have accommodation mechanisms.

Mr. LEWIS: Asia has surplus population, not Africa.

Mr. NASH: Asia, all right. Overpopulation there
is a problem and what it continues to do, empirically
anyway, is to subdivide tasks so that the net output is
not larger but the individual shares are reduced. The
modern sector exercises a pull, not only because of its
wages, but also because of the declining level of living in the countryside year after year after year in

places like India and Indonesia. I think Mr. Lewis has to build in the notion that these are "pathological" dual societies (urban and rural), and that they are not in any sense in a state of equilibrium.

For a long time there have been great pressures on the people in the countryside to break away and anything will pull them out.

Mr. LEWIS: All I am saying is that so long as they are on the family farm, they have some income. Now, you do something which brings them into the town. I am not worried only about the people from the farms. There is also the surplus in urban employments that gets thrown out because of higher wages; but, if you pull the people on the farms into the towns where they have no income, this becomes a social problem.

Mr. NASH: They are social problems back home anyway.

Mr. LEWIS: They are not anything like the same social problem back on the farm that they are in the town.

Mr. NASH: Well, that depends on the country and its political organization.

Mr. LEWIS: Let us put it this way, that when they are on the farms they are a hidden social problem and when they are on your doorstep burgling your house at night in the towns, they are an open social problem.

Mr. NASH: They are in many ways a more serious social problem in the country. In Burma, for example, or in Indonesia or Vietnam, one of the sources of the recruitment of insurgents is this rural population which takes off for dacoiting under political banners and keeps the government in a state of turmoil all the time. They are real social rural problems; you do not have to bring them into the cities.

Mr. LEWIS: I would not accept Burma in your list of countries that are overpopulated. I would agree if you have in mind India and Pakistan, for example, but not Burma.

Mr. NASH: Burma has this same kind of rural trouble. One of the reasons is that boys can leave the family farm without lowering its income and take five years off as a dacoit, as a PV Volunteer or as a Red rebel; this keeps the country in a terrible state of turmoil.

If you look for the sources of the peasant revolts in countries like Burma that are relatively prosperous,

you will find them in this "pathological" development
in the countryside.

Mr. BARANSON: I think this is also true in Colombia. The problem becomes insoluble in the countryside;
the greater pressures are there, and you cannot say
that urbanization, despite the problems it creates, is
more of an evil and more of a problem.

Mr. KREININ: I think Africa is different, and Mr.
Lewis's discussion is really more applicable to Africa.

Economic Development and Social Tension

Mr. ANDERSON: Without any reservations on your
economic analysis, Mr. Lewis, is the intensity of the
crises these countries are facing, which you sketched
out, serious?   Or, to what degree are the crises inten-
sified by the technologically reduced death rate of recent years and by the new technology, so to speak, of
political arousal that has been brought into these
countries that was not present in Europe a hundred
years ago?   To what extent does this intensify these
problems beyond this strictly intrinsic growth problem?

Mr. LEWIS: This ties up with something else that
was talked about before and I think it is important.
I said, essentially, that in certain countries which
are overpopulated, primarily some countries of Asia,
not Africa and not Burma, there is a surplus of disguised unemployment which is now coming out into the
towns, for the reasons which I analyzed, and that this
is a bad thing because it would be better if they (the
villagers) were to stay in the areas where they are
for the time being until there has been a sufficient
expansion of the capacity of the modern sector to absorb them and provide them employment.

I was challenged on this by people who, if I understand them correctly, take opposite points of view
and say, "No, it is a jolly good thing for these chaps
to get out and become unemployed in the towns because
unemployment in the towns somehow or other is not quite
as bad as unemployment in the countryside."   I do not
understand, really, how people can think that, because
it just does not accord with my experience.   One of
the things it does not accord with is precisely your
very last point about the political position.

It has been fashionable in some quarters to believe that economic development will bring social peace,
or even world peace, but most of us know very well that
economic development is a very disturbing process, and
on the contrary, produces the very greatest social tensions. It is only in the later stages of development
that you reach social stability. Economic development,
as Marx saw it around him--and exactly the same thing
exists in the developing countries today--produces very
great tensions, and produced very great political arousal in Marx's day and very great political arousal in
our day.

I think these countries would get along better if
the population and employment surplus remained in the
countryside where it could share in the income of a
large family pattern. The countryside does provide a
social security system, and it provides a place for
these people psychologically.

When you put them into the towns where the cultural patterns are not ready to receive them, the only
things waiting for them are the politicians and the
agitators. I think some of these countries are much
more likely to tear themselves in pieces if the surplus population comes into the towns before the towns
are ready for them, than if they had stayed in the countryside.

Mr. ANDERSON: It depends on what kind of disorder
you want.

Mr. HENDRY: It seems to me that from experiences
in Indonesia there are factors at work that go beyond
the economic situation. I am impressed by Professor
Nash's questions.

As you see people pour into Djakarta, for example,
a city of 3,000,000 people that was designed for
500,000, you get a feeling that these people are not
really concerned about whether or not they are casually
employed or unemployed. They come because there are
many other incentives. They simply like people. They
like mob scenes. They like to associate with other
people. They like the power structure of Djakarta.
They like to participate in the mob scenes.

There are bread-and-circus aspects to this thing
that I am not sure you can measure in terms of the economics of the situation. Also, I would not be convinced that the typical Indonesian would recognize that

he was unemployed, either in a disguised version of unemployment or an overt form of unemployment. He seems
to get by at a very low marginal or submarginal subsistence standard. I think my observation is that
there are many factors here at work other than the factor of the real level of wages these people earn in
these urban centers.

Mr. FATOUROS: I think there is a clear implication at least from a factual description of the results
of the transfer from the traditional sector to the modern sector in many of the underdeveloped societies,
that the modern sector will have to provide a high
amount of social welfare to the people who, on transferring from the traditional to the modern sector, lose
the implicit social welfare advantages they had in the
traditional sector. This makes necessary (and this
necessity is political as well as economic) a level of
social welfare, social security, and so on, which would
not compare with the much lower social welfare level in
Western societies at a corresponding stage of development. Would Mr. Lewis agree with that, as a factual
statement rather than a normative one?

Mr. LEWIS: As a factual statement, yes. Going
back to the point about politics, the towns are better
organized than the countryside to make claims upon the
government, and this is one of the reasons why it is
much easier for the government when the unemployment is
hidden in the countryside rather than in the towns, because the pressure that is then put on the government
to do something about it is terrific and they are
forced, as in Ghana, to create a Workers' Brigade or
start some kind of social welfare measures.

Modern and Traditional Sectors: Japan

Mr. GINSBURG: I wonder if some of the points Professor Lewis made about the contrasts between the modern and traditional sectors do not present us with a
taxonomic problem that needs resolution?

I think we probably have a reasonably consistent
common sense understanding of what is meant by the modern sector of an economy, but I wonder whether we have
the same conception of what a traditional sector is?
My point is that the definitions of the traditional
sector may vary so much as to make it very difficult to

generalize concerning the relationship, say, between
the two sectors. Let me illustrate with the case of
Japan, which I realize is far from an underdeveloped
country, but is certainly a developing one. Every year
approximately 300,000 people move into Tokyo alone,
from "non-Tokyo." By "non-Tokyo" I mean primarily
rural Japan, but also the smaller towns, though we are
not quite sure just where the migrants come from.

Now, what happens to most of these people? Most
of them, incidentally, are employable. They are literate. Japan has a 99-point something literacy, in spite
of the "devilish" language which makes Westerners think
that all these people just possibly cannot communicate
with one another. They are employable, and they are
young. I do not have precise figures with me, but
about half of these people go into tertiary activities,
and some of them certainly are quite marginal in terms
of the value of output that is associated with them.
Of the remainder, only a very small proportion, in spite
of their literacy, go into what we might call the modern industrial sector. The vast majority go into what
we would call the traditional sector. What is this
traditional sector of the economy like? I am talking,
now, about industry, not commerce. It consists, as we
all have read, of relatively small firms employing 25
people or less and mostly considerably less, paying
wages which are considerably lower than wages in the
modern sector.

Theoretically, I suppose, and I think that you
suggested this, because these wage differentials are
very great, there ought to be a massive flow of these
employables from the traditional sector to the modern
sector. There is some flow, of course, but it is not
as massive, perhaps, as the Japanese would like. Now
why don't they flow? They do not flow to the extent
one might speculate they might because of certain built-
in restraints in the Japanese culture pattern--which,
of course, includes the economy.

For one thing, there is a certain "stickiness"
about this traditional sector which can be defined in
part in terms of the kind of "extended family" type of
relationship between employer and employee which is developed there. Perhaps even more important, however,
is the institutionalized set of roles played by these
traditional-sector firms on the one hand and the modern-

sector firms on the other. The small firms of the traditional sector, which are much more labor-intensive,
I suppose we might say, than the firms in the modern
sector, are tied in with the larger firms by means of
contractual arrangements that are of very long standing. In other words, the small firms are linked with
the larger ones in supplying certain kinds of parts and
services.

We have all read about bicycles, for example, but
I am not just thinking of bicycles. The huge electron-
ics industry in Japan has taken on the same characteristics that the bicycle industry had decades ago, and
still has. This formalization of relationship has resulted in a relative stabilization of roles between the
two sectors.

Now, we are talking about Japanese society or a
particular attribute of it. It is something we do not
find in the newly developing countries, certainly not
in Africa, about which I know virtually nothing and
therefore can make such a gross generalization.

In Japan in the 1870's and later, there existed a
society which was predominantly rural in terms of population but which was urban in terms of its conception
of the way people ought to live. The city was something that was known, it existed, and it was indigenous,
not colonial; but there were in the cities artist-
craftsmen establishments supplying the elite, which
were organized much in the same manner that the small
firm in the traditional sector is now organized.

The traditional sector is Japanese; it is related
to the modern sector in describable ways, in ways that
are understandable to the Japanese. We do not find
this kind of phenomenon, so I understand, in the African countries or in certain of the Southeast Asian
countries, for example, where urbanization and industrialization have been associated both with colonialism
and with the import of foreign labor: Asians or Lebanese into East Africa, or Chinese and Indians into
Southeast Asia.

Let me ask Professor Lewis whether he thinks all
this is relevant to his schema and could be used to
distinguish among various types of cases.

Mr. LEWIS: It is very relevant, and I have
thought about it quite a good deal, because the problem with which I am concerned is in marked contrast to

the Japanese situation. The conclusion I come to is that there must be a difference in the trade union situation which makes it possible for people to flow into Japanese small-scale industry.

Wage Differentials and Mechanization

I do not know what the present situation is. Ten years ago in Japan I was told that it was quite common for small industrialists to be employing people and paying them half the wages that next door they were being paid by the big industrialists. Now, this means that we have a situation in Japan in which, as the surplus flows into the towns, a wage level is adopted which makes it possible to absorb these people in spite of the fact that a much higher wage level is being paid to some other people. It is the absence of this phenomenon that causes the trouble in the economies with which I am concerned.

If it were possible for the sugar industry in Jamaica to go on paying three pounds a week while the bauxite industry was paying fifteen, the sugar industry would not have mechanized. You spoke about the mining industry. The mining industry has enormous flexibility. Underground mining does not have this flexibility. A good deal of the mining in these countries practically all of the iron mining in West Africa and bauxite mining in the West Indies involves merely scraping the stuff off the ground, and you do not have to have bulldozers and so on to do it with.

The mining industry could employ four or five times as many people as it does.

Mr. KREININ: What, then, is the cause of the capital intensity?

Mr. LEWIS: Capital intensity is caused by the high wages.

Mr. KREININ: I do not agree with you.

Mr. BINDER: I am still intrigued by your recommendations--contrary to your viewpoint ten years ago-- for the holding-down of wages in the modern sector.

In one or two places near the end of the paper you used the word "should," indicating that the increased income to these industries was a rent factor and that this should go to the owner of the resource, which should be the state, or is the state in some cases. I am not sure which the term was.

There are a number of recommendations made, possibly including one that the state should be the owner of the resource, which is a highly questionable recommendation.

What I would like to explore is whether or not your "should" regarding the holding-down of wages in the modern sector refers to the explicit value of reducing unemployment in the economy as a whole or whether you are after other values going beyond that? If you are concerned only with the value of reducing unemployment or of limiting unemployment, the materials you have presented appear to demonstrate that unemployment has not fallen, but I am not quite sure that it has increased.

Mr. LEWIS: Oh, yes. I think, really, we ought to start at that end to see whether my impression of the places I have been to is supported, namely that open unemployment has been increasing.

Professor Harbison has just come back from Venezuela and he tells me that there they are terribly concerned and extremely puzzled. They have had a 9 per cent per annum rate of growth of the national output for a long time now and unemployment is just mounting by leaps and bounds.

He has been around the world in recent years. Our impressions are both the same, that this is a real phenomenon and not something we are dreaming up, but perhaps we could start at that end.

Chairman BLANKSTEN: With respect to some of the distinctions that are drawn here, for example, you talked about unemployment in the modern sector and another distinction that would occur to me would be that between skilled and unskilled labor. Would not these distinctions be especially crucially important in this kind of a problem?

Mr. LEWIS: This is all unskilled unemployment one is talking about, really. Let me give a particular example.

You ask me why one should be so concerned. Let me take a man who is now extremely concerned, and he is the Prime Minister of a state which came into existence yesterday or the day before yesterday, Zambia. Northern Rhodesia has one really profitable industry, the copper mines, and Mr. Kaunda and the copper companies are on very good terms at the moment.

Fifty per cent of the profits of the copper mines goes to the government of Northern Rhodesia in the form of a corporation tax. The copper mines employ very few people. The mines, as you know, in all of these economies employ very few people but they produce a tremendous amount of wealth.

If you were in the position of Mr. Kaunda and the few people that are employed by the mines at relatively high wages (I do not know what the figure is in Northern Rhodesia but I would wager that it is at least five times what the average person in Northern Rhodesia is able to earn) came up with a demand for a 20 per cent increase in wages, what would you do? Ten years ago Mr. Kaunda, being a Nationalist, would have been backing the demand solidly, but if you were in his position, would you now be backing that movement or would you be saying, "If the copper mines are making extra profits, these belong to the economy of Northern Rhodesia and we will use this money to build roads, to develop agriculture, to build schools, hospitals and so forth?" What would you do?

Mr. BINDER: The question is unfair. You see, if the issue is what ought to be done, then it is unfair to put me in the position of Mr. Kaunda or in the position of a miner. I have to stay in my own position and ask what ought to be done. That is why I wanted to have you refer your recommendations to a particular value.

Mr. LEWIS: What do you think ought to be done in your own position?

Mr. BINDER: Well, of course, I may feel that I do not even care that the state of Zambia continue in existence. You are setting a framework for your social responsibility which is that of the state of Zambia. Within the framework of that assumption one might say, then, that in order for the state to persist it might be necessary to have some source of revenue, but there are a host of other questions. For example, if unemployment is increasing in the non-modern sector and at the same time, by this capital-intensive development, the national product is increasing at the rate of 9 per cent per annum, is it not possible, or conceivable, that if you hold wages down in the modern sector, the national product will not increase so fast?

Mr. LEWIS: In fact, it might increase faster. The trouble with these economies is that they are increasing the national product by importing machinery. The thing does not make any sense whatsoever. Jobs which could be done by people are being done by machines which are imported, so wealth is being created to send away when the same wealth could be created by labor and kept in the economy. It does not make any sense at all.

Mr. BINDER: I am not certain that your assertion as to the "same wealth" is correct. Machines are far more efficient. I remember the Harbison-Ibrahim volume on Egyptian industry and the testimony of the managers of Egyptian industry that the machines are much more efficient than the men.[7] The managers want the machines and they feel that they can trust the machines more than they can the men.

Mr. LEWIS: Of course the profit is greater and this is why they put them in. Let me give you a concrete example. A major political issue in Jamaica today, and for the last five years, is the loading of bananas on the ships. Bananas are loaded on ships by hand in Jamaica and they are taken to Bristol where they are unloaded by machinery at half the price it takes to load them.

Wages have gone up and up and up in the banana-loading industry because they are chasing the bauxite wages and now it has reached the point where the banana industry of Jamaica is being squeezed. It is not itself a very efficient industry, and it cannot afford to pay these high wages for loading bananas. The farmers are threatening to load the bananas themselves rather than go on paying these wages, and they have demanded the right to import machinery. The machinery will do it much more cheaply than the people, but all that would happen is that income which could be used to support some people in Jamaica will instead be used to support the makers of machinery in Birmingham. Now, what sense does that make to the people in Jamaica?

7. Frederick Harris Harbison and I. A. Ibrahim, Human Resources for Egyptian Enterprises (a project of the International Relations Section, Princeton University; New York: McGraw-Hill, 1958).

Africa: Mining and Education

Mr. KREININ: I believe your recommendation is
sound, and apropos of Mr. Binder's point, it is equiv-
alent to restoring development which takes account of
factor proportions in the economy. If an economy with
surplus labor develops, taking account of relative factor endowments, it should introduce less capital-intensive industries, thereby increasing both output and
employment at the same time. This however, may not be
possible where mining industries are the main natural
resource. By their very nature mining operations are
capital-intensive and I am not sure that substitutability is possible there. That is, I am not sure that you
could mine very well with less capital-intensive technique.

If this is the case, then obviously the rent factor exists and should not accrue to labor. That is,
the share of labor should be the same share which
would have accrued to it had development proceeded
along lines that are more in accordance with factor
proportions. I think your recommendation would in a
sense bring that about by, so to speak, spreading the
investments over the economy, and it is for this reason that I do not think even the University of Chicago
people should object to it, because it essentially elim-
inates market imperfections.

Now, concerning the problem of unemployment in
Africa, with which I have some familiarity, I would say
that it is not really an increase in unemployment but
a transfer from disguised to overt unemployment. What
you said about the type of education that the Africans
receive is probably true, but that is only a minor factor. It is not only rural education that is not oriented toward retaining them in rural life, but the elementary education which prepares people for the professions is also at fault.

I was involved in technical assistance studies in
Africa and one of the proctors was very upset because
in order to be a certified bricklayer in Africa, students had to pass the London examinations, which meant
that they had to spend a third of their time learning
how to construct fireplaces; no bricklayer in Africa
will ever construct a fireplace.

This is just a side point, but I think the kind of

education they receive at the elementary level does affect the "school leavers" to some extent. It may not be the major part of the problem, but it cannot be ignored.

Alternatives to Capital-Intensive Mechanization

Mr. SCHWARTZ: Professor Lewis, you spoke before about, I think you called it the fundamental change, primarily in innovation, or at least in innovation with respect to relative factor supply proportions, which at present is bringing about situations in which smaller and smaller additions to employment result from a given amount of investment. I would like to ask to what extent you think this change has been, and to what extent do you think this need be, "so fundamental," and I have in mind three things, particularly:

First, to what extent have the countries promoted, and to what extent could the countries themselves promote, policies facilitating the adaptation of machinery that would be somewhat less capital-intensive, and somewhat less labor-saving, as I believe Japan did to some extent in the nineteenth century, the late nineteenth century?

Second, could not some international agency loans be shaped towards this purpose?

Third, to the extent that a fair amount of the new industrial expansion in these countries (certainly at this stage) has resulted from either foreign investment which has been trying to forestall the loss of a market, or exchange licensing aimed at a similar objective (and thus which is rather inevitable), could there not be more in the way of requirements that such foreign capital be permitted to enter only if certain changes are made so that some or all of it contributes to less labor-saving and more labor-using than formerly?

All three of these are possibilities. My supposition is that these things have not been done to a very great extent, but might there not be major possibilities here? What is so fundamental about the nature of innovations if you set up important financial incentives in an effort to redirect innovational developments, either re-adapting given machinery or developing new machinery? High wages in relatively labor-abundant

economies need not lead to the same degree of substitution of labor as in the past, if there are additional
varieties of machinery which permit the selection of
alternatives other than a highly capital-intensive operation when it becomes too costly to employ a highly
labor-intensive operation.

Mr. LEWIS: You do not have to create new machinery to solve this problem.   The incentive is very simple, and I am amazed that what I am saying apparently
is not accepted.

Let us take the bauxite industry in the West Indies.   The removal of bauxite in the West Indies is an
industry that is something like 50 years old.   If the
bauxite industry had not had to pay the rate of wages
which other industries have to pay, it would not have
mechanized so rapidly.   The sugar industry, which has
now thrown out half of its workers, is 300 years old in
the West Indies.   It has only mechanized at this rate
because wages have gone up so rapidly.   But apart from
those industries, I think we really need to investigate
the type of problem of which India is an example.

Compare what has happened in India over the last
ten years with what has happened in Japan, for instance,
or any other developing country that you can think of
in the nineteenth century.   There has been an enormous
investment in India, a big increase in output and so
forth, and extraordinarily little impact on employment,
and it is perfectly clear that if the Indians go on at
the present rate they will never catch up with their
labor surplus, and they will become worse and worse off.

Mr. FATOUROS: A footnote to the remarks of Mr.
Schwartz.   I think there have been some attempts to
induce labor-intensive development, first, in the case
of China where, of course, we do not know if there was
any choice; then, Algeria in a recent foreign investment law gives special incentives to industries employing a certain number of workers, although this may relate to the size of the firm as much as to its labor-
intensive character.

Mr. BARANSON: I think you have made a very basic
point on this matter of rapidly rising wages, and its
influence upon the inhibitions to development.   In the
first place, rapidly rising wages contribute to the
burgeoning of cities, and in the second place they aggravate the balance-of-payments problem; and as to this

business of technological choice, they intensify capital-intensive choices.

I would suggest that one of the differences between Japan and India is that Japan is a developed country in the sense that it can make a choice between a labor-intensive and a capital-intensive technology, and India has much greater difficulty in doing that. I think the reason is that Japan is more advanced industrially and socially capable of adapting various techniques. I was doing a study on Diesel engine manufacture, and in the case of Japan they could take a part and break it down into 21 labor-intensive processes--in the United States it is produced by two machines, two processes. India cannot do that. It does not have the engineers, it does not have the technical draftsmen, it does not have the relationship between the production plant and the bureaucracy in New Delhi.

Japan adapted labor-intensive techniques as an interim measure because it would take a year or two to buy more mechanized equipment, whereas India has difficulty in adapting either alternative.

I have only one exception to your thesis. I think your thesis is a very fundamental one--this whole business of rapidly rising wages and the fact that it is inducing aggravations to the development process--but I would not overlook the basic nature of underdevelopment and the fact that the choice is not so open as you would suggest about labor-intensive technology.

India cannot make the choice, even with the wage differential, and this is the important qualification I would make to your thesis, that the wage differential in itself is not the thing that places the choice and suggests that it therefore should be; in other words, if you hold down wages, they will then have the alternative of choosing labor-intensity. I think India is a long way off from that, much different than Japan was 50 years ago or today; it is a long way off from having a developed stage of society in which they can make the kind of choices you are talking about, despite wage differentials.

Mr. LEWIS: I agree with you where this choice involves innovation, where they have to sit down and invent a way of making the part in 20 pieces instead of one. That I would agree with. There are other choices, however, that do not involve innovation, and of course, they have made these choices.

In India some of the dams are being built by huge bulldozers and other dams are being built by people carrying buckets of mud on their heads. Choices do exist. I am not disagreeing with anything you say, but some of the choices that could be made are not made when wages go up.

Mr. KREININ: There is also a choice between industries, not only within industries. For example, why should India manufacture Diesel engines? Why not textiles, or something like that?

Mr. BARANSON: This is part of the business of developing a heavy industrial capability. You either do it or you do not.

Mr. BINDER: How would you set up a program for research whereby one could prove that higher wages led to capitalization rather than the other way around?

I get the idea that the culture of the manager in some of the underdeveloped areas is such, judging again from the Middle East and some reports on the Near East, that he prefers machines to people and that if it is not going to be too much more expensive he would rather have a machine than bother with all of these people, and the political aspects, of course, are important, too. If you do not have people, you just have machines, you do not have too many problems about managing the people. I have, therefore, a tendency toward hypothesizing that it is the purchase of labor-saving machinery which runs ahead of increasing wages.

Mr. LEWIS: This is true marginally, I would say, but to answer your question specifically as to how one would set up a research program, fortunately there are a number of industries in the underdeveloped countries which are quite old and which are mechanizing, and we can find out why they are mechanizing.

The governments in some of these territories are resisting mechanization and therefore the industries have to produce data. Take, for example, the West Indies. We know year by year exactly what the situation is with regard to mechanization in the sugar industry, because government after government is fighting it. We know year by year what the situation is in the banana industry, and we know year by year what the situation is in the bauxite industry, so it is possible to do research on particular industries and find out exactly why they are mechanizing.

Now, what you say is also an incentive to mechanization, that it is nicer not to have to deal with so
many chaps, but on the other hand, if wages were not so
high it would be more profitable to do it with more
chaps, and if capitalists are as rapacious as all that,
if it is more profitable to do with more chaps, they
will do with more chaps rather than the machines.

Differential Growth Rates

Mr. MORGAN: I wonder if I might go back to the
first data that Professor Lewis gave us on the growth
rates in the 1950's as reported by the United Nations
statistics; they are very high indeed. Four point one
(4.1) was the average for Africa, with a maximum 5.2
per cent in West Asia. My impression is that the average is higher than that for high-income countries in
general (with some considerable exceptions) and that
even after you subtract the higher rates of population
growth in low-income areas, you come out with the judgment that the gap in standard of living between low- and
high-income areas is no longer increasing perceptibly.
Perhaps it is even shrinking.

If so, the change is remarkable. The world is re-
versing a trend that has been going on for centuries--
three or four centuries at least. It is so remarkable
that it is almost unbelievable. One is impelled to ask
whether the data are accurate or whether we are being
fooled. Assuming the data are accurate, I should like
to ask a supplementary question. If it is true that
the trend has been suddenly changed in the 1950's, is
it possible that this might have been due to the up-
heavals of war, to the movement of armed forces and
refugees, which have brought a temporary stimulus to
growth, rather than a new secular trend?

Mr. LEWIS: Well, let us take the developed countries: It is true that the growth rate of the United
States and Canada and Great Britain is low, but the
growth rate of Western continental Europe in the same
period would be of the same order of magnitude or even
higher than the figures the U.N. gives for underdeveloped continents. The French growth rate is fantastic
and the Italian growth rate and the West German growth
rate are fantastic, also. I think if you take Western

Europe, it has been increasing at this kind of rate or faster, and it is really only Britain, America and Canada that have been below it.

I too was surprised by the high rates in the under-developed countries. West Asia one understands; these are the oil areas plus Israel. India is about 4 per cent, which is not bad. Pakistan, perhaps, is a little less than that. Malaya is very high. Thailand, it is reported, is doing quite well. Taking all this into consideration, I do not know of any reason to query the rate they have given for Southern Asia.

The rate I find difficult to comprehend is the African rate. The figures produced in the U.N. survey I was quoting from do not accord with earlier figures produced by the Economic Commission for Africa, but when somebody writes down a figure and says, "This is the rate of growth of the African economy between 1950 and 1960," you and I know that there has been a lot of messing about with figures. (Laughter.)

Let us take these countries that have achieved this high rate and see what it is associated with. The big failure is in agriculture. The growth of output of agriculture is probably 2 to 3 per cent, or barely keep-ing up with the population growth, but on the other hand there have been enormous increases in mining out-put throughout the underdeveloped countries, not merely the output of oil, but iron, bauxite and all kinds of minerals, and the rate of growth of manufacturing has been extraordinarily high. Very many countries have seen a growth of manufacturing output of 8 or 9 per cent. They are starting from quite low levels of manu-facturing, perhaps 10 per cent of the GNP, but it all comes into the picture, and therefore, it is not really difficult to accept a 4 per cent rate of growth, cer-tainly not in Asia; and it is certainly possible for some economies of Africa, where a 4 per cent rate of growth is not at all out of the question. Africa as a whole, it seems to me, is a little more difficult to accept on that basis.

Mr. HOLT: You presented a comparison, Dr. Lewis, with the kind of development that occurred in eight-eenth- and nineteenth-century Europe, where factories grew up in barns and schools and rather out-of-the-way places; I got the impression from this comment that it might be desirable in developing countries today if there were less ostentation in the buildings and less concern for glory for the politicians and the architects. Were you also implying that conditions could be improved if there were a greater proportion of investment in the private sector?

Mr. LEWIS: Well, these fellows certainly are too prestige-minded, and this has a very high cost.

Mr. HOLT: Would not one of the solutions be to transfer some of this investment into the private sector?

Mr. LEWIS: I am merely pointing out that money goes much less far today than it used to go in the underdeveloped countries because of the difference in the channels through which it flows.

Export Development

Sister THOMASINE: Dr. Lewis, two years ago at one of these conferences I asked Professor Ellsworth what he would recommend in the way of increasing exports from Latin America.[8] He came over to me afterwards and said, "I did not answer your question, Sister, and I am not sure now that I could." I wonder now if you could answer it? If the export industry should increase in countries which, we will say, are typically or maybe at least partially agricultural, what can they increase and to whom will they sell it?

Mr. LEWIS: Well, this is a different subject, is it not?

Sister THOMASINE: I know, but you said that they had chronic deficits, and one of the ways of reducing the chronic deficits would be to increase their exports. I just wondered if you had ever given that any thought?

Mr. LEWIS: Yes. I have given it a lot of thought. The development of Latin America in the last 15 years or so, like the development of India, has been based to a considerable extent on import substitution which has its limits because you must have imports for which to

8. Ref. to Prof. P. T. Ellsworth, Dept. of Economics, University of Wisconsin, commenting at Midwest Research Conference on Obstacles to Economic Development in Underdeveloped Areas, Allerton House, University of Illinois, May 18-20, 1962. Proceedings not published.

substitute.

Brazil has had a very rapid increase of industrial production based on import substitution. It has had very great opportunities for doing this. If you have import substitution as a basis for your development, you do not run into balance-of-payments problems.

Chile is a highly developed economy. It has run through its possibilities for import substitution and cannot continue developing at a high rate now unless it can export, because the only alternative to developing through exports is developing through balanced growth, and for balanced growth you must have all of the resources required to meet a variety of growing demands. This is impossible in a country like Chile, and therefore it must expect its development to lead to higher imports which have to be met by higher exports.

Therefore, countries that have run through the import substitution possibility simply have to get back to looking at the export market. Now, in Chile their principal export has been copper, which has been greatly handicapped for years by an annual inflation of 20 per cent, which is a very serious handicap to any kind of export industry. The other thing that they have to do, and the thing to which the Chilean economists attach the greatest importance, is to increase the productivity of their agriculture. As you know, the structural inflation theory is that as the economy develops, there is a greater demand inside the economy for agricultural products and it is the failure of agriculture to respond, because of the absence of land reform, as they see it, that creates the major balance-of-payments problem, and so on.

The whole situation would be eased if these countries could succeed in licking the agricultural problem, just to meet the home demand, let alone the external demand.

Now, what about the longer run future? This is really outside tonight's frame of reference, but you have asked the question. As you know, in the 1950's world trade has been expanding at phenomenal rates, 6 or 7 per cent per annum, much greater than anything for the last hundred years, but the expansion of the exports of the underdeveloped countries has not been of this order of magnitude, and also world trade in primary products of the kinds that the underdeveloped countries produce has expanded only by 3.5 per cent per annum.

Some people who are concerned about the future of the underdeveloped countries, and who have been trying to calculate what the trade of the underdeveloped countries would be at a 5 per cent rate of growth of national output, have come up with very large increases in imports as being necessary; and do not see where the exports will come from. The way they look at it is that in the past the main market for the underdeveloped countries has been the developed countries and if the developed countries are only going to increase their demand by 3 per cent, where will the underdeveloped countries manage to get the foreign exchange to pay for what they need to import?

For myself, I think this is a kind of myopia, because it leaves out the possibility of the underdeveloped countries trading with each other. As the underdeveloped countries expand, one of the reasons why their import need goes up is because they need more raw materials and food products of various kinds; these they could get from each other. Even if what they want is machinery, or insofar as what they want is machinery, there is an easy answer. Because the future of India depends (given the particular set of natural resources India has and does not have) upon India's becoming a major producer of steel and machinery. So even if the developed countries were to sink under the sea, you can foresee the underdeveloped countries building up a very large trade among themselves in commodities of all kinds, both raw material commodities and industrial commodities. This is the thing which, it seems to me, is left out in all of these calculations which tell us that the underdeveloped countries are really sunk because the developed countries have such a slow population growth, and so forth.

My general answer to you, therefore, is that if the underdeveloped countries did indeed look at their exports again (they have neglected them, they have allowed export costs to rise and rise and rise beyond what the world market will permit) those that need to would find that this was an opportunity for growth. But this is a separate and large subject.

Education, Employment, and Expectations

Mr. ANDERSON: Supposing you could design an educational system for these developing countries--waiv-
ing, now, the question of whether what you would design
would be politically acceptable--can you design an educational system which would function under the dual and
to some degree contradictory conditions that A, it has
to be run by half-trained and half-literate teachers,
and that B, it must produce a sizable cohort of people
who can match world standards for secondary school performance and entrance to universities?

If you consider that question, this idea that
there is some new content of education that is going to
solve these problems will turn out to be more difficult

Mr. WILLIAMS: I have a comment to make and a ques
tion to ask.   They relate to this question of the relationship between the expansion of education and unemployment.

First, this problem of urban unemployment seems to
be one that has been with us for an enormously long
time.   In Africa, taking on the one hand Ghana, which
has very extensive educational facilities, and on the
other hand Togoland, which has very limited educational facilities, it was in Togoland and not in Ghana that
the unemployed threw out the President.   Certainly,
even if one looks at the history of the Gold Coast itself, I think one finds continually the complaints of
colonial governors that the problem about having an
educational system is that you get a drift of people to
the towns even though the educational system is extremely limited and by contemporary standards an inadequate
one.

My own feeling is that the reason people drift to
the towns is because this is where opportunities are.
If you extend educational opportunities, what happens
possibly is that you get a slightly higher level, in
educational terms, of unemployed in the towns.   But it
is not that the education itself creates a problem.   If
one attempted to establish some kind of operational
hypothesis about this, and relate those areas in which
this problem of urban unemployment is serious to the
existence of educational facilities, I do not think you
would find a very good correspondence.

The only area in which I have any personal experi-

ence, other than West Africa, is Central America; my
feeling is that the problem of urban unemployment is,
let us say, as serious in Guatemala City as it is in
Accra, and yet Guatemala is characterized by an educational system in which, while very many people go to
the first grades, very few people go beyond the third
grade. I think that the primary impact of expanding
educational opportunity is not that it creates a greater degree of unemployment per se, but that it may possibly create a somewhat more highly educated level of
unemployment.

　　To establish the view that education itself creates unemployment, or is a great stimulus to unemployment, one would have to show that people who have received an education have a rather unrealistic notion of
the probabilities of receiving employment. Phillip
Foster of the University of Chicago has an interesting
piece discussing the expectations of Ghanaian school-
leavers which shows that in fact they had really quite
sensible notions of what results they might expect.

　　It is, of course, true that because the opportunity exists in the city, a person might go there for a
little while and even expect temporary unemployment on
the off-chance of getting a good permanent job later.
In this sense he is something like a graduate student
who will stay around Chicago or Cambridge rather than
go to Hopscotch Junior College, because he knows that
once he goes there he is not going to get away.

　　In the same way, I think some people who have had
some education will go to the city rather than go to
the farm, because if they go on a farm they know they
are not going to get away. In terms of the amount of
education, I think it is probable that increasing the
amount of education simply means that what you have is
middle-school unemployed laborers, as you now have in
Accra, instead of third-form unemployed school-leavers,
as you had in Accra 30 years ago.

　　Mr. LEWIS: What I was talking about was societies
in which the entry into education has shot up from 20
per cent to 80 per cent in ten years. I was not saying
anything against education or pretending that education
is the major cause of this unemployment. I was saying
that if you have a community in which, over the course
of ten years, you increase the entry from 20 per cent
to 80 per cent, you get into trouble because the ex-

pectations of the 80 per cent are the same as the expectations of the 20 per cent and cannot be fulfilled.

But over and above this, your view of the situation in Accra and mine are not, by far, the same. When
I was in Accra advising the government, the ministers
were extremely bothered about the stream of people that
were coming out of the schools, and this was the reason
why, at very great expense, they established something
called the Builders Brigade; it was primarily to deal
with what they regarded as a very serious problem. Exactly the same problem exists now in both the Eastern
and Western regions of Nigeria. It is not due to education. It is due to the acceleration in such a short
period of time, and it is only to be found in the countries where they have made this particular effort.

Labor Unions

Mr. NASH: I spent about a decade disinterring the
hidden sociology in every economic statement. (Laughter.)

Let me see if I have the sociology of Dr. Lewis's
recommendations correct. It seems to me that we have
a built-in political-economic villain in the form of
trade unions which not only keeps productive wages high
but accounts for this phenomenon of the less productive
modern industries chasing after those; your hypothesis
for Japan sociologically was that the trade unions are
schizophrenic; they push the worker up in the modern
sector, they keep him down in the lower sector. I
think that is one of your important sociological assumptions: that the trade unions in these developing countries must be in opposition to the government, whereas
in Japan they must be an arm of the government. Would
you comment on this?

Mr. LEWIS: I gave three different reasons why
this is happening, of which the trade unions were one.
The second was the social conscience, which is stronger
in the second half of this century than it was in the
first half of the nineteenth century, so even in situations where there are no trade unions, the employers
regard it as their duty to keep paying higher and higher wages if they can. The third situation is linked
with the second, that the nationalist governments of
new states have been putting pressure on foreign

employers. No capitalist finding himself in Northern
Rhodesia or Trinidad is going to refuse to pay high
wages if he can afford to do it, whether there are
trade unions or not, because the government is breath-
ing down his neck. That is the third reason.

Mr. BINDER: You squeezed out the middle one, now.

Mr. LEWIS: No. The second is an independent
fact, too. Why, in Japan, do the modern capitalists
pay such high wages if they do not have to?

Mr. GINSBURG: Well, there are Japanese labor unions, and they are increasingly effective, but they are
less effective than they may be in some other places
largely because there are other institutions within
Japanese society that regulate economic behavior. I
would say also that industrialists in Japan are paying
increasingly higher wages because they do require ever
higher levels of skills. Literacy is not enough.

Mr. LEWIS: I really do not think that the sociologist should be surprised that in the twentieth century
the social conscience of capitalists is different from
what it was in the nineteenth, and they behave differently. This is happening all over the world. This is not
true only in the underdeveloped countries. You mean
you do not find this in the United States?

Mr. GINSBURG: I find that they are as rapacious
as they ever were.

Mr. WHITEFORD: I wanted to ask a question to see
whether I was coming to a logical conclusion as the result of what you said. In the modern segment of the
economy, where labor apparently is well organized in
unions and is asking for raises, you would recommend
that the raises not be given in order that income or
profits would flow back into the government and be distributed on a wider basis.

This, it seems to me, and I am not an economist,
would be possible only if this were private enterprise
and if the tax level was high enough to put the money
back into the general treasury. Even so, you would run
a very great risk of still having considerable profit
so that an increasingly wider range in income would
develop between those who owned the companies and the
labor force which was operating on a set level of
income.

I come to the conclusion, therefore, and I want to
know if this is correct, that the only way really to

balance this situation and keep the money going back into the general economy is for the government to own the industries?

Mr. LEWIS: That is certainly a way, but do not forget the 50 per cent corporation tax and the possibilities of partnership arrangements between governments and new industries opening up in their countries and so forth, of which there is a great deal.

The thing we are talking about now is the attitude of governments in underdeveloped countries to their trade unions, which is one of political crisis, especially in Africa, but not exclusively in Africa. In Africa government after government put into power by the trade unions turns round and kicks the trade unions in the teeth. It is a real problem, and there is no simple, easy solution to it.

Chairman BLANKSTEN: I once attended a meeting in which we had such a spirited and heated discussion that we ran far overtime in the session until finally somebody said, "Let's forget about what we are here for, and let's get back on schedule." (Laughter.)

We should have adjourned about a quarter of an hour ago. I am not going to try to summarize the discussion tonight. I think we have done a good job this evening of opening up a number of avenues which I hope we will be able to pursue during the next day-and-a-half of our sessions.

UNDERDEVELOPED COUNTRIES IN THE WORLD ECONOMY

Chairman BINDER: The procedure that we are to
follow in these sessions will be that we will impose
upon the discussion leader to make the initial presentation, and we expect him to put forth some bright and
interesting ideas that concern him and his own research
in recent years, months, days, hours, and minutes, and
to present any questions which he may have on his mind
and matters of general interest to us bearing on the
topic. Hopefully, these ideas would have some form to
them but not close off the rest of us from plunging in
with ideas of our own and perhaps capturing the ball
and taking it off in different directions in terms of
our own interests. It is an open-minded kind of goal
that we have.

The role of the discussants, after the opening remarks of the discussion leader, is, of course, critically important in that they are to set some of the direction as well as having the wonderful opportunity of
getting the first potshots at the discussion leader,
and hopefully they will add increased form to our de-
liberations. After each of the discussants has had an
opportunity to add his own ideas to those of the discussion leader, then we will have an open discussion
which will involve not merely questions but also length-
ier statements of your own on the matters that have
been brought before us.

Now, Professor Karl de Schweinitz, the discussion
leader, studied at Dartmouth where he got his Bache-
lor's degree in International Relations and later took
a doctorate at Yale in Economics. He is a Professor of
Economics at Northwestern University at the present
time, and he has just returned from Japan where he has
spent a year doing research on economic development and
political change since 1868. He is the author of the
book, Industrialization in Democracy, which was

published by the Free Press in 1964.

The two discussants are Professor Raymond Randall and Professor Andrew Whiteford. Dr. Randall is a member of the Department of Government at the University of Indiana, and his interest is in the decline of rationalism in Indonesia. He has spent some time in Indonesia in the public administration project which is being run under the auspices of the Department of Government of Indiana University.

Professor Whiteford is the head of the Department of Anthropology at Beloit College. He is associated with the Logan Museum. He has just had a wonderful year in Spain, which research experience has just been added to his previous research experience in Latin America, Colombia and Mexico, where he has done extensive studies on urban affairs, particularly the delineation of social class.

Mr. de SCHWEINITZ: Thank you.

There is and always will be a tension between macrocosmic and microcosmic approaches to knowledge, between those who have a bird's-eye view of detail and those who have a worm's-eye view of system. While the one often seems to do violence to the empirical and institutional data of the real world, the other sometimes seems to be engaged interminably in collecting unfocused facts and information. Happily, the two approaches are indispensable for one another and so will continue in sibling rivalry, whatever one might say about either one.

I do not make these observations as a preface to an exegesis on research methodology for underdeveloped countries. Rather they are intended to prepare the way for a confession of my preference for the macrocosmic approach. The remarks that follow, therefore, should be compensated for this bias.

My bias, no doubt, is appropriate for the subject of this morning's discussion. "Underdeveloped Countries in the World Economy" is nothing if not a broad topic. Indeed I suspect that it is a kind of academic come-on designed to trap the wary professor. After all, who will admit he doesn't have something to say about it?

Let me start by paying my respects to economics. In recent years it has been belabored, both inside and outside the ranks, for failing to solve the enigma of

development. The realization that the non-Western
world has not responded to economic parameters in the
same manner as the Western world in its initial industrialization has somehow been disillusioning; the tools
of economic analysis no longer seem quite so powerful
as they did when confined to their indigenous habitat.

Yet without economics it would have been impossible to map the terrain of the underdeveloped countries.
The innovations of the 1930's, especially in the realm
of macroeconomics, have subsequently borne fruit in the
measures of income and product by which we now can establish rough approximations of stages or degrees of
development. It goes without saying that we never can
have enough data of this sort. It is essential for
knowing how we stand, whether we have moved forward or
backward, and for estimating the magnitude of the tasks
before us.

Moreover, economic models at least form a skeletal
framework to which one may attach the institutional
flesh, sinew, and muscle essential for its motion.
Analysis of saving, investment, and technological
change, for example, highlights the role of the entrepreneur in development. If he has, in point of fact,
not been sufficiently active in the underdeveloped
countries, or has not labored in an environment conducive to growth projects, economics can hardly be
held responsible.

But contemplating the growing number of underdeveloped countries in the world economy, I am struck,
if I may now be provocative, by the large gap between
economics and the other disciplines. It would, of
course, be far from the truth to say that the tasks of
economics have been completed, but there is certainly
a kernel of truth in the notion that responsibility for
explaining how the mechanics of development, so copi-
ously described by economists, are to be set in motion
now rests with the sister disciplines. Let me acknowl-
edge immediately that this statement is unfair.

I once heard Kenneth Boulding berating a group of
political scientists for not having solved the problem
of war, when economists had solved the problem of unemployment. There is not much doubt but that problems
of inducement and motivation are a good deal more difficult to explain than analyses of mechanisms. Nonetheless, this does not deny that the most important

areas of research in the underdeveloped countries lie outside economics.

Judging by the interest evoked among students of underdeveloped countries by the recent works of David McClelland and Everett Hagen, I gather that the views I have expressed here about the limits of economics are widely shared. The Achieving Society[1] and On the Theory of Social Change[2] provide a convenient point of departure for my remarks about research needs outside of economics. For while I applaud the imagination, verve, and industry with which McClelland and Hagen have explored the murky realm of the individual psyche, I am far from being convinced that we all ought to become psychologists or psychoanalysts. I suspect, indeed, that their work is informed by a search for first causes which can no more be tracked down than the fountain of youth. Further, their preoccupation with the why of development tends to divert attention from the how.

Falling back now on my methodological bias, it seems to me that the most fruitful area for research lies in the organizational, macrocosmic dimension, specifically in the area of politics. I have the impression that in the underdeveloped countries there is no lack of willingness to work, no fear of making money, perhaps even no scarcity of entrepreneurs.

The problem is the absence of an institutional context capable of focusing the potential energy and drives of individuals and groups on the production of the goods and services which generate sustained growth. Moreover, the stimuli for economic development are ubiquitous to the point of being overbearing. They no doubt are not so effective as they once were in transmitting the forces for autonomous industrialization.

The late Professor Nurkse has made us all aware of how the changing structure of demand in the advanced economies has tended to reduce the rate at which the

1. David Clarence McClelland, The Achieving Society (Princeton, N.J.: Van Nostrand, 1961).
2. Everett Einar Hagen, On the Theory of Social Change: How Economic Growth Begins (A study from the Center for International Studies, Massachusetts Institute of Technology; Homewood, Ill.: Dorsey Press, 1962).

markets for the primary products of the underdeveloped
economies grow, thus threatening them with a perennial
balance-of-payments problem. Nor are these countries
likely to attract private capital or a skilled professional, technical, and administrative migrant population. Yet, the demonstration effect broadcasts the
glories of material well-being to all and to at least
a few a burning desire to develop the potential of
their country's resource endowments.

The drive for independence itself in the formerly
colonial world is a manifestation of the stimuli for
development. However mistaken they may be in their expectations, the leaders of the new countries in Asia
and Africa believe that independence places destiny in
their hands and that they can consciously achieve what
so many of the old nations in the Western world did un-
consciously through the private market economy.

But why do I single out politics as the most important sector on the research front in underdeveloped
countries? Because, as suggested above, the responsibility for surmounting the obstacles to development now
seems to fall on government. Whether these obstacles
are sociological, economic, or political, the systematic use of the collective and legitimate power of society is needed to clear them away.

I should quickly observe that I do not necessarily
have in mind a Leviathan that dragoons and coerces the
civil community into growing and modernizing, as, say,
in Russia or China. But suppose that the difficulty in
an underdeveloped country is the vast gulf between the
elite and the masses which inhibits mobility and per-
petuates a social order that ascribes roles and depre-
ciates achievement criteria. Surely it is in the political realm that the initiative must be taken for
modernizing these social conditions. And certainly
there is plenty of evidence, as, say, in Latin America,
that when a feudal elite retains a monopoly of political power there is little progress in establishing the
pre-conditions of development.

Or how is the underdeveloped country to cope with
rural and urban idleness? Whether one attacks it from
the demand or the supply side, i.e., providing jobs for
the existing unemployed or training them for useful
skills, government, as a minimum, must determine the
investment priorities likely to bring about the desired

result.

And most ineluctable of all, how is an underdeveloped country going to tackle any of these problems if
it does not contain a widely held consensus which con-
fers legitimacy on government and thus gives it leeway
to deal with them in a systematic and rational manner.
In countries that are not yet nations and bereft of the
communion of national origins so useful in muting de-
bilitating conflict, the first order of business must
be the manufacturing of consensus. And this as often
as not leads to domestic policies and foreign adven-
tures which are not consistent with the needs of the
country for economic development, at least in the short
run. At a time when new countries are proliferating so
rapidly in the wake of receding empires, this surely is
the pre-eminent problem.

It seems to me that by now we have accumulated a
tremendous amount of material which throws light on the
relationship between politics and economic development.
We have, in the first place, the historical experience
of the Western world where industrialization took place
in political systems stabilized within nation-states.
Secondly, there is the brilliant performance of Japan
where the leaders of the Meiji Restoration achieved an
extraordinary tour de force in adapting traditional institutions to the formation of a modern state while
shedding those customs and traditions which interfered
with the economic mobilization of the society. Thirdly, the centrally administered economies in Russia,
China, Yugoslavia, and Eastern Europe provide varied
case studies of the consequences for modernization of
an explicit commitment to the use of the coercive powers of the state to create an institutional environment conducive to growth. The non-incremental, Utopian
deployment of political power in these societies can
reveal a good deal about the limits of collective action. Fourthly, in the underdeveloped countries today,
unhappily, there is no lack of examples of states which
must devote a large part of their energy and resources
to establishing the legitimacy of their political power.
In the Congo, Indonesia, and South Vietnam one observes
various approaches to this end, none of which can be
said to confer growth benefits on the societies.

Out of this experience it ought to be possible to
generate political theories of varying degrees of

generality which could guide us in evaluating the prospects for the underdeveloped countries of the world.
Indeed, if I were Commissar of Research, I would want,
for the time being, to place more emphasis on theorizing than on collecting new data in case studies.
I would urge Gabriel Almond to try again. I would also
urge the country specialists to acquire new countries
in new settings, i.e., Africanists to become Asianists
and vice versa, in the hope that this broadening of
interest and experience would stimulate the capacity
for generalization.

Finally, I would want my political scientists to
be insistent on the primacy of politics in their search
for the how of development and not be diverted by
multifactor explanations giving equal weight to all
factors. That may make good history, but does not always make good analysis. My instructions, then, are
for the theorists to mobilize the role of political
power and authority in explaining development, as
David McClelland mobilized the "need for achievement"
and Everett Hagen the "withdrawal of status respect."

Mr. WHITEFORD: In introducing opposing points of
view at this particular point in our calendar, we could
predict that Dr. de Schweinitz' emphasis upon the role
of government would be emphatically opposed by many
people--Barry Goldwater for example. We can, I think,
all accept with sympathy Dr. de Schweinitz' desire to
see political stability, and we can recognize this as
a necessity for economic development. Certainly the
situations in Southeast Asia, Latin America and Africa
point up the very great importance of this factor. We
can also agree, I think, with his recommendation or his
stipulation that such a government not be a dictatorship or some other kind of coercive force. This is a
particular bias in our own case as we are committed to
the fundamentals of democracy. Third, I think we can
accept his basic assumption that the government must,
as he says, contain a widely held consensus which con-
fers legitimacy to deal with these problems.

Certainly on these three factors we can be in
basic agreement, or at least I find myself in agreement
with him. He also wants to concentrate research on the
problems of how economic development and political stability can be attained and, at least temporarily, put
in a secondary-seat research which is focused on the

why. At the same time he proposes a de-emphasis upon
what he calls multifactor explanations.

This is the point at which I, with my own particular anthropological bias, would raise questions and
perhaps objections. Dr. de Schweinitz says that he has
been provocative here and in some respects I get pro-
voked, which is exactly what I think should happen, because it appears to me that, in some regards, he has
expressed desires for various things which may not fit
together; at least there is going to be difficulty in
attaining all of these things simultaneously, or even
in rather rapid succession, without their interfering
with each other. It appears to be assumed that the forces of government already have access to viable, depend-
able programs for the attainment of economic development; the only further need is for research to provide
guidance in instrumenting them. It is suggested that
we (the government) now know what should be done but
not how to do it.

Professor Lewis has given us examples from the
Barbados in regard to the unemployment situation. Here
unemployment became one of the major issues in the
election; the party which had made unemployment an issue won the election and after putting its plans into
effect discovered that it was dealing with something it
really had not understood before it came to power.
This is certainly one example of the kind of situation
which can arise where a governmental organization decides that it has in mind a valuable program without
knowing something about its actual roots. Perhaps our
own farm program would equally suggest such a shortcom-
ing. I am sure there is an unending number of situations that could be dredged up to give some valid suspicion to the assumption that the government really
knew what it was trying to do or that what it was trying
to do was actually in the best interests of the country.

The second assumption about which I would like to
raise some question is that the government should or
would dedicate itself primarily to economic development.
The question immediately arises: "whose economic development?" Is there such a thing as general national
economic development, or in every kind of economic development are there certain sectors or segments of the
population which become more economically developed
than others? Who is in the driver's seat and who is

going to derive the greatest amount of benefit from any particular economic development program which is put into operation?

There have been situations which raise questions in regard to this assumption of Professor de Schweinitz. For instance, in Latin America various governments have been forced into programs of land reform which are in the interest of national economic development, but which actually tend to reduce gross productivity. The governments, nevertheless, find themselves in a situation where the programs are <u>politically</u> necessary even if they do not attain the economic ends which it was hoped they might.

Part of this, of course, is involved in the attainment of the consensus that Dr. de Schweinitz desires, but the consensus which is attained might actually be pointed toward or be utilized for the development of other goals than the immediate economic goal which was the objective of the land reform program. He might well serve to prevent violent political revolution at the price of reduced agricultural production.

The point has already been made several times, and could be documented almost unendingly, that all the people in a given nation or in a given society are not equally concerned with, nor equally convinced that, the improvement of gross national product is an immediately valuable end in itself. In other words, the ends which the government is trying to attain have to be made sensible to a considerable portion of the population for any sort of a consensus to be developed. This is difficult.

The third point is Dr. de Schweinitz' assumption that we now possess adequate information regarding <u>why</u> and can concentrate on the <u>how</u>, and also his rejection, or at least temporary rejection, of multifactor explanations. I realize that multifactor explanations always give the impression at the outset of complicating the issue, but it also seems to me that one of the reasons they give this appearance is that the issues actually are complicated. Any attempt we make to eliminate multifactoral explanations tends to oversimplify the problems with the danger of distorting them out of their reality. My multifactoral anthropological orientation insists that it is only from multifactoral exploration and investigation that the eventual solutions will come.

If there are going to be real solutions, we are
going to have to take into consideration a very great
number of the forces which are operating in any society.
In order to develop the stability from which economic
development may come we must know why the peasant feels
he wants to own a piece of land before we can convince
him that there is perhaps a better solution to his
problems than simply possessing his own private plot.
The same thing applies to the sentiments, and I am talking about feelings--the visceral reactions--of the
hacendado who objects to giving up his land, or to the
Indian who prefers his old ways of life to new forms
under a government program.

What I am saying here raises the matter of the
psyche that Mr. de Schweinitz mentioned because, after
you get under the programs, after you get under the
structure, the sentiments of the people involved are
really of fundamental importance. We can only understand what motivates people, or why they reject or accept particular programs which government may propose,
by a thorough exploration of the cultural context within which these people operate. This is my anthropological bias right out in the open.

The only alternative to some kind of extensive
multifactor exploration, it seems to me, is some kind
of authoritarian regime. This is no more desirable to
Mr. de Schweinitz than it is to the rest of us, but it
necessitates some sort of authoritarian regime which
assumes that it knows what is best--on the basis of research or on the basis of some other factors--and decides to ignore the feelings of the ignorant populace.
This way a program can be put into operation very rapidly, and a great number of changes can be introduced--
perhaps successfully. We are well aware, as anthropologists, that, within the relatively short period of
a generation, a great many sentiments can be changed
also, but whether or not this is actually the "best"
means of attaining the sort of ends with which we are
concerned, is one of the issues raised by Professor
de Schweinitz. Perhaps I have overinterpreted him; if
I have, so much the better.

Mr. RANDALL: I am one of these people who is going to back into this from the microcosmic standpoint.
My experience in the field of development administra-

tion comes from a very specific experience in Indonesia
and a very enlightening and constructive experience immediately following that in the Philippines. Prior to
that I was only incidentally exposed to this area in
the form of public administration, but public administration as it is practiced by the federal government.

I am going to, if I may, give you some information
that is more illustrative of the thesis presented here
this morning than anything else. In terms of the decline of rationalism as I saw it in Indonesia, it was
very much a puzzle to me as an amateur economist. It
seems to me, however, that the Indonesians tend to
approach, since 1952 at least, since the fall of the
Wilopo cabinet, everything in terms of the context of
emotional nationalism. The only things that are really
efficient in Indonesia are the printing presses, and
they approach the problem of economic planning, for example, from a very immature standpoint. It reminds me
of the lady who went into the publisher and said,
"What is the length of the average novel?" The publisher said, "Fifty thousand words," and she said,
"Goody, goody, I'm done."

The Indonesians constructed their eight-year plan
on much the same premise. They got their independence
on August 17, 1945, so they constructed their eight-
year plan in terms of eight parts, seventeen volumes,
1,945 paragraphs. Now, this is a very puzzling kind
of thing. We were assigned the job of training individuals in the civil service of the Indonesian government to try to develop a rational administrative
base for the Indonesian government.

One of the things we ran into quickly was the emphasis upon ascriptive criteria as against achievement
criteria for selecting people to come to the United
States. We tried as best we could to break this down,
to try to get a broader base of selection for these
people, on the thesis that a participant training program should communicate both hope and promise to those
people who were not selected as well as to those who
were selected, that both groups should understand the
basis for either action in terms of the standards as
they were derived for the selection of these people.
This the Indonesians simply would not go along with.
They were using the development of high talent manpower in Indonesia as a means of building personal

empires, in my opinion, rather than in terms of building the country.

Now, in terms of a strategy that goes beyond what
we know now in the field of development economics and
development administration, I am much impressed, as I
follow it, with Harbison's thesis on human capital formation. Harbison has a three-fold strategy, if I read
him correctly. His strategy for the short run, or up
to three or four years, is that of in-service training,
of getting the expatriate institutions to do a good job
of training individuals within their organization and
trying to get a seeding effect from this training back
into the community at large.

We estimated in Indonesia, for example, that the
high-talent manpower need for the country in terms of
executives and entrepreneurs was in the neighborhood of
30,000 people, something on that order of magnitude.
Using the Harbison formula for a tactical supportive
group, this would then give us something of the order
of magnitude of 100,000 technicians. This in itself
prescribes a major effort in one of the areas mentioned in the paper this morning and that is that of institution-building: institution-building in the form of
universities to provide the foundation for future training, and institution-building in the form of training
institutions that are capable of carrying on this job.
Just recently, an institution-building consortium has
been established which will tackle this problem. This
consists of Pittsburgh, Syracuse, and Indiana, and the
direction for this institution-building consortium will
come out of Pittsburgh. I think it holds a great deal
of promise in terms of a new research approach and a
new perspective on the problem of development administration and development economics.

GENERAL DISCUSSION

Mr. de SCHWEINITZ: I would like to make a few
comments about Professor Whiteford's comments on my
opening remarks.

On the issue of whether government knows best, I
do not take any position on this. I simply observe
that in the world today relative to the world of the
nineteenth century government does seem to be playing

a much more important role and apparently this is because the conditions confronting the underdeveloped economies are such that one does not get autonomous growth generated in the private sectors. I do not mean to suggest that in consequence of these conditions you have to have central planning. There are any number of policy measures that can be devised to generate development, but it seems to me that it is hard to deny that in the underdeveloped world today, government plays a role which it did not play in the nineteenth century.

Now, as far as the multifactor analysis is concerned, as an economist I am somewhat interested in economizing effort, and I think, if we are trying to develop the predictive capacity of the social sciences, we have to look at the relevant variables and select some that we think are more important. Just as in the nineteenth century I have some sympathy with a historical approach to economic development, so in this century I have some sympathy to some kind of political determinism because it seems to be the role of government, and the uses of political power are so much more important now than they were in a day when it was more reasonable to wait upon the private sector of the economy to generate development.

Chairman BINDER: We have before us a number of issues to which I will try to call your attention. I see some of the problems that have been raised in this way:

The problems of development which we want to see in the light of world economy, it has been suggested, might better be seen in the light of world political developments.

The international political scene was not so much delineated but it was suggested as a possible source of some of the difficulties of development. Indeed, the approach to economic development was seen in this context with obstacles which suggest that there is perhaps some reality to looking at the political over against the economic rather than seeing these as two facets of the same thing. In other words, the question that has been raised here in the reification of the disciplinary and analytical differences between the political and the economic which I think was spoken to by Mr. Whiteford in his own phraseology.

The central problem, though, if I understood it

correctly, is that of an institutional framework by which development may proceed. The question which follows immediately from this is whether or not the international community, international agencies, the United Nations, or something like that, or simply the framework of international politics can supply an institutional framework which the underdeveloped countries themselves cannot supply.

The centrality of the role of government has been questioned and it has been suggested by one of our discussants that we must consider economic development as one possible value over against other values and that we must bear in mind the redistributive character of economic development, that some parts of the economy will be benefited over against others.

Unspoken explicitly but nevertheless implicit in our discussion has been the problem of trade between the underdeveloped countries themselves that was raised by Professor Lewis, the relations between the underdeveloped countries and the larger economic complexes, such as the European Common Market, and the possible success or failure of regional trading arrangements in Latin America or in the Arab world under the auspices of the Arab League.

The problem of whether heavy industry should precede light industry as a policy was touched on, politics, of course, having its bearing on this. Unspoken but quite implicit, I think, in the discussion has been the contrasting roles of private investors, of public, of other governments and international agencies--the three areas of responsibility, perhaps.

Finally, there is the problem of understanding how the world economy has changed. Professor Lewis has mentioned the sharp increase in foreign trade. I do not know how to read statistics, but it seems to me that there has been some sort of a boom in the price of raw materials--perhaps I shall be corrected on that by some knowledgeable people--in recent years and there has been apparently a great spread of technology and capacity for manufacturing into many countries, so that there is possibly some increased competition between the older manufacturing countries and some of the newer ones, requiring shifts in the orientation of the economies in the developed countries.

These, I think, are the problems that are before

us.

Institution Building and Economic Development

Mr. NASH: One thing about social science is that it is the kind of enterprise in which you cannot keep a rousing hypothesis down.   They keep cropping up.

I think in 15 years of work--and I think that is a real number--in the underdeveloped countries we have at least stopped talking about them as though they were a single species of poverty.   In some underdeveloped areas the government is not even capable of carrying out the minimal requirements for the administration of peace and order, and to expect that kind of apparatus to undertake anything in the way of economic development, I think, is silly.

In some places the government is consensual, legitimate, but not dedicated to development, so the first thing I contemplate is to leave the disciplines aside, scan the real world again and see what kind of poor countries there are out there.

As to recommendations about government, it depends upon what kind of governments and where.   If you have a theory as to what governments are viable enough to carry out projects in addition to governing, that would be of some use.

There is another thing I would like to comment on. There is still some echo or prerequisite thinking of framework, of institution building, and I think that is retrograde.   Most of the cultural and social change that goes along with economic development is coterminous in the product of development.   There is the kind of thinking that says, "Let's change the society's culture and then we will develop."   I do not think that has ever happened historically.   Every country has developed its modern institutions in the act of modernizing, and you cannot build them first and then set them in motion.   I think those two links ought to break at least one side of the box.

Mr. HARING: I want to question Mr. Nash on his comment that you do not build institutions and then set them in motion.   Certainly there are such things as economic systems which governments legislate into being.   True, governments may not consciously legislate them into being, and I would say historically they

have practically never done so, fully consciously,
knowing all that is going to happen or foreseeing it.
Governments may often legislate economic systems into
being by implication rather than specifically.

A laissez-faire government--if there is such an
animal, the term is no good--but a government that
thinks of itself as a laissez-faire government is simply delegating to others various areas of responsibility. Such delegation, even if it is unconscious, even
if it is implicit, is nevertheless real because responsibility is made to lie with the community as a whole
and the community as a whole is headed up in the government, which is a sort of a shorthand definition of
government.

It seems to me, therefore, that the government,
always, inherently, in any situation, at any time and
place, is the primary piece of the puzzle. But this
does not mean that governors understand this to be so.
I am looking back, now, with the benefit of hindsight.

More specifically, with respect to this building
of institutions, the public school system in the United
States was not built, I take it, with the notion of
modernizing the country to prepare for later stages of
the Industrial Revolution. I am sure that was not in
mind. There were other specific objects in mind that
we know about, rather romantic notions of democracy and
community and the common man, equalitarianism, and this
sort of thing, which all got into it.

This is all history, but nevertheless, is not the
net effect of this to have built institutions that made
possible the later stages of industrial development? If
I am right, then it seems to me what we do is look back
to find out not merely what was consciously in people's
minds, but what actually took place whether they knew
it or not (insofar as we think we can know it) and then
apply the lessons. So it seems to me that we do not
have a terribly difficult problem with respect to the
relationship of economics to politics.

Mr. NASH: I did not mean to imply that political
activities were not consequential. When I referred to
building an institution, I meant that people do not sit
down and design and in the real social world build the
institution they design. They are always in inadvert-
ent consequences of a purpose of action, to lift a line
from another intelligent sociologist. Governments are

in some countries extremely consequential, and I think, if we traced it out to the real world again, we would find that in most places, India excluded, the consequential acts of government have been anti-developmental rather than pro-developmental.

Regardless of the intention, the institutions they have built have resulted in the clustering of industry around capital cities and a whole brokerage system, licensing and money problems. The source of change, the things that stimulate and affect governments themselves, are the sources of stimulative effect of whole populations. The government is not a separate kind of animal anywhere that is moving to its own drum beats, so we have to get wider social causes than just what they write in five-year plans, because nobody acts on them very much.

Mr. HOLT: I certainly would agree with Professor Nash if he is holding up a straw man of a country concerned with development deciding that it has to have a full-blown educational system and this institutional development and that institutional development before it can get under way with the business of economic growth. On the other hand, if you are looking at the analysis of historical cases of development, it seems to me that you can observe certain developments in Tokugawa, Japan, which were institutionally prerequisite to the kind of changes that occurred at the time of the Meiji Restoration. We could do the same thing for England in the seventeenth and early part of the eighteenth century.

I think part of our theory has to recognize that there are certain kinds of policies and certain kinds of developments that require a certain base and that the lines of development are in some ways sequential lines. If you are going to try to get to C, which is development, and you are at A, somehow you have to go to B, and if you attempt to go directly from A to C, you will probably be met with continual frustration.

In this sense, not in the sense of deliberately building institutions, some concern with requisites or prerequisites would seem to me to be realistic.

The Effectiveness of Theory

Mr. BLANKSTEN: I have three things I want to say

in reaction to Professor de Schweinitz' paper. The
first has to do with what has been called here the
reification of interdisciplinary differences, and it
strikes me that in a large sense he has done this. The
question that seems to me to be central when we gather
together people of different disciplines focusing on a
common problem is--What is it we should be doing together?--and it seems to me that what Professor de
Schweinitz has given us here in the relationship among
disciplines, especially between economics and political
science, is a kind of a division of labor in which one
discipline says to the other, "You provide the stimulus and I'll watch the response." (Laughter.)

I am not sure that this is the best way we can
work together on an interdisciplinary basis, even
though, looking back over some of my own work in this
field, I suppose I have to admit I have been somewhat
guilty of this. I like to assume that economic development is taking place and I have looked for the political implications or the political response. My
first question would look toward some more fruitful
mechanism for interdisciplinary research here.

The second general point I want to make had to do
with the kind of research that Professor de Schweinitz
is urging on political scientists. I think that there
is a kind of fallacy in the notion that the role of
government is central in economic development, therefore it is up to the political scientist to do the research on what it is that government should do to give
the economist something else to watch happen. Do you
really believe that the most important research contribution that political scientists can make is the production of data for policy recommendations which will
enable governments to institute programs for the stimu-
lation of economic change?

My third point, and with respect to this I feel
more like a devil's advocate than in what I have said
so far, has to do with the relative priorities between
further theoretical work on the one hand and the gath-
ering of data on the other. We have now for many years
been saying what Professor de Schweinitz says when he
urges that we place more emphasis on theorizing than on
collecting new data in case studies. I agree with that,
but it seems to me I have been agreeing with it for at
least 15 years. When I read back and try to count the

number of conferences I have been involved in and the number of times those of us interested in underdeveloped areas have undertaken some project--it seems to me that it must be at least the last 15 years--that we have all sat down together and said, "Look: we need more theory." As I say, I agree, but how long do we stay in this same box?

I notice that Professor de Schweinitz, in making this suggestion, says "for the time being." Looking at the title of this Conference, one of the things I understand we are going to try to do is reappraise some of the work in economic development. After something like 15 years of talking this way and thinking this way, is this kind of relationship between theory and data collection still the same, or do we move anywhere; and are there new ways of formulating this relationship; and are there new kinds of things we might do in each of these areas?

These are my three simple questions.

Sister THOMASINE: The innumerable theories and some of the policies that have been proposed over the last 15 years can and should be reassessed, especially in the case of priority, and I think Professor Lewis's reassessment is fruitful in the economic field. We do now know things we were just guessing at then. As yet we do not know too much, but we do know a few things that we were just guessing at in 1945 and 1947. That is one part of the awakening of the economist, it seems to me, as regards economic development.

Currently, however, economists have become extremely aware of the non-economic factoral approach. The institutional question that has just been raised seems to me to point to this other aspect, namely, that institutions can prove to be obstacles in the way of economic development. Institutions, and I am thinking of the one to which I belong, need a good nudge once in a while, and yet certainly institutions have to be preserved.

Mr. ANDERSON: I would assume that within the limits of the state of the art, the economist can lay down a list of some of the kinds of policies that need to be adopted by a government. For example, "Wage rates shall not be more than X percentage above such-and-such." From the political scientist I would like to hear some considered judgments on certain issues,

distinguishing two things. One is the question that
has been raised this morning and that always comes up,
namely, what is the effect on economic development of
having the entrepreneurs preponderantly civil servants?

Then there is an entirely different kind of question that relates to the bearing upon economic development of the degree or kind of political arousal of population, of the ways in which the interests of the sectors of the public are articulated in relation to
government policy or are not, and so on. These are
fairly specific issues which I may be stating in rather
amateurish words, but I think the political scientists
here ought to tell us about them.

Mr. HARING: With respect to this matter of civil
servants, I would like to ask the economist: what do
you think of the Russian experience? Did anything
suffer, aside from the damaging trial and error, which
is always involved, but did anything suffer from the
main actors being on the government payroll?

Mr. LEWIS: I very much want to follow up what
Professor Anderson said because in advising quite a
number of these countries, I have come to the conclusion that by comparison with the politics of economic
development, the economics of economic development is
really trivial; I say that remembering what John Stuart
Mill said about economics.

The really serious problems unsolved are the political problems and unless we solve the political problems we cannot hope to see the kind of economic development we would like to see. Now, I keep wondering:
what do the political scientists have to contribute, or
what are they contributing in this field? One of the
things one takes for granted is that these countries
need to establish a decent civil service. The governments do not take it for granted because the party and
the civil service are in many of these countries locked
in struggle. But one must look further than this.

As I look around at these new countries, I see
very many that have fallen into the hands of rogues.
An enormous proportion of the governments of new countries consist of rogues who are feathering their own
nests. Now, political scientists have been studying
for two or three thousand years what is necessary in a
society to prevent rogues from getting into political
power, and they ought really to be able to contribute

and help to create institutions--I do not know whether
I can get away with saying this--institutions, frames
of mind, or something which will be helpful to these
countries, but I have yet to hear a political scientist
in Ghana, Nigeria, Bolivia, Burma, or anywhere say
something useful about how to create a viable political
society.

The economists keep on saying what they think is
right to create economic development, but what do political scientists have to say to Ghana, or Kenya or
any of these places?

Mr. ANDERSON: In fact, don't most political scientists today defend the rogues?

Mr. LEWIS: Yes, they do. They tell us what wonderful guys they are. (Laughter.)

Mr. HOLT: I think you can defend the rogues, and
you can defend the rogues in terms of the experience
of economic development in countries in the nineteenth
century. I object to economists and others saying,
"Many of these problems of development are political
problems. We would like to hear the political scientists tell us about them." Typically, they define the
question too narrowly; they want the political scientist to tell them how to control the rogues. They do
not ask the question: what is the appropriate role of
the government for political development and what kind
of people do you have to have in crucial governmental
roles?

Mr. LEWIS: I would like to look at the situation
in India. India has tremendous economic problems and
it has even more tremendous political problems. Economists have done a tremendous amount of work on the
Indian economy and have said a lot of useful things to
the Indian government, many of which India has put into effect with the consequence that we are told India
had a per capita fall in national income consistently
from 1900 to 1950, but has had a $1\frac{1}{2}$ to 2 per cent rise
in per capita national income consistently since 1950.
Economists make mistakes, but they clearly have something to say to India. Much more important than the
Indians' economic problem is the Indians' political
problem--the possibility of survival in India of something political that is worth preserving--but I have
yet to hear a single note from a political scientist
of any use to the Indians in solving this important

problem.

I feel sad about this. I would like to hear this note, because I think it is much more important than anything we economists have to say. India is just an example. The same is true of all these new African states that are coming forward. They can send to the United Nations and ask for assistance and they can get some sound economic advice. If they send to the United Nations and ask for a political advisor he will tell them something about creating a civil service system, but that is a minor matter in the larger context of the political problem.

Mr. KING: I wonder whether it is fair to expect a political scientist, or anybody else, to go to a country and do anything more than "tinker" with the civil service?

Supposing the only legitimate answer to Mr. Sukarno would be to say, "Step down." This is surely a solution open only to the Central Intelligence Agency if it is indeed open to them. To get rid of the rogue, they have to identify him, and this has caused trouble before.

This leads me to a generalization. When you ask whether the people in underdeveloped countries are or are not ready for democracy, you are asking the wrong question. It is not whether the people are ready or not for democracy; it is whether the leading group or elite is willing to accept it. If the elite, as in this country, decides that they would not back Mr. Washington for king, then Mr. Washington would be president. I seem to have aroused something.

Mr. LEWIS: You can say that about Sukarno but you cannot say that about Nyerere. It is not the most desirable thing in Indonesia that Mr. Sukarno remain, but anybody who knows Mr. Nyerere knows that it is the most important thing for Tanganyika that Mr. Nyerere should remain. Mr. Nyerere is in serious political trouble. He needs political advice. The Russians are willing to give it to him and the Chinese are willing to give it to him. What do we have to offer?

Sister THOMASINE: Could it be that people trained in the Anglo-American tradition in politics have a certain reticence about giving advice?

Mr. WARREN: My own training is not in economics or in political science. Often, as I listen to the

discussion, I wonder why I am here, but I see, that underlying the topic of this morning's discussion, and
underlying the topic of the Conference, is a desire--
and no one discusses this--a desire on the part of some
one, or the members of some group, to induce change in
someone else or in some other group.

In all of the discussions we have treated countries as units, and have discussed how these units, by
some means or another, should be changed in the same
way that personality is viewed as the unit by the psy-
chologist; and in changing the individual you must con-
sequently, in some manner, change the personality.

Mr. de Schweinitz' point of view, then, of approaching culture change or social change or economic
change through government is perfectly plausible, because this is the expedient approach. This is the way
to connect one of our units or one of our countries to
another country, or one country to another country, because this is the only line of communication that is
possible.

You cannot connect one government to another government and hope, then, that the second government
will respond in some way as a result of its connection.
You can attempt to bypass the government, and we tried
this, too, in Radio Free Europe, for instance, hoping
to induce change in the people by going around the government, but in most cases all of our efforts to induce
change in the so-called underdeveloped countries in the
world must be through their governments, or else it
seems to be illegitimate in some manner or another.

We have other tactics of inducing change but up to
now government seems to be the most appropriate way of
doing this, so until we find some other way of hooking
our unit or our country to these other countries, or to
the people of these other countries, and inducing
change, then the governmental approach, or the approach
through the political scientists, seems to me to be the
most expedient approach.

Mr. MORGAN: It struck me what a fine example of
humility we from different disciplines have been suc-
cessively giving in arguing that some other discipline
than our own holds the key to the problems of the underdeveloped countries. One after the other of us has
done this, and probably often rightly.

In this connection: economists argue plausibly

that rogues in economics have often been quite useful socially--despite themselves. There have been exceptions to the rule, of course. But there is a good deal to be said for it. It is in contrast, much harder to find support for the social usefulness of rogues and scoundrels in other lines of activity, notably government.

Several of us here are refugees, in a sense, from Indonesia. Experience there brings the issue to mind. The government there does count in economic life, and its pursuit of political advantage has had disastrous economic repercussions.

We have the notion that patriotism, or nationalism, is the last refuge of a scoundrel. It is more clearly the first resort of the scoundrel in politics, frequently with baleful effects on economic affairs. Perhaps the specialists here in political science can suggest to us how the burden of nationalist policies can be made lighter. How can we substitute rationality for nationalism?

Mr. ANDERSON: Last night we were given an economist's dictum which I will vulgarize as follows: strong, autonomous labor unions stultify development--economic development.

Now, is a political scientist willing to give us a similar dictum which I will vulgarize: a universal suffrage electoral system will preclude the possibility of sound governmental policy for economic development. Why don't the political scientists come out and tell us something here? You are talking about international politics.

Mr. NASH: I am not a political scientist, but I want to take on part of the burden that Mr. Lewis laid at the doorstep of those beleaguered gentlemen.

One of the major questions being asked is, how do you form a polity--a civic consensual polity--that can get on with the job of economic development. I have been reflecting on it offhand and I think most of the polities that have gotten on with economic development have had a shared and bloody experience. To get consensus, and to get a feeling of being members of a nation who would take a discount in real income for the benefit of the nation you need patriotism, which probably comes from some shared bloody experience--literally bloody.

I think of the differences between Mexico and
Guatemala. At any time during the 30 years the Mexicans were running around from 1910 to 1940 shooting up
each other in the countryside, the prospects for economic development looked very, very slim. When they
finally got consolidated as a pretty dictatorial one-
party system, they did pull the country into one of
the fastest growth rates in the world, and I contrast
that with my experience in Asia. In Burma the country
got its independence surprisingly. Aung San outfaced
them in England and there was no battle, no bloody
national feeling, no shared climactic situation; only
a symbolic leader who got them independence with an
aura as a result of which he could not do anything but
celebrate that one act. He was a ritual leader who
continually celebrated the act of independence. He
did not do as much harm as the new celebrant in that
job, but it did not make much of a nation out of Burma.

His main contribution was to impress political
scientists like Hugh Tinker, who wrote articles about
serene statesmen, while the Irrawaddy was silting up,
rice was going down, and U Nu was building sand pagodas.
To Westerners he looked as though he had Buddhism and
serenity and nice things to say, but he did not do
much for his country except build sand pagodas.

If I were a political scientist, I would say,
"Well, what you need is a shared experience which will
confer on those who live through it the kind of nation-
hood and brotherhood which they unfortunately did not
have by language or any of their other experiences."
That advice, of course, is useless, but that is the
way the historical experience looks to me.

Mr. BARANSON: I want to comment on that. It
struck me before that this business of timing is a
very important thing. Think about the feasibility of
city planning in our own country 50 years ago under a
Tammany Hall regime in New York City. It is no use
trying to apply a medicine that is devised for an in-
hospitable situation. This is comparable to taking
modern medical techniques and going into the hinterland of Haiti where voodoo and magic are practiced.

Much of the talk today ran something like this:
"I have a nice kit of practitioner's tricks and all
you have to do is reorganize the society for me and I
can go to work on it." There is one other comment I

would like to make. Today's discussions reminded me of
Isaiah Berlin writing about Leo Tolstoi in <u>The Hedgehog
and the Fox</u>. Berlin commented that whenever Tolstoi
talked about God, it was like putting two bears in a
cage. I think the political scientist and the economist today are somewhat like the two bears, although I
am not sure which one is Tolstoi and which one is God.
(Laughter.)

About two years ago, at a conference in Cambridge,
Hans Morgenthau and Albert Hirschman played Tolstoi and
God. They were reviewing Latin America. Morgenthau
suggested that the problem was essentially political.
Hirschman said that the economists, however, were the
ones who were providing some answers. There they were
arguing over whose problem it ought to be, and today it
is interesting because there is a little more modesty.
Each is trying to push it off on the other. But it
really is not a question of who should own the problem
but one of joint effort toward determining who should
solve it.

One last point: I think part of the difficulty
brought out today was that many people are looking for
totalistic answers based on theoretical precepts involving a certain time sequence, social predisposition,
or a set of values. As for implementing the theory
they say, "I leave that to another discipline. Someone
else can figure out a way to work out the details. I
have done my share in providing the broad theoretical
framework."

I think this is putting us all in a narrow box.
It seems to me the political scientist has provided us
with ways for analyzing social pathologies rather than
with prescriptive solutions. There are a lot of things
in medicine today that we do not understand--cancer and
other pathologies--but the medical sciences are not
committed to a cradle-to-grave solution for all pathologies inhibiting growth.

There is a whole range of development pathologies,
and I think there are opportunities for tackling these
problems piecemeal. I think the problem in this sense
is a little more manageable, if the totalistic approach
is a little more toned down, both from the standpoint
of the political scientist and the economist.

Mr. SCHWARTZ: I would like to dissent respect-
fully from the arguments of the economists, and suggest

that in addition to the fact that some of the other
disciplines may not have provided us with sufficiently
good tools for analyzing development, there is another
problem and that is one that the economists are responsible for, namely, a certain lack of follow-through.
By this I mean the following: it seems to me that sometimes much is left undone with respect to expediting a
more optimal allocation of resources. The consequence
is that there is either a reduced income for a given
period of time or there is not the rapid rise which
might have taken place. As a result, the already existing political and social pressures are accentuated
and aggravated.

I have in mind particularly the situation in
Argentina. It became very popular a few years back to
say that the causes of the country's economic problems
were, in fact, political, and these days you hear some
rather good economists saying that the basic problem is
sociological, but I would like to point out the following: In the 1959-1962 period there were a number of
economic decisions with respect to which it is now
clear (though in many cases it was quite clear even
then) that what was being done constituted an ineffi-
cient allocation of resources, and threatened to seriously limit the potential increase in Gross National
Product in comparison with what might have been a-
chieved had different decisions been made. Secondly,
to take a point which I think Professor Lewis has developed elsewhere, whatever the potential increase in
GNP, it might not take place rapidly enough, given certain underlying political difficulties, to enable the
government to remain in power. This, of course, is
something else again.

In 1959-1960 some Argentine officials recognized
a number of the problems, and pointed out that the
policies being pursued were going to cause a severe
balance-of-payments problem. But their warnings were
largely ignored, and not followed up by other officials.

A recent report of the Economic Commission for
Latin America states that in some of the basic equipment industries which developed, costs are only 10 to
15 per cent higher than world levels, while in others,
costs are 80 per cent and more over world cost levels.
Thus, whatever the basic political constraints, you are
going to get better results if you focus more on the

allocation of resources.

Frondizi concentrated on development of the oil industry but did not make sufficient allowance for the fact that large amounts of natural gas output would probably accompany the oil production. This is what happened, and much natural gas escaped. One economist had pointed to this possibility, and continued doing so during the course of the rapid increase in petroleum output, but he did not receive much support from the appropriate authorities--or other economists.

What I am saying is that you came to a situation in March of 1962 in which the working class had experienced a considerable redistribution of income. This redistribution of income might have been at a higher level of average per capita income if there had been a more efficient allocation of resources--quite consistent with the kinds of political decisions which the country wanted to make. Then the March election results might well have been different and the subsequent crisis might never have arisen.

What I am trying to say, in other words, is that if enough good economists look after the details of the plans they draw up, and point out where there are poor allocations of resources, there could be more satisfactory results; but if they do not stay with it, then you are not going to get the kind of economic development that is possible (even with the constraints) and you are going to aggravate the political and social pressures; I think the economists have fallen short of what might have been expected in this respect.

Incentives and Job Prestige

Mr. MIRACLE: I think I detect from this discussion an underlying assumption that economics has done pretty well over this interval we are appraising and we do know the economist's answers. Professor Lewis was talking about this a little while ago; I wonder if he would agree that the proper study of an economist is response to economic incentive? If so, I suggest that we know very little yet.

We have lots of hypotheses that some people are trying to attack one way or another but we do not really know very much and we cannot tell the political scientist, the sociologist, the government planner or

others very much about how farmers in Africa will res-
pond--particularly to price changes of economic incentive. It may be that there is a lot more to it than
economics. Maybe you would want to argue that it is
not strictly an economic question, but it is an example of the need for theory or for measurement, or both.

Getting back to the original paper, I am a little
bit disturbed that, as a spokesman for the economists
here, the leading paper suggested that political scientists should start with more theory. It seems to me
very often that in economics, at least, measurement,
empirical work, case studies and all sorts of things
have been the source material from which good hypotheses and good theories develop, and I wonder if this
could happen in political science as well as in some
other disciplines?

Mr. LEWIS: The area in which the economist's
understanding of development is least, not merely of
development in underdeveloped countries, but equally
of development in developed countries, is what causes
people to invest. Why are investors aggressive in
Germany and not aggressive in Great Britain? Or rather, let us ask, why are they aggressive in developed
countries in general and not aggressive in underdeveloped countries? This is an area where one would like
to see a tremendous amount of work and where no doubt
the psychologists and the sociologists will make their
contributions, but even this problem is not as grave a
problem as we think it is.

When I look, for instance, at the African economy
I do not see any shortage of people wanting to invest.
I see the same things that I see when I look at the
history of Europe. I see lots of little people seiz-
ing opportunities and becoming big people in the process, a man starting out by doing a little trading and
then going into the trucking business, for example,
and becoming a big man in the process. All I see is
that African entrepreneurs, who are numerous and aggressive, do not have at the moment the capacity to
run large-scale enterprises. They cannot run a big
mine employing 3,000 people.

This is not a major problem. This is something
which can be learned. Some of what is necessary can
even be taught by a business school. The man who will
eventually come to own a large mine, working his way

up from nothing, can not be taught in a business
school. But large mines will employ accountants, a
personnel manager and other kinds of people who are
necessary to run large organizations, and who can be
taught in business schools, so even in underdeveloped
countries I do not think the problem of entrepreneurship is such a difficult problem as we make it out to
be.

Mr. KREININ: I think that the problem of incentives is not only related to investment behavior but
also to the behavior of individuals. I have inter-
viewed quite a few Africans and people who extend technical assistance to African countries. They consistently indicated Africans do not like to do manual work.
In terms of social status in Africa, doing something
with one's hands--perhaps somebody may want to correct
me on this--is the worst thing that can happen to a person. Almost every African who goes abroad six months
to study a technical subject such as chicken-feeding
wants to sit behind a desk.

I have come across a couple of practical nurses
who refused to do any manual work while being trained
abroad. When they were asked why they said, "Well,
when we go back we are not going to work." "What are
you going to do?" The only thing they could say was,
"We are going to replace the Belgians. The Belgians
didn't work. Why should we?"

So you come up against the social status scheme
about which perhaps the sociologists can tell us something.

With reference to the civil service, much prestige
is attached to being a Minister or a high official such
as a permanent Secretary or Undersecretary of a ministry. I was amazed to see the number of medical doctors
in Africa who occupy positions of responsibility in
government when there is a fantastic doctor shortage in
their countries. Apparently, although I am not sure of
this, there is more prestige attached to being a government official than to being a successful entrepreneur. It is certainly superior to being an engineer.
And an engineer, of course, would not dirty his hands.

I think, therefore, that a question that might be
addressed to the psychologists and the sociologists is
what to do about this scheme of social values that is
interfering with the development no less than the

political problem.

Mr. ANDERSON: I am always a little astonished that a group like this of white-collar men raises such questions. I think we have sufficient evidence to demonstrate that if a country, by whatever process, gets an appropriate wage structure related to the relative supply and demand of different kinds of skills, people will respond with amazing alacrity. The problem in many of the new countries is that the governments are absolutely determined that there shall be no flexible wage structure, and of course, the government personnel set the wage structure, putting their kind of jobs on top, so you get this result.

Sister THOMASINE: I would like to make a comment about the relationship between education and the attitude toward work. This applies also to our discussion about Japan and India.

Irrespective of the mystery of why some people like to work and some do not, we know there are a number of reasons for both, nevertheless the Japanese educational system certainly has fostered a healthy respect for the engineer and the technician that I do not think the Indian system has done.

Interdisciplinary Research

Mr. BLANKSTEN: Mr. Chairman, I have been sitting here as a defensive, sensitive, self-conscious, embarrassed political scientist listening to everybody complaining about political scientists and telling us the things that they would like to see political scientists do for them. I suppose I should confess that in listening to this I have made kind of a list for myself of the things all of you people say you want political scientists to do for you. I look at this list and I am bewildered.

You want us to figure out what difference it makes if civil servants are entrepreneurs, how to control rogues in politics, how to get India out of its political jam, how to analyze pathologies. Then we were told we ought to be doing philosophy for you people and we ought to be doing history for you, and all of this reminds me somewhat of a session in which I participated many years ago when a group of political scientists invited people from other disciplines

in to give us talks on what they would like to see
political science do for them. I remember at that time
a talk by an anthropologist who had been doing work
among the Indians in the American Southwest. He was
really bitter about the way the political scientists
had let him down in his project with the American Indians, because he said that what we should have done
was to tell the anthropologists how to find which part
of the United States Government contained the Bureau of
Indian Affairs, so that they could go and contact the
government on certain problems. I remember feeling at
that time, "Gee, if I had only known!" If we only had
realized that what he wanted was the United States
Government Directory, or something like that, we could
have helped him.

It just seems to me that this simply highlights
what I think is an error in this exercise of delineat-
ing the differences among what disciplines ought to be
doing. It seems to me that the great positive way to
approach interdisciplinary questions is not to divide
up all the questions and work at divisions of labor and
so on, but rather, to define the common thing we are
trying to resolve together. What is the common problem we can all add something to? I guess the burden of
my sermon here is that I do not think we are doing this.
It does seem to me that the great need in this kind of
a session is the identification of the kind of things
on which we can fruitfully work together rather than on
those we can split up and push out of the way.

Mr. KREININ: Couching the problem in a somewhat
different framework might better identify the issues
with which we are confronted. I learned two things
just now: first, that perhaps the focus in the field
of economic development should revert from emphasis on
capital-output ratios to relative-factor endowments.

Second, there is perhaps some optimum of disturbance to equilibrium. Economic development is not essentially a stable thing. The emphasis on stability
that prevailed in this morning's discussion is misleading because, after all, economic development is an un-
stable situation. You want to disturb the equilibrium.
Equilibrium will lead you nowhere.

We have been shown that not every disturbance is
optimal and it may often be excessive. The idea that
the underdeveloped countries can jump over the in-

dustrial revolution and borrow techniques which are 200
years too advanced for them is a misleading notion.
Perhaps they do have to go through some agonizing experience just as the developed countries did. There is,
therefore, some kind of an optimum disturbance, an
optimum stimulus that needs to be given to the economy
for it to develop in a reasonably smooth way. All this
was limited to economics. I suspect that in terms of
the interdisciplinary approach we are examining today
there is an optimum stimulus in fields other than economics.

Perhaps in the field of politics the optimum
stimulus is zero, namely, the domestic political situation should be stable to provide a stable framework.
With respect to sociological-psychological effects,
what is the optimum stimulus? We speak of the demonstration effect. Well, some demonstration effect is
good; too much of it is bad. Some of it would stimulate people's desires to develop, so to speak. Too
much of it might lead to balance-of-payments difficulties. Here you have again the question of what is
optimal in the particular field.

Perhaps, then, we should ask ourselves, what is
the optimum stimulus in various disciplines and tie
them together. We should not emphasize stability; instead we should emphasize disequilibrium, but the question is how much disequilibrium.

It is in that context that I think an interdisciplinary approach might be very useful. We have learned
from economics that there exists this kind of an optimum stimulus, but what about other fields? What about
sociology? What about psychology? What about political science? This is a question I would like to pose.

Mr. FATOUROS: Historically the task of government, and not alone the task of the political scientist,
has not been how to get the rogues out of government,
but how to control them when in government. I think
the word used by Mr. Blanksten, "control," was very
appropriate. The problem is how to control and canalize the actions of people who, for reasons of their own,
which may or may not be morally or perhaps esthetically
satisfying, want to have political power and want to do
certain things with that power. The question is how to
canalize their actions somehow, perhaps by creating
various counter-balancing forces and the like, so as to

make it possible to achieve a certain desirable result.

A second point is that I seem to detect--I surely hope I am absolutely wrong in this--a kind of arrogance in the air in the way in which we look at problems and decide that since we have solved the technical problem (the technical economic problem or perhaps the technical political science or public administration problem), after we have separated it from every other problem, and after we have looked at it in the exclusive economic context or in the exclusive political context, we can say, "Well, the solution would have been that, but, of course, there is a whole background to it with which we are not dealing at this particular moment." I think that we should not adopt this kind of attitude, especially today, in the United States, where we are facing certain critical problems which are neither exclusively economic nor exclusively political, but are both at the same time. People are starting slowly to realize that the war on poverty and the civil rights problem cannot be dealt with either on an exclusively economic level or on an exclusively political one. Economic development is closely related to the effective participation of all members of a community in the community's political and economic processes. As long as the dominant political structure in any region deprives people of political representation, the "war on poverty" cannot be won, and as long as the economic realities are ignored, the civil rights struggle is ineffective. Similar, though not identical, considerations obtain in the international context. We should focus, then, on the unity of the problems rather than on their partial aspects.

Perhaps sociologists might be able to look at problems from above, though I am afraid that they, too, would look from a specific sociological viewpoint. And there is obviously a psychological problem as well as a moral one. It is possible, if we look at a problem, to say always, "Well, we can solve this if only we limit it to our own terms of reference"; of course, there is a metaphysical problem behind the whole question. If the philosophers would give us an answer, then we might have our solution.

To summarize: we are oversimplifying the situation when we look at each partial solution and are happy with it, instead of trying to see how we can put

all the partial solutions together in order to arrive
at some solution which is obviously imperfect, certainly imperfect, perhaps very often a failure, but still
is a general, all-inclusive solution.

Mr. WIT: As a political scientist, I have been
groping for some meaningful response to the query:
"What can a political scientist provide?" I think the
last speaker has suggested an element, which is that
problems are societal, not just political.

In addition to that, it seems to me that, when
one asks the question we are faced with two types of
problems. One is that we have been operating on the
assumption that consensus is essential, and simultaneously, we have been talking about the fact that
many of these societies lack consensus and are not
nations. This suggests, then, that for many of these
countries, about the only thing the political scientist
could provide would be essentially a dictatorial system, a philosopher-king who would somehow or other
come out with all of the types of solution--in terms
of adequate policy, that could effectively implement
the economic solutions which we have been told are
simple. I think also of Ivor Jennings and some of his
impressive efforts to provide rational political answers in countries like India, Pakistan, and Ceylon,
and of the inadequacy of these answers.

I do not think, then, that it is a fair question
to ask of the political scientist that he come up with
"the" solution. We have certainly all recognized the
diversity of the problems. We--the political scien-
tists--cannot say, therefore, that there is a given
philosopher-king who should handle the polity, or create a polity, in a specific way. All we can do is to
analyze the ways in which the polities arise and some
of the aberrations one finds. We do not even know the
norm of "good governments" because customarily we work
in terms of an Anglo-American norm and this, as Sir
Ivor has demonstrated effectively, is not really applicable. Therefore, I do think, and I agree with
Professor Blanksten, that we have to talk in terms of
how we can mesh the efforts of different disciplines
rather than how one discipline can "solve" what is not
soluble within its own jurisdiction.

Mr. BARANSON: One aspect we should consider in
the day or so we have left is whether we are basically

concerned with practitioner's knowledge. There are
many economists who have no taste for the problems of
this world. They are more concerned with theory for
its own sake, and I think this applies also to certain
political scientists.

I think it is a fair and responsible challenge to
political scientists to pose practitioners' questions,
where you have to diagnose and prescribe. In "diagnos-
ing" Sukarno, I would first like to know to whom we
attach the diagnostician? Is it to the CIA? Is it to
the opposition party? Is it to U Thant? If the question is one of political power and social change, where
do you begin?

Recently at Indiana University we were approached
by AID on staffing a development advisory group in
Brazil. AID was very frank. Harvard was already over-
extended in Latin America and elsewhere. The Yale
Growth Center wasn't interested in a practical advisory
group in Brazil. They don't want to muck around in
politics and a real situation like that. For economists there are practitioner sets of knowledge that
deal with the problem of growth and development and
they sorely need the advice and assistance of political
scientists.

In Brazil we will not be able to move one step unless we have an economist who knows enough about the
political reality of the kind of advice he gives and
knows where to begin, and how to tackle the economic
problems in a meaningful and effective way.

I do not think that the state of the art in the
applied sciences is that underdeveloped and I am certain
that there are in fact bits and pieces of theory and
practice that apply to the problems of this world.

Mr. HENDRY: I would like to identify myself with
the claque of humble economists who have been foisting
their problems on the other disciplines. I would like
to address myself to Mr. Blanksten's apparent aim of
establishing an interdisciplinary approach, which is a
kind of general equilibrium approach, under which somehow we can now all pull together and come up with a
general model for handling development problems.

My own feeling is that this would not be a very
fruitful direction in which to head. I would prefer,
instead, more of the kind of thing Mr. Baranson has
been suggesting, identifying from an economist's stand-

point what kinds of things are inhibiting the development he would normally like to see, and then asking
the political scientist or the sociologist or the anthropologist, "What is your advice on this particular
point? Why, for example, is the civil service not
following through on this particular policy?" This is
where the communication between the disciplines is
rather poor, and where the economist constantly finds
himself unable to give an answer out of his own experience and out of his own training.

    Mr. KING: The Singapore government has a politi-
cal science training course, and George Thompson, the
director, is trying to teach this sort of political
philosophy. He is trying to instill a concept of government that is consistent, let us say, both with
democratic processes and with economic development.
The Singapore government is committed to the democratic
process, but you must still take in all the civil servants as they come to you. You train them, you argue
with them; they move out and you bring them in again
next year, and you can say the same thing over again.

    You can urge the dedicated, "If you want to solve
the problems of democracy in Malaysia, go to Nanyang
University and spend your career there, giving up any
possibility of progress in your own profession, and
argue with these people." Some day you will see these
students in positions of responsibility reacting to at
least some of your ideas. Some of my University of
Hong Kong students are now in relatively responsible
positions in Malaysia. They may be messing up things,
but I feel I have had a role in the way they are messing them up.

    One other point. I am worried about this idea
that economists have solved the simple problem of knowing how fast economies grow. From the technical statistical viewpoint, my experience suggests that this
is not true.

    Mr. WIT: This goes to the heart of the matter,
in one way. A couple of days ago I also spent a few
hours with Mr. Thompson talking about what he is doing,
and I could not for the life of me find out exactly
what it was he was transmitting other than, apparently,
the attitudes of the ruling party of Singapore, and in
general imposing upon the civil servants of Singapore
the notion that they have to stop looking toward Europe

and have to start thinking of themselves as Asians.
So, he is making a gesture toward nation building and
he is acting as a conveyor belt for some of the attitudes of the dominant political party, all of which are
rejected by the opposition party. He is therefore in
the position of being accused in Singapore at the moment of being either a British agent or at least an
agent of the political party in authority. But he is
not really providing political "solutions" to Singapore's problems.

Mr. FATOUROS: That is politics, not political
science, is it not?

Mr. WIT: He is running a political center and his
mission, you see, is the mission of providing advice,
political advice. He has latched on to a vehicle.
Really, this is all we have been saying all along;
there is no all-encompassing "scientific" political advice that one can provide for development in these diverse types of situations. It must be adjusted to the
local scene.

Mr. LEWIS: We must not object because political
advice is "political."

Mr. WIT: We have been asked for scientific solutions, and what I am saying is, as I have said before,
that the political scientist does not provide scientific solutions.

Mr. KING: No, no, no. You were not asked for
scientific solutions. If you are asked for solutions,
give them a philosophy as to how to run things. This
is what Thompson is doing.

Mr. WIT: He is taking the official philosophy
and--

Mr. KING: Because he agrees with it.

Chairman BINDER: Order, gentlemen, order. At
this time I would like to ask Mr. de Schweinitz to mak
a few remarks.

Mr. de SCHWEINITZ: Well, I consider it a singula
achievement that the political scientists here have nc
disaffiliated yet and we can look forward to seeing
them at this afternoon's session.

I must say that I was elated with what the economists have said here. I like what Mr. Hendry said. I
am not impressed with Mr. Blanksten's notion that what
we should be doing here is looking around for an area
where we can work together fruitfully. If I understar

it, what we are trying to do here is to establish some
priorities in research. Early in the session Manning
Nash talked about the prerequisites of economic development being passé, because they give the impression
that you first establish them and then the economy
takes off into economic growth; he points out that economic growth and cultural change are taking place all
the time. With that I quite agree.

We live in a general equilibrium world where
everything affects everything, but it seems to me that
this does not help us much in the matter of priorities
of research. What one has to do is to plug into the
system somewhere and you have to decide what particular problems are most important. I would insist, along
with Professor Lewis, that politics is certainly a most
important area, but I also would insist that politics
is not the same thing as giving advice. It may include
this, but it is a good deal more than that. I think of
politics as an attempt to explain phenomenon, and whether or not out of the explanation or out of the political theories you develop you derive advice is another
question. Perhaps we can look forward to this afternoon and Mr. Holt's clearing up, once and for all, all
these questions that have been raised and thrown in the
direction of the political scientists.

Chairman BINDER: I do hope that everyone will
maintain the present level of excitement, enthusiasm,
embarrassment, humility and tenseness that has come out
of this morning's session, because I have a feeling
that the session this afternoon will be very much a
continuation of the kind of discussion we have been
having this morning.

I hope that this afternoon we may get over our differences and find some areas of agreement. I am bound,
however--if you will forgive me--I am bound as a political scientist, rather than as Chairman of the morning
session, to make a few remarks. I have restrained myself up to this point and I have been embarrassed,
tense, angry, humiliated, and everything else, along
with the rest of the political scientists, and in more
ways than one.

I will try very hard to avoid making a speech. I
have not had too long to think about these things, anyway, but I do want to make just a few remarks that
might at least give you some idea of how I might

respond if I had two hours in which to respond to many
of the terribly irritating things that have been said
this morning.

Now, for one thing, there has been no clear distinction made between the role of the statesman and the
role of the scholar. This is not a new problem in political science. It is not something that has come up
just in the last 15 years in which we have been concerned with economic development in underdeveloped
areas. This is a problem that has been with civilized
society from the time it has been recorded, and I think
it is naive to think that the problems that have been
at issue here are things that have just turned up day
before yesterday. If these are questions that have
been contained in the great writings of all time and if
they have been contained in the works of the great political philosophers, it is a matter for us today to be
very much concerned with those things even as were our
forebears.

American political science is not 50 years old.
It is part and parcel of this great long development,
and some of us do have better memories. However, this
does not resolve the problem. It has come down to us
as our heritage of the development of philosophy as
well as political philosophy over centuries, millenia
in fact, and I do not believe we have a solution to the
problem that is posed just by this issue of the role of
the statesman as against the role of the scholar, because they are not merely different roles but they are
different philosophical approaches, which I might present to you in the form of the opposition of the notion
of purpose in politics and the notion of process.

Now, behind the notion of purpose is the idea that
we can control the way in which political things work
themselves out. Behind the notion of process, as far
as I am concerned, is a sense that we cannot control
these things because human beings are not given to that
kind of control, but we can perhaps examine and analyze
a process. I do not know whether economic and political development is something that we can design in our
minds and fulfill by a purposeful policy or whether it
is something we can examine as it occurred in the past
and hope for in the future.

Nothing that has been said here gives me confidence that we can apply the notions of purpose as

opposed to the notions of process.   There are political
scientists of both kinds in the world and I think there
are economists of both kinds in the world.   Now, if you
believe that this is all given to us in terms of some
a priori notion of what we would like to have, and if
we therefore designate a policy and presume that anything can be accomplished by an effective government
then, of course, you approach it from the point of view
of purpose and you say to the political scientist, "Why
in heaven's name have you not told us how to accomplish
this purpose?"

If there are political scientists who do not believe we can control all these things, but who do believe in the radical heterogeneity of the human being
as opposed to all other kinds of things under the sun,
then we do take the point of view that we can examine
processes and it is for that reason, I think, that the
subject of this morning's session was accurately stated
to be the underdeveloped countries in the world economy,
and it was for that reason that I did indeed ask about
some of the changes that have occurred in this world
economy.

Development in these underdeveloped countries is,
at least in part, dependent upon what happens in the
world economy, and what happens in the world economy is
in the nature of a process within which the economies
of underdeveloped countries find themselves.   They cannot control it; they can only react to it.   It is not
given to a Sukarno or to a Nkrumah to control the pattern of change of the world economy, nor is there any
organization, the United Nations or anything else like
that, that stands above the world economy which can
tell us how that world economy is to be controlled.   It
is a non-controlled process, and I think that this is
a decent and dignified kind of thing for social scientists to examine.

SESSION III

THE INTERNATIONAL POLITICS AND DIPLOMACY
OF DEVELOPMENT

Chairman BLANKSTEN: I have a fairly clear signal
that a more exact title for this afternoon's session
would probably be "The Political Scientist Strikes
Back."

The discussion leader this afternoon is Robert T.
Holt, political scientist from the University of Minnesota. Professor Holt has been involved in problems of
political development and change in underdeveloped
areas. He has been doing, from my standpoint, some of
the most interesting work in this area and as he left
this morning's session in a somewhat angry frame of
mind, I told him I hoped he would stay in that frame of
mind until this afternoon. He said to me, "Don't
worry--I'm always in this frame of mind," so I am sure
we can depend on that.

The first of our two discussants is Mordechai
Kreinin of Michigan State University. He is an econo-
mist whose chief research interest has been in the
field of international trade. He has also done work on
Israeli technical assistance to various countries in
Africa, Asia and Latin America.

Our second discussant will be A. A. Fatouros of
the Law School of Indiana University. He is a graduate
of the National University of Athens. His chief research interests have been in legal aspects of international economic relations. He has been especially
interested in the general set of interrelationships
between international law and economic development.
Now for the more substantive action.

Mr. HOLT: When Professor de Schweinitz finished
his brief ten-minute talk this morning, I sat back
rather smugly in my chair. Last night, you remember,
at the close of his paper, Professor Lewis was looking
to the political scientist for answers to many ques-

tions and Professor de Schweinitz this morning talked
about the major problems of development being not economic problems but political problems. For a minute
or two I imagined that I would be running with the ball
behind the powerful interference of de Schweinitz and
Lewis and I thought things would go pretty smoothly.
After about 15 minutes of discussion this morning, however, I began to realize that this perception was a
little bit false. There was a hole in the line, all
right, but it was really a mouse trap and some 280-
pound linemen were ready to jump on me as soon as I
picked up the ball and began to run.

When I agreed to talk on the problems of diplomacy, I said that I wanted to emphasize some of the
theoretical and conceptual problems of approaching
this topic rather than talking in any specific empirical detail about one or two given cases. After the
discussion this morning I would like to reorient myself even further away from the direct problems of
diplomacy of development and see if I can address myself to that problem along with some of the problems
and some of the questions that were asked of the political scientist primarily by the economists earlier in
these sessions.

There are a couple of introductory remarks, however, that I would like to make because I am sure they
will in some way explain why the economist and perhaps
other scholars interested in problems of development
have been somewhat disappointed in the answers they
have received to questions that they perceive are part
of the legitimate domain of political science. The
first point I would like to bring out, and perhaps
there are many of you in this room who are not aware of
this fact, is that of all the academic disciplines in
the United States, political science is the one in
which there is the least consensus about the nature of
the discipline and the problems of the discipline. In
the study on graduate education in the United States
that Berelson did several years ago this comes out very
clearly.[1] The amount of dissension, the lack of agreement, and the lack of consensus in political science
set this discipline apart in a rather marked way from

1. Bernard Reuben Berelson, Graduate Education in
the United States (New York: McGraw-Hill, 1960).

the other academic disciplines in the social sciences
as well as in the natural sciences and the humanities.
This means that when you ask a question of political
scientists, you are likely not to get one answer but
you are likely to get a dozen answers and you probably
will find more controversy among political scientists
of different persuasions answering the same question
than you would find among the people that have asked
the political scientists this question.

Now, this has had some rather remarkable effects
upon the kinds of work that political scientists have
done on problems of development. Because we are operating within very different theoretical frameworks
within the discipline itself, because there are different people taking some very different approaches,
the work that we have done has not been very additive.
We tend to have a scholar over here within his frame of
reference who has done a little bit and another scholar
over there with his frame of reference who has done a
little bit, but the work of the two does not fit together. When one begins to address oneself to some of
the tough problems, for example, of the practitioner
who is interested in what kind of advice to give to a
foreign government of a developing country, one finds
that the body of knowledge in political science is not
an integrated body of knowledge. No clear answer
emerges; indeed, many times conflicting answers are
forthcoming.

The second point I would like to make about political science and its concern with problems of development is that the political problems specifically related to economic development have not received much
attention. If one, for example, looks over the four or
five volumes that have been published by the Princeton
University Press for the Social Science Research Council Committee on Comparative Politics and examines the
footnotes, one will find that something less than one-
half of 1 per cent of the references are to problems
of economic development.

Most of the scholars who have been concerned with
problems of development have been concerned with the
way in which a democratic polity is built and emerges
in developing countries. If one asks them questions
that are oriented specifically to the political implications of economic development problems, one does not

get a response based on much research. There is only
a very small fraction of the time and effort and energy
and interest of a political scientist that can be
geared into the work of the economist. Now, I am personally very critical of this but, nevertheless, I
think this is a relatively fair assessment of the
state of the discipline.

The third point I would like to make has to do
with the role of the scholar, really the various roles
of the scholar. In my own mind I like to make a pretty
clear distinction between the scholar who is interested
essentially in the scientific tasks of description, explanation, and prediction, and the scholar who is more
a social engineer, who is interested in practical advice for the practical problems of the governments that
are confronted with horrendous problems of development.

Now, in my own experience, the kind of personality,
the kind of training and the kind of interests that an
individual has to have differ for these two roles. My
own concern is with the scientific problems. I am interested in trying to explain and predict patterns of
development, and I feel that it takes another kind of
political scientist, with other kinds of skills, to
take this theoretical knowledge and transform it into
the kind of knowledge which is necessary if one is going to give practical advice to developing countries.

There is a fourth general comment I would like to
make in reference to Professor Lewis's paper. It was
one of the first systematic treatments of the problem
of unemployment in the modern or industrial sector of
a developing economy. In his paper, Professor Lewis
referred to certain problems of domestic capital formation, certain problems of international trade deficits
and the balance of payments. It is possible for him,
within the theoretical framework of economics to present a pioneering paper on a specific topic, and yet it
is very clear, that this paper would link with another
paper that would be done on problems of domestic capital formation, or a third paper that would be done on
problems of international trade and development. This
is possible because of the logical theoretical structure in economics that enables a scholar to identify a
discrete problem like unemployment in a developing
country and focus upon that problem without having to
worry a great deal about the way his work will fit into

the work of other economists relating to developing
areas. There may be disagreements, of course, but the
arguments are essentially carried on within the context
of the same conceptual and theoretical framework.

I do not think that political scientists (or anthropologists or sociologists, for that matter) have
the kind of conceptual frameworks that allow them to
identify discrete researchable problems, to do work on
them, and to have the results of work on various problems linked together in a mutually acceptable theoretical framework.

While I am a great admirer of the degree of sophistication and integration of economic theory, I
think that it has been bought at a price. Economic
theory tends to be very isolated from the theories in
the other social sciences. One of the reasons is that
the economist, in order to increase the sophistication
and integrity of his theories, has made assumptions
about certain sociological, political, and psychological factors, and these assumptions constitute parameters of his theory. While these assumptions may aid
the development of economic theory, they tend to hinder
the establishment of firm theoretical relationships between economics and other social sciences.

I was impressed with Professor Nash's comment last
night when he said he had spent a decade revealing the
hidden sociological assumptions that underlie a large
number of economic propositions. One can identify
these assumptions and even demonstrate that they are
wrong, but this is at best only a small beginning to
establishing some kind of common ground where economics
and the other social sciences can meet. Until such a
common meeting ground is established, the economist
with his much more deductively powerful theories will
ask the political scientist specific questions that he
cannot answer.

The absence of a theoretical consensus in political science, the relative lack of concern with problems
of economic development, and the different interests
and qualifications of the scientist and the social engineer, combined with a proclivity on the part of many of
the best political scientists to concentrate on scientific concerns, are three reasons why the political
scientist finds it difficult to deal with many of the
problems of development that are thrown at him in other

fields. Perhaps an understanding of these characteristics of the field will help relieve the frustration that many have expressed in this conference over their failure to get the kinds of responses they feel they deserve from political science.

The first two characteristics also help to explain why I would agree to discuss the topic of diplomacy and development with you only if I could deal conceptually and theoretically with the problem. The absence of a theoretical consensus and the lack of concern with problems of economic development make it impossible to deal with the problem within a widely accepted theoretical framework, and I must start by sketching out the framework within which I operate.

I start out working with a variation of a Parsonian framework which employs a set of assumptions concerning the functional imperatives (or requisites, as I prefer to call them) of any social system. I will mention these only briefly because I am sure that most of you are familiar with Professor Parsons' work. Professor Parsons and some of his associates have postulated that there are four functional requisites that any social system must meet if it is to continue to operate.

The first one of these that he identifies is the functional requisite of adaptation. Every social system has to adapt to its non-human environment, and from Parsons' point of view and from my point of view it is this functional requisite that is concerned primarily with what in the social sciences would be labelled as economic.

A second requisite of any social system is the requisite of goal attainment. There is a set of social system goals and there must be the kind of structural organization within a social system that guarantees that at least a minimal level of these system goals will be achieved.

A third functional requisite is the requisite of pattern maintenance. I differ in my interpretation here rather considerably with Parsons, and I look at pattern maintenance as being primarily concerned with the needs of the social system to conform to the values and prescriptions that are prescribed by the cultural system. (Note that I make a very rigid distinction between a social system on the one hand and a cultural system on the other hand and treat the two as environmental, one to the other.)

The fourth functional requisite that Parsons deals with is the requisite of integration. In effect, I argue here that in order for the functional requisites of any social system to be satisfied it is necessary to have a minimal degree of role differentiation among roles that are in fact interdependent. One of the functional requisites of the system is to provide the minimal amount of integration that is necessary to bring about coordination among these roles that are necessarily differentiated but are also independent.

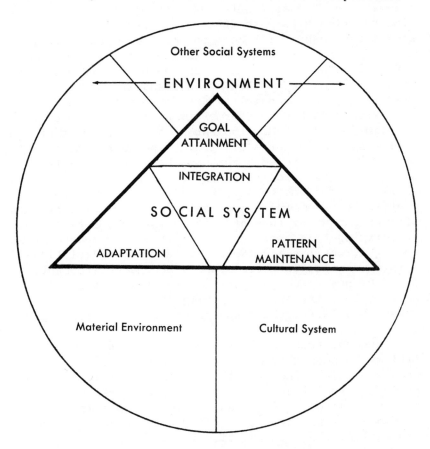

Fig. 1.--Adjustment of social system to environment. [Compare with paradigm in Talcott Parsons and N. J. Smelser, Economy and Society (New York: Free Press of Glencoe, 1956), p. 19.]

Certain aspects of this formulation become clearer if presented diagramatically. In Fig. 1 the large triangle represents the social system at the societal level. Within the large triangle, small triangles represent each of the four functional requisites. Notice that each of the first three requisites I mentioned has an external boundary and is relevant to an aspect of the environment. As already mentioned, the non-human environment is relevant to the adaptive functional requisite and the cultural environment is relevant to the pattern maintenance functional requisite. The goal attainment functional requisite is primarily concerned with relationships with other societies, but also has some relationship with both the non-human and the cultural environment. The integration requisite has no external boundary. It is concerned primarily with the integration of roles that are necessarily differentiated if the four requisites are to be satisfied.

With this kind of formulation, we can look at the problems of social development as the adjustment of the social system to three different aspects of the environment. Some of the work that has been done in anthropology, for example, the work of Julian Steward, would emphasize problems of social change and social development in terms of the adjustment of the social system to its non-human environment. In a sense, my formulation is carrying this work one step further. The crucial social structures are those that develop in relationship to changes in three aspects of the environment, plus the needs of the system to maintain integration among roles that are necessarily differentiated if these three different kinds of environments are going to be dealt with.[2]

Because functional frameworks have often been criticized because they do not aid the analysis of social change, I might indicate the way in which I treat economic and social development. For any given state of the three aspects of the environment, there is a limited range in the variation of concrete structures that can satisfy the four functional requisites. I refer to the patterns of concrete structures that satisfy the

2. This scheme is discussed in detail in Robert T. Holt and John E. Turner, The Political Basis of Economic Development (Princeton, N.J.: Van Nostrand, 1966).

functional requisites in any given type of social
system as the <u>social structuring</u> of that system. Social change is viewed as changes in this concrete
structuring that occur in response to the changes in
the environment, with the additional consideration
that there are limits imposed on potential changes by
the state of the system at any given time.

Now, I would like to make just a few comments
about the problem of diplomacy in development. When
we are dealing with relationships to other societies
and the impact of the type of international system
upon a developing country, we are quite clearly dealing with the goal attainment functional requisite.
The crucial questions concern the kind of structural
adaptations that are necessary to deal with certain
kinds of relationships with other societies, and certain kinds of relationships with the international
system. One of the interesting historical observations
that I think one can make about the problems of development that arise out of the nature of the international system and of the kinds of contacts with other societies deals with the kinds of procedures that are involved in the satisfaction of the various functional
requisites. In other words, there may be differences
in the kind of structures that can satisfy certain
functions, but there may also be differences in the
procedures that can be followed to achieve these particular objectives. It is possible, for instance,
that a democratic government and a totalitarian government might do pretty much the same sort of thing. The
differences may be largely procedural differences in
the way in which the requisites are satisfied.

It seems to me, from a look at the development of
countries in Europe in the nineteenth and early twentieth centuries, one finds that the nature of the international system imposes some important limitations upon the kind of procedural alternatives for governments
in these countries. I think it is interesting to note,
for example, that in those countries which evolved
democratic systems in the nineteenth and the early
part of the twentieth centuries that later developed
into <u>stable</u> democratic systems--these countries had
their early development in a period in which foreign
policy problems and foreign policy crises were relatively unimportant; Great Britain, the Scandinavian

countries, and the United States are cases in point.
By contrast, the countries, particularly in western
Europe, where the development of basic democratic institutions coincide with a period of prolonged foreign
crises, the democratic systems in the twentieth century
have not been particularly stable. France, Germany,
Spain, and Italy are good examples.

Now, I think the political scientist can address
himself to a whole set of reasons why it is exceedingly
difficult, if there are major foreign policy crises,
for democratic institutions to develop. One set of
reasons deals with the necessity, in periods of foreign
crisis, for the government to increase its role in the
direction and control of the economy for the purpose of
mobilizing resources that are necessary in the defense
effort of the country. One of the propositions that
would emerge out of my work is that in the very early
stage of democratic development it is improbable to
have a political system which is engaged in this kind
of regulation that does not have what I refer to as a
highly resolved authority structure of policy making.
That is, you cannot have a basic policy structure in
which there is a whole host of representative veto
groups that can block the development of a given policy.

In a modern, twentieth-century democracy it is
possible to have representation and to have a resolved
authority structure of policy making, as one can see in
the case of Great Britain, but in the very beginning
development of democracy, when the kind of disciplined
democratic political parties that exist in Britain today have not yet evolved, this kind of combination is
most improbable. Prolonged foreign policy crises lead
to increased government direction of the economy, which
in turn will tend to limit popular representation.

A second set of reasons concerns the problem of
ethnic groups and the integration of ethnic groups into
the larger community. This, of course, is a problem
for democratic polities at almost any stage in their
development. The problem is greatly magnified during
periods of international crisis if some of the ethnic
groups within a country have close ties to the foreign
power with which there is conflict. Even in the United
States in the period of the First World War we encoun-
tered this particular kind of problem with the German
minority. It would seem to me that it is quite improb-

able that the kind of democratic institutions that are
associated with the protection of ethnic minorities
would develop in a country which was confronted with
prolonged international crisis and in which ethnic
minorities were associated with an antagonistic power.

I would like to leave the problems of international relations and their impact on the developing country for a moment and pursue some other aspects of the
development of democratic institutions that take me
back to some of the issues raised earlier in this conference. In his paper last night Professor Lewis
indicated that in order to deal with unemployment in a
developing country, it may well be necessary for a
strict limitation to be placed on the ratio of wages
in the developed sector to wages in the non-developed
sector of the economy. In a developing country, organized labor is likely to be one of the most articulate
and influential interest groups in the society. If
free elections are held, organized labor is going to
have a voice in deciding what group will form a government. It is unlikely that organized labor over a long
period of time will tolerate the kind of restrictions
on wages recommended by Professor Lewis and it seems
relatively probable that such restrictions cannot be
imposed unless labor is denied some of the normal democratic freedoms.

Although I would like to argue this point in more
detail, there is another issue that was raised in our
earlier discussions that I feel more compelled to comment on. Several times during this conference the
economists (and others) have indicated their dissatisfaction with the kind of answers they receive to the
questions they throw at political scientists. I oftentimes object to the questions because they seem to me
to emerge partially from the false assumptions about
the political system which are too frequently made by
the economist. The questions are too frequently of a
very technical nature. For example, "How can we de-
vise a civil service system in a developing country
that will keep the rogues and the rascals out of positions that are important in the control and regulation
of the economy?" But how do we know that we want to
keep the rogues and the rascals out? Even more important, how do we know we want to have civil servants
in important positions of economic regulation?

Most economists do not ask these kinds of questions, often because they have answered the political
questions on the basis of an economic analysis. Let me
give an example of what I mean. Many economists would
concur with the remarks of both Professors Lewis and
de Schweinitz that the most important problems of economic development are political. I too would concur,
but I object strenuously to the kind of reasoning that
leads most economists to this conclusion. It is usually based on the proposition that a high degree of economic planning and consequent government regulation of
the economy are necessary if development is to take
place. This proposition, in turn, has been developed
from an almost exclusive concern with technical economic considerations.

For example, a theorist of the "big push," like
Professor Rosenstein-Rodan, argues that the technology
of the mid-twentieth century that is available for import into the developing countries is much more capital-
intensive than was the technology of the nineteenth
century. He argues that the production functions associated with this technology are far less homogeneous.
He emphasizes particularly the indivisibility of capital. He concludes from his analysis that resource allocation must be far more centralized today than it was
in the nineteenth century if industrialization is to
proceed rapidly and that a good deal of this centralized resource allocation should be in the hands of the
government. It is reasonable further to conclude that
the government must play a major role in resource allocation and that the major problems of economic development are political. But the kinds of questions that
the economist throws the political scientist from this
kind of analysis are purely technical problems. For
example, "How does one organize a civil service so that
it can handle these important resource allocation problems?"

Let us go back and look at the whole problem of
the most desirable role of the government in planning
and managing the economy from a broader perspective.
There are a number of very relevant considerations that
are not typically considered by the economist because
they lie outside the confines of economic theory.
First, it has been clear in a number of historical
cases of economic development that have been studied,

that there is typically a minority group within the
society that has provided a disproportional percentage
of entrepreneurial talent at very crucial pre-industrial and industrial stages of development. Take, for
example, the Nonconformists in England, the "old
believers" in Russia, the Jews in areas of Western
Europe. I think an argument can be made that if the
government takes over ownership and active control and
regulation of important sectors of the economy in
developing countries, representatives of those minority
groups that have been absolutely crucial in industrialization experiences in the past may be squeezed out of
entrepreneurial roles. If there is a high probability
of this happening, it would be an argument against government management of the economy.

The second point I would like to make is that one
of the problems that is involved in any developing
society is the establishment of a set of social structures which enables the motivation of individuals to
be geared to societal goals. This, of course, was
what John Stuart Mill was concerned with when he
talked about "The Invisible Hand." The profit motivation of the individual stimulated behavior that was
manifested through the particular kinds of institutions and structures that were established and which
contributed to the achievement of the goals of the
total system. I think that the kinds of manipulation
of wage rates that have gone on in the Soviet Union,
in complete opposition to basic Marxian goals, indicate that even in this kind of economy there is a
problem of the way in which individual motivation is
geared to, and is put in the service of, the goals of
the system itself.

In a developing country what is the most desirable
career for a young man with a high pecuniary motivation? If the government in his country is actively
involved in economic regulation, it may be to take a
job in the government bureaucracy and put his favors
up for sale. In other words, the fast avenue to wealth
may be the sale of favorable decisions to the highest
bidder. The money which is accumulated in this way is
not likely to make much of a contribution to domestic
capital formation. It is more likely to find its way
into a foreign bank. I would argue that as there is an
increase in the amount of government regulation, there

is an increase in this kind of behavior which will tend to inhibit rapid economic growth.

Let me conclude by saying that the political scientist may well not provide the economist with satisfactory answers to the question, for example, of how to organize the government so that it can best manage the economy, because he feels that the question is not a proper one. Until the economist can make more realistic assumptions about the non-economic aspects of behavior, I doubt whether he will be asking the political scientist the right kinds of questions. The kind of framework that I sketched out is one that I think can lead to a fruitful analysis of the problems of developing areas and which can be an aid in the fruitful interchange between economists and political scientists. But because of the characteristics of the field of political science I mentioned in my introductory remarks, there is little likelihood that I will find much agreement among other political scientists.

Mr. FATOUROS: I find it extremely difficult to comment on Professor Holt's paper, partly because I am not sure I have been able to follow every aspect of it, but especially because it seems to me that this was a presentation of what political scientists are doing or should do, saying in a sense, "Well, that's what my profession is doing. How about yours?" I am not sure that there is really very much to comment on in that respect, especially since the discussion itself was an example of the kind of thing that can and should be done. Any complaint as to why a particular point was not discussed can be answered very legitimately by saying, "Well, I did not discuss everything. I left out some things by necessity," which is, of course, true.

I would perhaps add another set of topics for research, trying to find out what the factors are that affect integration in any society as such, and in the international society as a whole. This is a topic that can be studied both in the domestic and in the international context. In the international context, for instance--and this was touched upon very lightly--we have the problem of intergovernmental contacts and contacts through a variety of other semi-governmental, or possibly non-governmental, agencies--using the term "agencies" in a very general sense, in the sense of institutions. In addition to trade, you have cultural

contacts; you have all kinds of other contacts. In
fact, we can hypothesize in advance that the range of
this kind of non-official contacts is much broader
among the developed economies than among the underdeveloped ones. If you go, let us say, to an international
association meeting somewhere, you have a very good
chance of meeting some French participants who do not
represent the official policy of the government of
France. There are very few chances of meeting people
who do not represent the more or less official policies
of the governments in the developing countries. This
creates a problem of communication. I am not saying
this to correct what was said before, but rather as an
elaboration of a particular point.

In the domestic context, I suppose what has been
called nationalism--that is, the modern kind of nation-
alism--is certainly one of the integrating factors, one
of the factors that make it possible to ask citizens to
do things that may not be to their immediate interest
at that particular moment.

Perhaps the whole legal or social order, both international and national, can be seen in these terms:
an effective legal order exists (and I say a legal order in the sense of an order in which most of the expectations of its members are normally fulfilled)
where every member of the order has an interest in the
continuing existence, in the persistence, of the order.
This I think applies both to individuals and to states.
The moment an individual (or state) finds that it is
not to his interest to continue supporting the order,
you will have, in the domestic context, a revolutionary
situation, and, in the international context, pretty
much what the attitude of at least some of the developing countries has been. The interest I am talking
about does not have to be of a particular kind only.
This should be made clear. It can be an interest of a
moral character, an interest in the order's existence
because in the particular society certain values are
shared by all its members, it might be a purely material interest, or it may be both at the same time.

With respect to the integration of the international society, looking at it from the outside, so
to speak--not from the point of view of the individual
state but from the point of view of the international
society as a whole--this perhaps is the main problem

today: how to make it clear, or how to make it true, that the individual states, which are the active a- gents in that society, should act in a manner tending to strengthen the international society, again not necessarily out of moral considerations, but because it is to their interest. This was taken for granted in the nineteenth century, when all the subjects of the international society were, more or less, Western coun- tries. It was taken for granted because they shared certain common interests as well as certain common val- ues.

In fact, this particular point of view is some- thing that I find is lacking in trying to look at the problems of economic development or the international society from a global point of view. I am not thinking in terms of expressions of wishes--"How nice it would be if things were nice," and so on--but of trying to develop the kind of analysis of factors and of situa- tions which would assume, let us say, the necessity of avoidance of frictions within the world society in the same way in which we assume that necessity within the national society.

There is a further point which I could make if I were to discuss the problems of a legal, juridical, approach to the whole subject. I should say, perhaps, and I suppose it is self-evident, that I think there is a basic necessity for taking into account the legal factors in the problems of economic development. In fact, one of the problems I sometimes find in economic discussions (especially economic, perhaps, rather than political science discussions) is that certain legal attitudes and legal institutions are taken for granted. It is assumed that the Western legal institutions and the Western legal framework are not merely the best, but even to some extent the only ones, something I am afraid that lawyers, too, are very much wont to do, but which they somehow are trying to get away from.

Mr. KREININ: I was very much impressed by the attempt to provide a framework here. I think that for people in disciplines other than political science it was difficult to absorb everything on the spur of the moment. As Dr. Holt was talking, I was simply trying to relate a few things from my experience to that framework, because a framework is only as good as the content you can fill it with.

Let us suppose that the government gets involved in development because entrepreneurial ability is in short supply in the country. While some people sitting around this table will dispute this, I maintain that there is such a shortage and that it is one of the reasons why government needs to participate in development. Let us further suppose that along with the development process the nation also adopts democratic institutions. How compatible are these two aims? The government can follow a labor-intensive line of development--and I am trying to relate this to Professor Lewis's remarks last night--which would mean that the investments are spread throughout the economy, raising the level of living of everybody by a small per cent every year.

Alternatively, the government can adopt a show-piece type of approach which would involve the concentration of investment capital in a few capital-intensive industries, benefiting directly only a small segment of the population.

What are the government chances of getting re-elected? Very few people would be impressed by an imperceptible increase in the standard of living of everybody under the first course postulated above. But showpieces appeal to many voters. Therefore you will find that often the drive toward industrialization and away from agriculture--much more than is warranted by factor endowments--is caused by the fact that the government has to seek votes afterwards. Examples of showpieces constructed partly in order to attract the votes are a large hotel in Enugu, which, as expected, is filled to 20 per cent of capacity, and similar hotels in Lagos and in Ibadan, as well as capital-intensive industrial complexes which employ very few people.

An interesting phenomenon in that context is the settlement projects in Africa. As you know, the Africans are seeking ways to reorganize their agriculture, and one thing they have been trying to adapt from the Israelis is the Moshav system, which is essentially a multipurpose cooperative. Containing about one hundred families, it combines both elements of cooperation and of private-investment initiative. It affords the utilization of large-scale efficient methods, and at the same time retains private initiative. It is the

combination of these two features which is attractive,
and the FAO considers it very applicable to Africa.

In Israel they also developed regional settlement
units whereby about ten Moshavim are scattered around a
rural center, and several such combinations surround a
regional town. The Nigerians, the Burmese and others
have been trying to copy that kind of settlement.
While in Nigeria, I inquired about the purpose of such
settlement schemes--which cost large sums of money.
Are they really going to cure agriculture in Nigeria?
The answers were usually couched in terms of the demonstration effect and the effect on the school-leavers in
the country who might be attracted back to the farms.
I asked further, "Aren't they going to absorb all the
agricultural budget of the country, leaving no funds
for extension?"

Curiously enough, all the extension service people
were for the settlement project. I asked them why, and
they said, "This, in a sense, is much like an industrial project. The government needs a showpiece. It is
not about to allocate the money for extension because
extension is considered a failure. Extension will not
revolutionize agriculture. On the other hand, the settlement project can be pointed to at election time and,
although in itself it is not going to cure the agricultural problems of Nigeria, it has made more money available to agriculture, including extension, because some
extension is tied into the settlement project."

What I am trying to say, essentially, is that the
democratic process can drive the government to engage
in a highly capital-intensive development effort in industry as well as in agriculture, where it is not warranted by economic conditions.

GENERAL DISCUSSION

Chairman BLANKSTEN: Thank you, Professor Kreinin.
Let me, before we launch into a general discussion, attempt to focus what has been said here. In an attempt
to respond for political science, so to speak, to some
of the things that were said this morning, Professor
Holt has pointed out that the omnibus nature of political science as a discipline has tended to be such that
we have less of a central theoretical core than do many

other social science disciplines. Therefore a uniform kind of response is more difficult to make for political science than for many other disciplines.

One kind of response that could be made, although this would likely not be held unanimously among political scientists, is that, through some kind of systems analysis such as the functional requisite analysis that Professor Holt attempted to sketch here, we could have a central systematic way of responding to many of the questions that are put to political scientists.

We did not get an awful lot said about the international politics and diplomacy of development, but it may not be stretching Professor Holt's point too much to say that the system of analysis which he outlined for us could also provide ways and means for thinking about that kind of problem as well.

Let me now throw the floor open to general discussion.

Political Science, Theory, and Practical Democracy

Mr. KING: I want to focus on the objection that you had to the presentation of political problems to political scientists in a set form with rigid constrictions. It seems to me that this is the way problems must be presented. I was told yesterday, for example, that in the development process we must not have primary education of a certain type, or that primary education creates problems, that the people cannot go into town and so forth. Now, today I am told that they cannot have democracy.

These are, it seems to me, the very things these people are after. Thus we are presented with problems with constraints. We are not necessarily asking a political scientist to set up a political system which will permit economic development, but to set up a democratic political system or to set up some other specified kind of a political system.

We are told, for example, in Thailand, "We want economic development but we want Buddhism. Don't tell us that Buddhism does not lend itself to development. Fix it so we can have both."

Now, let us look at democracy and ask the question, "Is it incompatible with development?" I am told that democracy, as opposed, presumably, to other systems,

leads to capital-intensive projects. Now, this seems
to me to be false. Dictatorships are notorious for setting up capital-intensive projects. This is a standard
economic objection to such regimes. For example, there
is the Merdeka Stadium in Djakarta. Granted, there is
also a Merdeka Stadium in Kuala Lumpur. You have stadiums under both systems. The biggest one is in Indonesia, but then they have more people there--100,000,000
people.

Political parties and labor unions have been mentioned. Certainly some political parties lend them-
selves--or unions--to policies which are destructive of
economic development. Others are controlled in such a
way that they further and foster the process of economic development. In Thailand you cannot impose irrigation water rates on the farmers. Why? Because the
government, which has no contact with the people
through the democratic process, is afraid of the reaction of the farmers. In Malaya where you do have this
sort of contact, you can convince the people, through
their political representatives, that water rates on
irrigation are essential.

I am not here arguing in favor of democracy or
against it. I am simply saying that the economists are
faced with this problem: "Here is a country which is
not suited to economic development, which is not suited
to GNP growth; please fix it so the gross national product grows." If we were not faced with this contradic-
tion, there would not be any problem. We all operate
within constraints. I may have misinterpreted Mr. Holt,
but the tenor of his arguments appeared to imply that
democracy is an unfair constraint to put upon the political scientist. I would maintain that such a constraint may be a difficult one. But I would also maintain that in the world today there is no conclusive
evidence that democracy is peculiarly unsuited for the
development process.

Mr. HOLT: First of all, I do not object to the
stating of questions within very narrow constraints.
What I would like to say is that one should not expect
to get an answer within those constraints because I
think oftentimes the question has been phrased to the
political scientist without consideration of the economic variables and the political variables that might
change those constraints.

The second point I would like to make briefly has to do with the reference to dictatorship and democracy, because I think this is an area in which there has to be a great deal more precision in our analysis. When I was talking about democracy, I was emphasizing its procedural characteristics. When you talked about dictatorship, you were associating a particular kind of procedure with a certain set of government functions, particularly control over resource allocation. I would say these are two different dimensions. You can have dictatorship with a very limited range of government involvement in the economy. You can have democracy with a great range of government involvement in the economy. The factor that is involved here is the wide range of government involvement in the economy, which I think tends to lead to these capital-intensive projects whether it is democratic or dictatorial.

As to the third point, about, "After all, we have to have democracy but we want you to tell us how to go about getting it," I would simply say that social systems are not that flexible. There are certain kinds of conditions under which you can say, "You cannot have economic growth of 4 or 5 per cent at the present time; there is a set of prerequisites that has to be met first and there have to be slower growth rates first. There is a set of institutions and there is a set of structural changes that have to come about; what we will try to do is to establish a non-democratic system, but the kind of non-democratic system that has the highest probability of giving rise to a democratic system after several generations."

What I would argue here on the basis of my work is that if you superimpose the mechanisms of democratic government--universal suffrage, et cetera, et cetera, et cetera--at too early a stage of economic development, you actually increase the probability of a totalitarian dictatorship and you might be much better off aiming in the direction, let us say, of the kind of authoritarianism that existed in England in the 1820's or in Japan under the Shogunate. If you introduce universal suffrage and freedom for labor unions too early, what you are probably doing is introducing the features so conducive to the manipulation of masses that are associated with the totalitarian dictatorships of the twentieth century.

Mr. KREININ: I would like to ask a question of Mr. King. What actually is the meaning of democracy in a country in which 90 per cent of the people are completely illiterate and really do not know what they are voting for?

Mr. KING: The first question is really whether some of these places should be countries, is it not? We are again faced with constraints. Have we, perhaps, given some areas their freedom too soon?

Mr. KREININ: Well, we cannot do anything about that.

Mr. KING: That is true. But to return to the question of democracy with an illiterate citizenry, I would say we have to play a game here--a game which is played in so-called successful democracies--where the leadership will play the game of democracy and yet not give in or not knuckle under to the demands of the mob, but rather lead the mob.

This can be done. Let me make it clear, however, that my idea was to say that if people demand democracy, if they want it, then, if the political scientist is to perform his role properly, he must come up with an answer within this constraint which will satisfy the people. I am not necessarily suggesting that democracy is everywhere equally applicable, but I would suggest that in most places it is. I am aware of the standard problems. Nevertheless, I maintain that it is the leadership that must play the game, the democratic game, and make it work.

Mr. NASH: In most of these countries which are underdeveloped the best they can do is sort of a weak-kneed tyranny. Totalitarianism is an industrial phenomenon.

Mr. KREININ: You mean a benevolent dictatorship? Is that what you mean?

Mr. NASH: No--just a capricious kind of tyranny. Totalitarianism--

Chairman BLANKSTEN: Perhaps what you mean is "authoritarian" rather than "totalitarian."

Economic Nationalism: Monuments and Development

Mr. NASH: What I think looms even larger in the developing countries is the idea of economic nationalism, whatever the political system. One of the things of the twentieth century--one of the developments in this century--is that governments are considered, even in free enterprise systems, the custodians of the GNP. Whatever the numbers are, it is their fault in any kind of system.

If you have economic nationalism with a thinly Westernized elite, you have obvious kinds of consequences. Some of these I have looted from Harry Johnson and some I have invented, but, given economic nationalism and the fact that the government is the custodian of the GNP, you will get symbolic behavior irrespective of the type of political system because they are going to put up something that is a symbol of the nation, whether it is stadia or pagodas. You could think of all sorts of things.

The second thing you will get is a drive toward nationalization insofar as the government can nationalize. It will nationalize against Western interest groups. The third thing you will get is indigenousization, a conscious attempt to put the economy in the hands of nationals and run out Chinese or Lebanese or whoever are around with entrepreneurial skills.

Fourthly, from a strictly economic point of view, you must get mal-allocation of resources and mal-placement of industry, because you have to place them politically. Israel is a good example and provides an illustration I like. The cost of these frontier settlements you mentioned probably makes them one of the worst investments in the world. If they took that money and put it in AT&T, Israel would be a much richer place--but not a country. I think some of these mal-allocations, from an economic point of view, are part of the price you have to pay for the process of building a nation.

Possibly the symbolic behavior may have long-range payoffs that are not immediate. The symbolic behavior of the Mexicans in building large museums and restoring the Indian heritage and making people proud of it has, I think, had that sort of payoff. In the short run these nations are stuck with economic nationalism irrespective of political systems and some of them might have great payoffs.

Mr. ANDERSON: I would like a little more instruction on the process by which the public acquires the idea that these factories or dams or stadia are things on which the government is going to stake its prestige. I do not quite see how the effect of building these monuments filters down to the semi-literate or wholly illiterate peasants in Kenya. That is a puzzle to me.

Professor Nash has, I think, in part answered the related question, although I am not wholly satisfied with his answer. Why does economic nationalism seem to keep prosperity indefinitely postponed so far as the citizens are concerned and lead them to be willing to accept showy symbols while leaving their bellies empty? I do not see that economic nationalism gives any explanation for this. I think there are other factors that have not been mentioned.

Mr. GINSBURG: I do not think the masses really care about these matters. It seems to me that the significance of large public works is greatest for a very small elite which has acquired its notions about the significance of these things from contact with the West and usually abroad. It takes a good deal of persuasion, I suspect, even in Indonesia, to convince the general populace that a great stadium is a good thing, that the enlarged airport is a great achievement; and I think this point has a bearing also on some questions that were raised about industrial managers in the Near East preferring machines rather than people.

It was said that these managers do not like all those chaps around. That's true. They do not like all "those chaps" around because they are more alien to them, that is, to the common laborer than they are to the machines, since they have gone to engineering school in France or Britain.

Chairman BLANKSTEN: Are there studies of the perception by these people of these monuments? I suppose there are not.

Mr. MIRACLE: There is at least one study that has been done in Latin America of what information gets down to the grass-roots level and what people at the grass-roots level perceive, and it is precious little in this particular study. They know the name of the local soccer hero, who is Pelé, and apparently has had a Russian monument given to him; and they do not often know who the president of Brazil is--of course, some of us do not either because it has changed so frequently-- they do not know what the country's leading export is, what a dollar is, and a lot of things like this.

Now, I would very much like to see some of this research done in Africa because I think it is tremendously important in development to see what the communication pattern is from the planners and their advisors, be they Americans or others, to the people who are locally involved in these situations.

But I wanted to try to answer part of the question that Professor Anderson raised. I think the important thing about the big showpieces is that they are so visible, not that people necessarily want them, but when they come to the city they can see them. Secondly, I do not think the people at the grass-roots level are sacrificing as individuals as much as we are led to believe by our notions of hungry people or empty stomachs.

There may be such sacrifice in education, but there has been much talk about two-thirds of the world being hungry, there are "freedom from hunger" campaigns, and so on, which is like the rate of growth of GNP in that it needs to be clarified and worked on. We do not have nutritional studies which demonstrate that Africa is hungry; perhaps India or some other place is, but what I am saying is, perhaps these people are not giving up so much. Perhaps as far as they are concerned this stadium is a net addition that was not there in the colonial regime, and they are happy to have it.

Chairman BLANKSTEN: Why is it assumed that people, upon being shown these things, will react positively to them?

Mr. BINDER: If there is a good game going on in the stadium, they enjoy it. After a lot of rioting in East Pakistan they built the stadium and it was a lot more fun to watch other people fight with one another in the stadium than to fight with one another outside.

Mr. GINSBURG: Some studies have been made of perception in environment, but it is not the kind of environment that has been talked about here. It is environment that is partially natural and partly man-created and which people have to deal with as resource complexes when they are planning particular kinds of development projects. For example, we have two students in East Africa who have been studying the attitudes of certain tribal groups toward water as a resource and toward the control and manipulation of water resources for developmental purposes. They have not yet found anything remarkable but this at least is one field of investigation in which pioneering is being done, and I think it quite important.

Mr. WERNER: I want to comment on this stadium business. I am not so sure that there is not a lot of mileage in such a proposition. I do know that in Indonesia the Sukarno regime went to great lengths to publicize it. The majority of small children do attend primary school and in every primary school they were required to write little essays on what this meant to the country. Further, groups of people were invited, at their own expense, to come from all over the nation to Djakarta, to see it.

With respect to the foreign communities, this thing was publicized at great length and perhaps every foreigner who could possibly have any connection with it or see it was informed by a variety of means that Indonesia was a great country to be able to build this thing, and put it together. The fact that it was built with foreign aid was carefully concealed as much as possible, and instead emphasis was given to the fact that this was a symbol that they were putting the country together effectively.

I am not so sure that they did not try to really use this as a political tool to impress the population--both domestic and foreign.

Mr. MORGAN: To supplement Professor Werner's comment, I want to add that I think I would trust the extremely sensitive political antenna of a person like Sukarno, for whom I think no praise could be excessive as an effective politician in office--I mean this in a negative sense as well as positive--rather than surveys. I think Sukarno knows what he is doing politically, at least with respect to showplaces.

Mr. HOLT: With regard to keeping himself in power? If you are talking about sensitive political antenna, I assume it pertains to keeping himself in power.

Mr. MORGAN: Yes. That is what I mean.

Mr. HOLT: That is one kind of a problem. But you can also, it seems to me, address yourself here to the problems of what kind of political system is he evolving, and what is the impact upon economic development, and this is something else. Here he may not know what he is doing at all.

Mr. MORGAN: I do not think he has any interest in

economic growth at all.

Mr. KREININ: I think there are two points involved. First of all, it is rather unfortunate that we
have placed so much emphasis upon the stadium. It is
true that the stadium is a symbol but it is merely that.
What I was trying to suggest was the frequent occur-
rence of developments of capital-intensive industry--
the idea that every country ought to have a steel mill.
I am not talking about stadiums; rather, I would prefer to discuss steel mills, which are more than symbolic.

Number two, I tend to agree with Professor Werner
that these projects do have some impact. In the settlement project case, farmers are brought from all over
the region to observe the project and learn from it.
Additionally, it is not very important whether it actually makes an impact on the population. What is really
important is that the leaders believe it has such an
impact; this is really what guides them. It may be
that if after a certain number of years they are proven
wrong, they might change their minds. So you have some
interaction here between the degree of actual impact on
the people, on the one hand, and the perception and
anticipation of the leaders themselves on the other.

Generally speaking, I think there is some impact.
In addition, there is another prestige factor, an external one. If a leader wants to acquire international
reputation, he needs to have some kind of a capital-
intensive complex to show the visiting dignitaries from
other countries.

Mr. BINDER: Other developing countries?

Mr. KREININ: Other developing countries, that is
right.

Mr. WARREN: I hate to add historical depth to
this discussion, but if we would consult Robert Adams,
for instance, at the University of Chicago, he would
tell us that every civilization, beginning with
Mesopotamia, has been involved with impressive visual
symbols of one kind or another; the pyramids in Egypt
and in Mesopotamia and in Central America, and so on.
Evidently there is some connection between the level of
social complexity and these symbols.

They may also have other important functions as
Mr. Kreinin suggests, for instance, steel mills. Steel
mills are very impressive visually, and to take it back

again to the concept of the pyramids, they have other functions as well, which involve the supernatural and so on. Perhaps we are attributing certain developments to contact with Western culture which are really part of some other kind of phenomenon, namely, social complexity.

Mr. WERNER: Might I just add that in our own history we did some of these things, such as building the city of Washington, or at least laying it out and starting it at a time when we could have put that money to other more economical uses.

Chairman BLANKSTEN: I hate to be a divisive force here, but may I mention stadia at state universities? (Laughter.)

Is there anything further to be said about monuments, stadia or steel mills?

Mr. ANDERSON: I am still bothered about something. I thought it was said that in these countries the governments stand or fall on the basis of these spectacular projects. I still have not understood how it comes about that the public who vote will make the government stand or fall on those projects rather than on something which is economically more presumably relevant. This issue I do not think has been dealt with yet.

Mr. NASH: I do not think it was asserted that they stand or fall on the monuments. The governments I have seen in the underdeveloped countries stand or fall on the inherited charisma from the struggle for independence and these people are the Western elite, the remnants of the civil service, and a few soldiers who are the country. For example, in Burma this government gets elected, because U Nu, if he ever gets out of jail, could win any election any day. He enshrines and embodies the independence movement, and he is a devout and pious Buddhist, and he appeals to the peasants, and he will win any free election. He does not have to do anything but be U Nu to win.

Now, one of the things about being U Nu is to build monuments. He does it. What drives him, I do not know, but these elites are all driven to build monuments, not to get votes. U Nu does not know how to run a country, it is pretty obvious, but one thing he can do is build a monument or build a pagoda--the World Peace Pagoda, a beautiful thing.

Mr. HARING: I agree with what Manning Nash has just said. Building monuments is political language, and there is nothing you can do about it. A politician is going to talk the politician's language and this is a part of it.

Mr. HOLT: First, I do not know why we should associate a government staying in power with economic development. I think you can make a good argument for the fact that probably the way in which you encourage economic development is to rotate governments every 18 months. You are talking here about the problem of monuments and pyramids, and you are talking about it in the context of political advice. Perhaps what you might want to do is to tie in a United States foreign aid program with a restriction on building monuments even though it may contribute to the overthrow of the government in a short period of time.

What I was suggesting earlier is that you tend to decrease the probability of expenditure on monuments as you reduce the government's role in economy. That is the point I was trying to make. This would be the kind of recommendation in this regard that I think would be relevant.

Mr. WHITEFORD: I would like to follow up on this comment because what we are talking about, really, is communication. With the pyramids, with the stadia and with all these other things, what you have are communicative symbols by which the government or the party in power says to the people, "We're strong, we're powerful, we're able to do all of these impressive things." Some of them may be completely worthless so far as what they will do for the people of the country. Others may be very valuable, but certainly the evidence seems to suggest that many of these projects, for example, the building of the steel mill at Paz del Rio in Colombia, are symbolical kinds of development. While we were in Colombia a couple of years ago, the newspapers had a great deal of information about land reform and potential land reform, and yet, when we talked to the people, the response was almost completely negative. They told us either that nothing was going on or that it was all government talk.

When we crossed the border into Venezuela, we were impressed by the fact that all along the road we kept seeing large signs, big billboards that were 15 feet

high and 20 feet across, at frequent intervals which
advertised the land reform program. I do not know
whether there was any more land reform going on in
Venezuela than there was in Colombia, but certainly the
people in Venezuela had every opportunity to be more
informed about it or at least impressed with it; I
think the billboards were the same sort of things as
stadia. These were the means of communication by which
the government was saying to the people, "We're doing
this," or "We're doing something." Frequently it does
not have very much to do with whether it is something
important, direct or economic, at all.

The Diplomacy of Development

     Mr. GINSBURG: I am interested in the behavior of
states in an existing world system which is not closed
but is partly open, because over a quarter of the world
(i.e., China) is not now involved in what we normally
think of as a closed system. Nevertheless, there is a
world political system that we can describe, or at least
attempts have been made to describe it, and states play
certain roles within it. What I would be interested in
knowing is how the political scientist, if you like,
can help us appraise the behavior of states that are
developing or underdeveloped. This appraisal might be
on a rather abstract and perhaps theoretical level--or,
better, on an empirical level first and then on a theoretical one. How can we incorporate our observations
into a systems analysis of the sort that can also be
used for the examination of the internal political organization of these new and developing states? Most
important, how should, all other things being equal, a
state that wishes to develop rapidly behave in the
world system if it wishes to maximize its opportunities
for economic growth?
     Mr. HOLT: I think your first question here is
really one of the very fundamental ones. It is not a
question, however, which is very much in gear with the
earlier kinds of considerations of this conference. I
think there are two or three observations that could be
made. Let me talk about one of them. It seems to me
that an argument can be made that as industrialization
proceeds in the developing countries, some of the traditional structures which were very crucial in the

social integration of that society tend to break down. One of the problems that the developing society is confronted with is the problem of developing new symbols of loyalty and the problem of developing new social structures to deal with the problem of integration.

I think that one of the ways in which this can be done is through a certain kind of aggressive foreign policy in which you identify an external enemy, so to speak, and try to solidify, or resolidify, the community in which certain of these integrated mechanisms have broken down, on the basis of a new kind of orientation.

If you look over the sweep of history, you find some kind of empirical association of extreme nationalism and aggressive foreign policy with the periods of the most rapid economic growth. The United States at the time of the Spanish-American War, Germany in the twentieth century, France under Napoleon III are examples of what I am talking about.

Mr. GINSBURG: If this is an empirical observation, then I can think of enough exceptions to it that I wonder how valid it is.

Mr. HOLT: I think the way I would state this, and what I was trying to say more precisely, is that you may be increasing the probability of this kind of international behavior in a period in which relatively rapid industrialization is breaking down some of the traditional structures. Certainly there are exceptions to it, but I would think of this in terms of increasing the probability of this kind of behavior.

Mr. GINSBURG: Are you talking about states that want to develop, or poor countries?

Mr. HOLT: I am talking about states that have gone through a certain initial stage of development to the extent that many of their traditional structures have broken down. I am not talking about a state that is just thinking about doing it; I am thinking about states that have gone partially through the process of it. That is what I mean by "developing."

Mr. FATOUROS: Of course, it is true that the identification of a foreign enemy is very often a matter of self-assertion, rather than aggression. For instance, if when we talk about the identification of a foreign enemy we are referring to the so-called anti-colonialist attitude, there are several ways of interpreting

this attitude. The attitude itself is really far less
aggressive than self-asserting. There is a difference,
I think, in the kind of manifestations that follow from
each kind of attitude.

I would agree that in some cases there is an aggressive attitude as a component of development. That,
of course, is a common and very old factor in foreign
and international affairs. On the other hand, the role
of the developing countries in the present state of the
world society is becoming increasingly important; this
happens in part for reasons which may seem at first
glance without substance; for instance, simply because
they have formal statehood. But this formal statehood
does represent or make evident, to a considerable extent, substantive problems, such as the problems of the
welfare of the people involved--the people represented
by the state. It is probably possible to say that, in
a great number of cases, developing countries, or their
governments, react in the same manner as a developed
country would react if it were in a similar situation,
but, in fact, the developed countries are not in a
similar situation. On the other hand, a great number
of developing countries are in situations which are
fairly similar to one another.

For instance, take their attitude on solving economic problems, regardless of whether they are correct
or not in terms of economic theory. I am thinking especially of the problems of international trade or the
problems of international economic assistance. Simply
because their interests are common in this particular
connection, this leads to the development of a kind of
bloc, that is, a unified, common attitude toward certain problems. This is a new factor in present-day
international politics which it is important to examine: how far the perception of the similarity of their
problems leads to similar conclusions and therefore to
similar attitudes toward the developed countries, on
the one hand, and toward the Soviet Union, on the other.

We can go very much further in that direction. We
can examine how far it is possible in international
politics to talk today in terms of bipolarity; although
I do not know if this is exactly what we have been talking about here. I think the presence of the developing countries has made a difference, to a certain extent. Their presence leads to a restructuring of the

world society. Again, and this is somewhat more tenta-
tive, something that should perhaps be studied: how far
is there a common perception of their interests even
when they are not similar, or how far is there different perception when the problems are similar.

Sister THOMASINE: Let me carry that a step further and perhaps along a little bit more practical
lines. Most of us are aware that last year at the various world trade conferences the underdeveloped countries outvoted the developed ones. There have been
some very humorous remarks with respect to that situation, but perhaps that sense of identification between
nations which normally would be rivals will have a
positive world political result, something akin to what
Mr. Lewis mentioned last night. Perhaps the underdeveloped countries will soon be more in a position to
trade with one another and to uphold their part of the
world economy.

Foreign Aid and International Development

Mr. BINDER: I have put together some notes regarding this problem of the international aspect of development. It seems to me that if our discussion is
to be articulated with the scheme we have on the black-
board [see Fig. 1, p. 91], it of course has to do with
the structural aspects of that environmental sector
which is labeled "Other Societies," and one of the
problems with which we would have to concern ourselves
would be the changing structure of the international
system to which the domestic system has to adapt it-
self--in that goal attainment triangle, I suppose.

Some things may be done within the country in
terms of economic activities--adaptation proper--and
some things may be done in terms of political activity
domestically, and some may be done in terms of economic
activity outside of the country itself with the establishment of economic and trading blocs among the developing countries themselves, or in terms of more effective trade relations.

I would like to call to your attention three possible configurations of an international structure, terms
that are in general use, although I suppose in this
form Morton Kaplan may be more responsible for them
than anyone else: these are a bipolar system, a loose

bipolar system and perhaps a multipolar system.   What
I am really talking about is the decline in bipolarity
in recent years, the result of a fragmentation of the
blocs. The question that I am asking, for no one in
particular to answer, because it is a question we all
have to face, is this: what is the consequence for economic development of developing areas of the changing
structures in the international system?   It changed
from what seemed to be a bipolar system to a multipolar
one.

Under bipolarity itself I am not entirely sure
that the competition between the two great blocs--over
the extension of assistance to the developing nations--
was a really necessary kind of competition. That is, I
do not know whether it was vital to the United States
and vital to the Soviet Union that they be the first
ones in with assistance to the developing countries.

In other words, I am suggesting that I am not sure
that the developing countries were necessary to the defense of the West or to the defense of the East against
one another; and we might well have been able, in terms
of a very narrowly construed self-interest, to turn our
backs on the developing countries. But we did not. We
assumed, for perhaps logically inconsistent reasons in
terms of the rest of our foreign policy, that we ought
to and must assist the developing countries. We decided, in other words, that bipolarity required our assistance in the developing areas.

Now, as the Western bloc loosened a little bit before the Eastern bloc had shown evidence of this loosening, I think there developed a pattern which was essentially bilateral--in some cases multilateral--of economic assistance from subordinate bloc members of the West,
Britain, France, Holland, Belgium, and Italy. Bilateral,
and in some few cases multilateral, assistance came from
subordinate bloc members of the Western bloc to the members of the New National Internationale, if you will,
or the Third World. The reasons for this seem to have
something to do with the search for prestige on the part
of subordinate bloc members of the West. They seem also
to have something to do with the desire to loosen the
Western bloc by increasing the power of subordinate bloc
members through their relations with the developing
areas, and perhaps to strengthen or to restrengthen such
organizations as the British Commonwealth and the French

Community.

These kinds of activities broaden the pattern of trade and the possibilities for development on the part of the new nations. They also give them a little bit of schooling in maneuver, in how to play off one possible donor against another possible donor. They have much more opportunity to maneuver than when they only had two, the United States and the Soviet Union, and in fact, in the earlier days of the postwar period it was only the United States that was really helping and it was merely a threat of possibly working with the Soviet Union that was used as an inducement. I think the real schooling in maneuver happened in what we might call a middle period.

Now, I do not think that this kind of economic activity really was the effective thing in loosening the two blocs, but it was part of a tendency which developed while loosening was going on and it has increased, I think, now that we can look around and say that we do not really have a bipolar system any more. At least the two blocs, if there are only two blocs, are extremely loose and there is lots of room for maneuver on the part of the nations of the Third World among the various bloc members. For example, you can now set China against Russia in this framework of economic assistance, and I guess African nations particularly are able to do this.

At the very same time, with the explosion of a nuclear bomb by the Chinese Communists, this points up the possibility that some of these developing nations, unable to fulfill the aspirations of their citizens, may well be able to blast the rest of us to kingdom come, or at least set off an exchange of nuclear explosions that will lead to that. In viewing the Third World, therefore, we can ask what our attitude ought to be and what our attitude must be.

We can ask the question again: do we need to help these countries now that we see that the world is not going to divide up into two groups which will seek to eliminate each other? Do we have a more stable international picture which will permit us to say, "Well, we don't have to worry about the disposition of every single people in every single country in the world?" Or do we have a situation where any country having control of nuclear weapons can blow all of us up so that

we have to be concerned, vitally concerned, with the
domestic tranquility of any little pipsqueak of a country anywhere in the world, because they might get hold
of a nuclear bomb and heaven knows what will happen?
Therefore, any tiny country of a million population or
something like that can hold an atomic bomb against our
head and say, "If you don't help me, I'll blow myself
up." And the rest of us have to do something about it
and offer economic assistance to try and straighten out
the problem.

This has not yet come to be, but nuclear weapons
are indeed a great equalizer and may return us to a
situation of intense concern with the economic welfare
of even the smallest and seemingly most inconsequential
country. There is a possibility, which I think is even
more likely, that nuclear warfare is pretty nearly impossible because much as we may need psychiatric aid,
we are not that far gone. Therefore, once again one
may argue, "Well, who cares? We have a lot of problems
to worry about even with some of the larger countries."

It is not at all clear to me from this changing
pattern of international relations and the changing
distribution of nuclear weapons, and from the loosening
of the blocs, that we ought to go on in the same way as
we have in the past. For 15 years we have been saying
something about economic development and maybe now we
can just forget about it. We have not solved the problem but perhaps we do not have to solve the problem any
more for these countries. We certainly have to ask ourselves whether, given these new circumstances, the problem remains the same; and I do not think we have asked
ourselves this question here.

A third possibility is, of course, that the struggle between East and West, between right and wrong, between good and bad, between up and down, will continue
by other means and not by means of bloc formation. It
may be fought out in terms of cultural and economic development. Perhaps we ought to redouble our efforts
and recognize that this is a real front, and not try to
shoot the moon, and not increase our nuclear stock-pile,
but indeed, turn our efforts entirely away from military development, or largely away from military development to the seeking of means for winning friends in
the Third World.

I think there is one last consideration I would

like to put before you and that is that the remarks
made by Professor de Schweinitz this morning were
largely correct that it has been the political environment of this previous period of bipolarity or would-be
bipolarity which led us to bring these countries into
being. Someone had said, perhaps they should not be
countries. This may be true, but is there now any
residual moral obligation that we have, despite the
changed structure of the international system, to keep
these countries in being even though they came into being for reasons that had to do with the previous structure of the international system?

Mr. BARANSON: It strikes me as very interesting
that this whole business of power relationships involves a gamesmanship of development. I think it is
interesting to recall that during the nineteenth and
early twentieth centuries, nationalism and self-deter-
mination became pawns in big power politics, and sometimes ran away with events--Sarajevo and World War I
are an example. In more recent times, Vietnam is a
live pawn in the international power struggle.

The fact is that we have come up with some odd
forms of development gamesmanship. For example,
President Kennedy talked about "peaceful evolution" in
Latin America. He wanted to see change, to get the
process started but then he hoped to laboratory-control
it so it would not go too far left and upset our power
position vis-a-vis world communism. This is indeed a
game involving pawns that have their own volition and
dynamics and it becomes especially intricate with the
United States viewing economic development in terms of
political goals entailing controlled social change.

For the game we are trying to play, our understanding and know-how are themselves highly underdeveloped.

Mr. NASH: I think we have shifted the terms. We
were earlier talking about elites trying to get through
a process with their peasantry, and then we got up to
the big powers who, I really think (except for the
Alliance for Progress, in which I do not believe much
more than do most Latin Americans), are not sincerely
interested and do not sincerely act for economic development goals.

We act in Korea, Vietnam, Cuba, or whatever. We
like economic development and it would be nice if it

would pay off; but the main reason is political and not
for the internal necessary benefit of the government
being aided.

With respect to Cambodia, the Cambodians are not
hungry, they are not striving for development, and yet
we have given them $350,000,000 in the last ten years--
there are only five million Cambodians--and their GNP
stays exactly the same. This is an amazing business.
It takes great skill to absorb all of that without improving your GNP. (Laughter.)

The problem of economic development and international relations, I think, has not really been joined.
The big power relations to the poor, non-prosperous
countries tends to be political and mainly oriented
toward self-interest. I throw that out as a view of my
own. Perhaps, as a footnote to what Professor Binder
said, maybe the world situation has changed enough that
the attention the powers give to the non-prosperous
countries could really be in terms of economic development, but I think the situation from 1945 to 1960 was
such that we could not seriously be interested in economic development so much as in allies or non-trouble
spots.

Mr. FATOUROS: Do we have, really, to separate the
two or the three so clearly? That is, is it really
completely inconsistent to have at the same time, the
goals of having a friend in Asia, and avoiding a trouble
spot, and assisting economic development? If you could
assist economic development, and in this manner avoid
a trouble spot and have a good friend--I agree that this
is a very big "if"--but if this were so, then this would
be a set of consistent objectives for American foreign
policy. The problem is, how far is it true that assisting economic development does not serve the two other
purposes, and especially the one of avoiding a trouble
spot? Of course, the problem is made worse, because no
alternative is suggested, at least I have not heard yet
of any possible alternative.

Assuming that international economic aid does not
assist economic development in fact, or does not assist
it in a proper way, that it does not gain friends and
does not avoid trouble spots, what else can be done?
The problem is that the only alternative that appears
probable is a much worse trouble situation, as far as
trouble is concerned--a purely negative situation, from

the point of view of the Soviet Union, or the point of
view of the United States. I do not see any positive
gain in this for either party. In fact, I have the
impression that part of the trouble between China and
the Soviet Union can be stated in these terms. The
Soviet Union is saying, "We have to help them. We
don't know what will happen if we don't, but we cannot
avoid helping; we cannot take a different attitude
toward the underdeveloped countries," and China is saying, "No, we prefer revolution." I have then the impression that one of the strongest factors in favor of
economic aid as a tool of American foreign policy is
really the fear of the alternatives rather than a positive and clear objective in extending foreign aid.

Mr. HARING: It seems to me that it is the frame
in which this whole picture sits. The kindergarten
facts of the nation-state system are an analogue or
parallel to the laissez-faire system. In place of economic men you have self-interested nations, and these
are amoral nations, as they were amoral economic men
in the laissez-faire system.

Secondly, economists know better than anybody why
the laissez-faire system could not perpetuate itself.
It broke up and went bankrupt for dozens and dozens of
reasons we all recognize.

The nation-state system is in the process of going bankrupt in this same sense and we can predict, I
think fairly safely, that this sort of power politics
system just cannot last, it is impossible.

We all know this in our bones but we do not see
any way out of it. When you think of laissez-faire
states and so forth, one can do some pretty good guessing as to why is going to happen.

Then, regarding economic development, if you
change these amoral economic man-nation-states into
social creatures, there develops a concern for each
other's affairs that has been forced upon them whether
they like it or not. So, of course, they (and we) are
going to be concerned with the economic development of
the rest of the world for these reasons. The reasons
become political as the nation-state system goes bankrupt. This is a long range trend, and I see it as being inevitable, although somebody may disagree.

International Economic Cooperation

Mr. MORGAN: I have three brief questions I want
to ask. Quite honestly, I would be glad to have answers from anybody, and I suppose especially from political scientists. One is suggested by Professor
Lewis's comment that economic problems are relatively
simple--I have heard people from the International Bank
say the same thing--and the real problems are of another kind; also his observation that there are lots of
rascals in power. I wonder whether political scientists, or others, could develop any generalization on
whether you are more likely to have rascals in power
in low-income countries that are developing successfully, as compared with those that are developing more
slowly or not at all? That is one question.
Second, it has been fashionable in recent years to
be concerned with the possibilities of regional cooperation. The United States Government has the problem of
the extent to which it should favor and encourage this
concern. Generally the attitude has been favorable.
And yet such efforts have fallen on dubious days, if
not perhaps evil days.
I would generalize that the East Asia cooperative
movements were mainly stimulated by the rise of the
Common Market in Europe. They were visualized as defensive efforts against it. As the Common Market has
seemed to be less malevolent and less threatening, and
perhaps as political events have had their turbulent
way in the East, these efforts have diminished.
The very successful East African organizations are,
I think, now weaker than they were some years ago:
Kenya, Tanzania, and Uganda are having their problems
of getting along together. The Latin American Free
Trade Association seems to be having its own problems.
Can we generalize to any extent about the dynamics of
cooperation among such areas?
Mr. Lewis, of course, suggested increased trade
among low-income areas as a way out of some of their
burdensome economic problems.
My third question is a practical one. At the
Geneva meetings one of the main recommendations from
low-income countries was that they would like to have
trade preferences granted to them from high-income
countries. The French have been awkward about this and

have supported the notion of concessions by mother countries only to their previous colonies--five or six bilateral arrangements.

The Germans have lately supported a more general arrangement in which all high-income countries should give trade concessions on imports from all low-income countries. My question is: which is the better policy?

Chairman BLANKSTEN: Does anyone want to respond to these questions?

Mr. KING: On this question of the dynamics of economic cooperation and with special reference to Southeast Asia and ECAFE, my experience suggests that economists are playing it down. When I worked for the World Bank any mention of a common market for Asia or Southeast Asia was immediately met by the response, "This is premature." If you were to then ask, "Well, when does it become mature? When is the time?" the response was, "We don't know, but any thought before the right moment would be quite out of line."

In Southeast Asia there is, of course, fear of Japan dominating the market. Nevertheless and despite many professional economists arguing against a common market--showing that these countries do not trade with each other and there is no point to it--still the Manila Declaration at the ECAFE meeting went ahead to say that such a market ought to be created. Then political considerations prevented the furtherance of the limited goal of discussion of such matters. Here again you get this problem of a constructive policy versus a political-monument goal: they would rather have a Maphilindo [Maylasia-Philippine-Indonesia Alliance], they would rather have a Bandung atmosphere. Here again is a contrast with the little steps which may not be very dramatic: an extension service versus a stadium, a conference that examines steps toward a common market which may be 20 years off; versus the emotionalism of the Bandung, or uncommitted powers, or New Emerging Forces!

I see a parallel here between the domestic and the international policies of the underdeveloped countries. I also see similar consequences: the threat of anarchy, the threat of the government giving up development internally, the threat of the developed nations getting fed up with the international scene and questioning the desirability of the whole assistance program.

I am sorry to have brought up stadiums again. Please forgive me.

Mr. SCHWARTZ: A minor note: the common market or free trade association arrangement regarded by economists to have the least chance of all--the Central American one--of which they spoke least favorably, even compared to LAFTA [Latin American Free Trade Association], has worked relatively well. It has certainly worked far better than LAFTA, probably for reasons which are basically political, not economic.

Mr. KREININ: I would underscore the point--that the enabling condition in the drive probably ought to be political. But I think the movement toward integration in underdeveloped countries was triggered by European integration, where you and I know that the benefits from integration, the economic analysis of integration, and the entire economic conditions leading to integration, are completely different. You are almost comparing incomparables.

When you come to Latin America, therefore, you should ask yourselves, even in strictly technical economic terms--let alone the political problems which probably are the determining factors--can these countries integrate? They face an overwhelming transport problem. It is cheaper to ship to the United States than to ship across the mountains to a neighboring country. They maintain extensive exchange control. What is the meaning of eliminating tariffs and quotas when you still have exchange controls and multiple-exchange rate systems?

Even the technical conditions for integration do not exist. Of course, the benefits to be derived from integration in the case of underdeveloped countries are different from those derived from the European Common Market or another industrial area; they ought to be analyzed differently.

Chairman BLANKSTEN: I would like to point out that about the only problem that has been mentioned in both sessions today, to which no one has responded, is the question of rogues and rascals in government. On the theory that it takes a rascal to catch one, I have asked Bob Holt to speak to that. Would you care to comment on rascality?

Mr. HOLT: As I understood your question, Professor Morgan, it was whether or not there is a greater

likelihood that you have rogues and rascals in a developing area or a rapidly developing area than you do in
one that is relatively stagnant?

Mr. MORGAN: Yes.   I was assuming that there would
be more rogues and rascals in low-income areas because
of low education generally and other factors of background.

Mr. HOLT: When you talk about rogues and rascals
you certainly have to identify the particular normative
context in which you are identifying rogues and rascals,
and this may differ very much from society to society.

It seems that when you have a relatively stable or
stagnant kind of situation, you may get one kind of
rogue.   For example, if you have a new clique or a new
dynasty coming into power, you may have rogues at the
beginning of this period and in their positions of power they proceed to redefine the mores of the community
so that the same behavior which at one time would be
defined as being that of rogues and rascals, at a later
period--when they are still engaging in it--is considered to be a legitimate kind of undertaking.

When you are dealing with areas where there is
rapid economic development and rapid political change,
you certainly are increasing the frequency with which
you are recruiting people into political roles, and you
are tending to broaden the social groups from which you
are recruiting people.

Often you have the phenomenon that the people who
are coming in are not aware of the mores that govern
the particular status which they are occupying and they
act as rogues and rascals for a while until they learn
these particular things.

From the point of economic development, however, I
would like to make a further comment.   When you are
dealing with a situation in which the state is perform-
ing a relatively active entrepreneurial role, I think
there might be some economic advantages in having rogues
in these particular political-economic kinds of roles.
I think one of the important things to point out, however, is that there are rogues and then there are
rogues.

I think it was Plunkett of Tammany Hall who talked
about the difference between honest graft and dishonest
graft.   He said that it was perfectly all right (it was
honest graft) if they told their friends that the city

was going to condemn certain property and take it over
for building, and they should buy it up because they
would get rich within 18 months if they did. That is
honest graft. When the Republican machine over in
Philadelphia, however, sold the copper roof off the
poorhouse, that was dishonest graft.

When we are looking at this problem it is necessary to identify a certain kind of roguish behavior
that may be of economic advantage at a certain period,
as contrasted with another kind of roguish behavior
which really inhibits growth.

Mr. NASH: Sometimes I read political scientists,
and Robert Dahl, I think, in his book[3] on how American
cities are governed has some good clues for the kinds
of systems under which rascality can flourish. He
traces the change in American politics at city level
from the machine kind of ethnic interests to the more
pragmatic, unheroic politics, which characterized
Boston, Philadelphia, and New York, and are beginning
even in Chicago. His main theoretical apparatus is a
good one.

There is a system of cumulative privilege. If one
group has monopolies or quasi-monopolies on the resources, the education and the government, they can be
"grafty," and as political systems evolve, one of the
things which keeps them honest is not that they get
moral or they get revelation, but it is a dispersion of
privilege among groups who can do each other a lot of
good or a lot of harm. No one group can do itself too
much good or too much harm, so their interaction keeps
them honest but does not lead to a change of heart.

He [Dahl] spells it out for one of our wicked old
cities, New Haven, and I think the analysis can be
lifted for the purpose of this discussion.

Mr. HOLT: I was not talking about a change of
heart. I was talking about a change in the norm or a
change in the structure.

Mr. NASH: I think the mechanism of cumulative
dispersed privilege is the clue. How you get that
started, I do not know.

Mr. HOLT: If you read political scientists on

3. Robert Alan Dahl, Who Governs? Democracy and
Power in an American City (New Haven: Yale University
Press, 1961).

this, or if you read sociologists like Merton on the
economic functions of the [political] machine in New
York, you begin to get some sort of view of the economic contributions that are possible.

Mr. NASH: I do not believe in that kind of structural functional analysis. I just want to know why
that machine was there. If it gave coal away, the
latent function, I think, is childish. Just why, in
that kind of social system, do you have a machine?

If you say you have a machine and it stays there
because it gives buckets of coal away, that is nice and
interesting. Of course, Merton lived through the
Depression.

Mr. HOLT: No. I was emphasizing here the comments about the functions it performed for big business in New York rather than the coal it gave away.

I merely said that it was useful, if you are talking about certain kinds of economic development.
Whether these are functional interpretations or not, I
do not care.

Mr. NASH: I have already exhibited my anti-func-
tionalism.

Chairman BLANKSTEN: Before we adjourn this session, let me simply draw attention to what seemed to
me to be some of the chief problems with which we have
been concerned this afternoon.

In the first place, in discussing the system of
analysis that Professor Holt put before us, we had a
basis through functional requisite analysis to look at
certain kinds of questions, such as, what kinds of
systemic properties set the limits within which governments can move in such directions as those related to
economic development, and the question of democracy,
and the question of dictatorship, and wherein governments could operate in the developmental kind of context.

We discussed also, somewhat within that systemic
context, the problem of monuments, stadia, steel mills,
and so on. I have a feeling we did not get all of the
mileage, theoretically, out of this problem that is
probably possible.

Certain things seemed obvious: that these were
quick visual symbols that seemed to perform the function of mobilizing support or consent behind certain
regimes. There was, I think, an interesting point in

the communications theory regarding the functions of these monuments, and so on. Much of this, I think, can be handled in terms of the kinds of theoretical consid- erations which we opened up, but as I say, I have a kind of unfinished feeling about this monument and sta- dium problem. I think there is still more pay dirt in that which I do not think we reached.

We did, for a wonder, late in the session finally get to talk about international politics and diplomacy of development. Much of this, it seems to me, also lent itself to systemic analysis along the lines Pro- fessor Holt opened up for us, especially if we thought in terms of the environmental sector in the scheme with which he presented us. This helped us look at such things as the development in underdeveloped areas of common attitudes towards certain international problems, and helped us to understand some of the processes by which friends and enemies in the international commu- nity are identified.

Professor Binder also pointed out that it helped with certain problems in relating bipolar and other kinds of international assistance to such problems as foreign aid and technical assistance, and changes in nuclear capabilities among various countries in the international system.

We talked, somewhat in this context, about various types of economic cooperation. I had the feeling that that did not lend itself as readily to fitting within this same systematic frame as some of the other prob- lems, but that may also be because of the context in which we came to it.

Even rogues and rascals seemed to lend themselves to some kind of systematic analysis. The notion of the dispersion of privilege appeals to me in this direction.

SESSION IV

ECONOMIC GROWTH IN NEWLY SETTLED
AREAS AS CONTRASTED WITH OLD SETTLED AREAS

Chairman HENDRY: The discussion leader tonight is
Professor Theodore Morgan of the Department of Economics of the University of Wisconsin. I suspect it is
not necessary to go into the details of his wide experience in the problems of developing countries, but the
range with respect to geographic area is Ceylon, Indonesia, and Kenya. Professor Morgan has referred to
himself earlier as one of the refugees from Indonesia.
He has also acted as consultant to the Ford Foundation
and the World Bank.

The discussants include Professor Baranson of the
University of Indiana, International Development Research Center, whose main research interests are in
technological transference problems and primary regional interests in Latin America and Central America.

Our other discussant is Scott Johnston of Hamline
University, the Political Science Department. His major area of interest is in the Middle East, and I believe his research has centered on the development of
political parties in Israel.

Mr. MORGAN: I think the first thing I should do,
and briefly, is to try to put sense into the title,
"Newly Settled Areas as Contrasted with Old Settled
Areas." The problem is that of the effect of European
exodus during the last several centuries into other
parts of the world. Europeans went, in part, into areas that were already densely settled. These are called
old settled areas. They went to India and to other
parts of Asia, and to some relatively densely settled
parts of South America. They also went to areas that
were either initially or eventually, through disease or
fighting, thinly settled: among these, Australia, New
Zealand, North America, and perhaps a few other areas.

Obviously, there has been a tremendous difference
in the experience of economic growth in these areas. I

suppose the extreme contrast is India and the United
States. At this point you may feel it is all too easy
to explain the contrast.

I. First of all, I should like to say a few
words about the context into which explanations fall.
One tries to explain economic growth; those of us from
different disciplines have different kinds of emphasis.
What sorts of causes do we talk of: human resources,
natural resources, produced capital, technology, the
value system, social organization, political factors,
and no doubt still others. I think we would agree that,
broadly considered, all of these have relevance; they
are all influential. The question is not, therefore, a
matter of "either-or." It is more subtle. It is a
matter of the relative importance of each of these and
perhaps of their interrelationships, both in timing and
in causation.

There is involved also the extent to which these
are necessary or only conditioning--only supplementary--
causes of growth. There is the extent, Gerschenkron
will emphasize, to which you can get around blocks to
growth. You may have a society growing despite what, a
priori, you might have argued to be effective blocks to
development. This is the pattern. What I say is not
to throw out X or Y cause. It is simply to argue for a
particular supplementary cause as being--on prima facie
evidence and not final evidence--an important cause.

II. I do not want to spend very much time on the
two main usual explanations of diverse standards of
living in, let us say, Australia, New Zealand, Canada,
and the United States, and perhaps Hawaii, South Africa,
Uruguay, and Argentina; as compared to India, Pakistan,
Ceylon, Indonesia, Burma, Malaya, the Andean countries,
the Near East, and most of Africa. A Ricardian economist would think of the ratio of labor and, in the
longer run, also of capital to natural resources. And
so Marshall[1] suggests in his chapter on "Economic Progress" that the "field of employment" any place offers
to capital and labor depends first of all on its natural
resources. But he does not consider the resources-pro-
portion explanation as the central one. Instead, he

1. Alfred Marshall, Principles of Economics: An
Introductory Volume (8th ed.; New York: Macmillan,
1949).

picks out trade as the chief cause of the modern prosperity of new countries. "The causes that determine
the economic progress of nations belong to the study of
international trade...." (I suspect that to all of us
who are not economists, that sounds very limited indeed, and probably that reaction is right.) Within the
heading of trade Marshall emphasizes the flow of capital which exchanges goods and services moving into an
area against the promise of an outflow later of local
products.

Nurkse talks of the nineteenth century as a period
in which international investment scored its greatest
triumphs with strong emphasis on the great importance
of international investment for the growth of what I
call here the newly settled areas. Millikan, Rostow,
Rosenstein-Rodan, Leibenstein, Nelson, and the studies
that Chenery--well, Chenery's office, really--the labo-
rious and impressive studies that his office is making
for AID--place emphasis upon import coefficients and
export projections for predicting foreign aid needs,
and their possible and hoped-for tapering off as time
goes on.

The savings-investment emphasis is presented in
Nurkse's Wicksell lectures,[2] and in an excellent study
by Douglass North, Economic Growth of the United
States.[3] It is developed in Haberler's Cairo lectures[4]
as a cause for growth in a dynamic context. Contrary
to Myrdal and Prebisch, Haberler finds a number of ways
in which trade, over time, stimulates the growth of nations. Perhaps I should list them: it provides them
with capital goods, machinery and materials; it facili-
tates the flow to them of financial capital, dissemi-
nates knowledge, serves as the means for importing
skills and talents and checks monopoly. This is an

2. Ragnar Nurkse, Patterns of Trade and Development (Wicksell Lectures, 1959; Oxford: Basil Black-
well, 1962).

3. Douglass C. North, The Economic Growth of the
United States, 1790-1860 (Englewood Cliffs, N.J.:
Prentice-Hall, 1961).

4. Gottfried Haberler, International Trade and Ec-
onomic Development (National Bank of Egypt, Fiftieth
Anniversary Commemoration Lectures; Cairo: National
Bank of Egypt, 1959).

impressive list. Meier follows much the same position
in his attractive book, International Trade and Development.[5]
      III. The theory of investment in physical capital
as the central cause of growth has been subject to cri-
ticism by Schultz and his fellow investigators, also by
Abramovitz and others at the National Bureau of Economic
Research, and by Solow and Denison in econometric and
statistical studies which suggest that physical capital
explains from one-eighth to one-quarter of growth, and
that the "residual" or non-measurable inputs account
for from one-half to seven-eights.
      Tables 1 and 2 (pp. 136-137) compare, for the half-
century before World War I, the value of investment
capital and of human capital outflows from Europe to
overseas. I have spent so much time on them that I
have, perhaps, a myopic view. I think they are worth
considering seriously.
      You can get--this is a judgment--data good enough
to give you orders of magnitude on the value of the
flow of immigrants as compared to the value of investment flows. To illustrate: what is the economic value
of an immigrant? First, estimate the working life span
of individuals once they arrive in this country. This
is taken from life-expectancy tables for the period in
conjunction with data on the age at which people came
to this country. Find average earnings in this country
and discount them back to the time when they got off the
ship at Ellis Island. The data we have from both British and American sources is that, on the average, some
102,000 people per year were coming over from the U.K.
They are valued, in addition to their discounted product here, at the cost of bringing them up in England.
      Then you can do the same thing for the value of in-
vestment flows. Their current amount comes from Imlah
data.[6] Their contribution to product relies on margin-
al-capital-output-ratio estimates taken mainly from Kuz-
nets' studies. The range is wide; undoubtedly the

      5. Gerald M. Meier, International Trade and Devel-
opment (New York: Harper and Row, 1963).
      6. Albert Henry Imlah, Economic Elements in the
Pax Britannica: Studies in British Foreign Trade in the
19th Century (Cambridge, Mass.: Harvard University
Press, 1958).

actual range might well be wider than that.

Mr. HOLT: Are those annual figures?

Mr. MORGAN: That's right; averages per year for the period.

Mr. HOLT: In what, 1964 dollars or in 1800 dollars?

Mr. MORGAN: Valuation is taken as of the time of the inflow of capital and migrants. The median point is around 1890, approximately, in both cases; not quite that, but almost.

Consider the viewpoint of people who emphasize the importance of investment inflow into the New World, or into overseas generally, as explaining economic growth. Here is an attempt, if you like, on the side of heresy to ask, "Is that really true? Can we get some figures that will measure the value of immigrants side by side with the value of capital inflow?" What is the outcome of the comparison? I think one should conclude that the orders of magnitude are in general roughly the same in Table 2.

But for the U.K.-U.S. the orders of magnitude favor the immigrants--they were economically more important. You might well say that if the figures are worth taking seriously at all, the greater importance of immigrants to the United States was probably not a matter of chance. The relative importance of immigrants probably is genuinely a part of the reason for the unique economic growth of this country.

These figures, by the way, do not give a complete comparison. They take no account at all of backflows to Europe and the U.K. from immigrant remittances on the one hand and amortization and interest on the other. These are not included because I could not find data for them. To that extent these figures are imperfect.

If it is true that the immigrant flows have a value equal to or greater than that of investment flows in the half-century before World War I, then I submit that there is no doubt at all about the relative economic magnitudes of these two flows a half-century further back, or a century further back. Investment outflows from England and from Europe were hardly beginning before the early part of the nineteenth century, but people were coming to this country and elsewhere voluntarily or involuntarily, a long time before.

IV. The next point to mention is that sizable

Table 1.

Average Annual Value of Immigrants
and
Value of Investment Flow
into the United States
from the United Kingdom,
1870-1914

(Rounded to nearest $10 million)

A. Value of immigrants

    1. 101,800 immigrants, valued at
        their 25 years' product, discounted,
        of $8,702........................$890 million

    2. 101,800 immigrants, valued at the
        cost of their rearing in the
        United Kingdom, $1,306.............133 million

B. Value of investment inflow

    3. Investment inflow, valued at its
        discounted net product.........150-500 million

    4. Investment inflow, valued at time
        of flow............................70 million

Table 2.

Average Annual Value of Immigrants
and
Value of Investment Flow
into All Overseas Areas,
from Europe,
1866-1915

(Rounded to nearest $10 million)

A. Value of immigrants

    1. 456,000 net immigrants, valued at
       their 25 years' product, discounted,
       of $5,801......................$2,650 million

    2. 456,000 net immigrants, valued at
       the cost of their rearing in
       Europe, $1,088....................496 million

B. Value of investment inflow

    3. Investment inflow, valued at its
       discounted net product.....1,030-3,530 million

    4. Investment inflow, valued at
       time of flow......................500 million

foreign investment seems historically to have come relatively late in the development process. The logical
argument is that it is justified only when you have a
foundation already built, when you have an economic and
social structure that makes the bet a good one.

Mr. FATOUROS: In "foreign investment," do you include direct and indirect?

Mr. MORGAN: Yes. The data here comes in large
part from Berrill's paper given at what we think of as
the Rostow meeting of the International Economic Association.[7]

Mr. NASH: Was there any U.S. investment going out
of the country at this time, too, do you know?

Mr. MORGAN: There undoubtedly was some. I don't
have any data on it. I assume it was very small.

Mr. FATOUROS: There was some in the late nineteenth century. According to the U.S. figures there
was some in Latin America--direct, rather than indirect.

Mr. ANDERSON: What is indirect investment?

Mr. FATOUROS: Portfolio investment, securities.

Mr. MORGAN: Floating bonds, for example.

V. Now, a word or two on trade as an engine of
growth. This explanation has had various emphases:
Nurkse thought that the engine was running down;
Prebisch thinks that the engine always has worked badly, because it has always been transferring part of the
gains from technical progress from the low-income to
the high-income countries; Haberler feels that it has
worked effectively and is working effectively now to the
extent that it is allowed to work.

Evidently the expansion-of-trade mechanism as an
important cause of growth must have worked imperfectly.
There has been many an export boom, but among the countries of the world only a few, outside of Europe, have
become developed. Economies have gone on developing--
the large continental areas of the United States and
Russia being the chief examples--without necessarily
having external trade booms.

It is interesting to note, side by side with the

7. K. E. Berrill, "Foreign Capital and Take-Off,"
in W. W. Rostow, ed. The Economics of Take-Off into Sustained Growth; Proceedings of a Conference Held by the
International Economics Association (New York: St.
Martin's Press, 1963), pp. 285-300.

trade or export boom theory, the Chenery cross-section study of 51 countries in the early 1950's. The results of this study turn the expansion-of-trade hypothesis upside down. The main single cause of industrial growth, amounting to about one-half the total causation, is, according to Chenery's findings, input substitution.[8] It is replacing goods that used to come in, the squeezing out of trade as the growth of local production outruns the growth of local demand. At a certain stage in their growth countries become less specialized, according to this study. Of course, the 1950's experience need not necessarily be valid for earlier years, yet it is suggestive.

Where trade expansion does not lead to growth, you can set up your special explanations. Robert Baldwin has an interesting analysis in Economic Journal.[9] You can think also of Rosenberg, or Hagen, or of Meier or Sinai's hypotheses to explain why external stimulus does not take hold within an economy.

VI. What I would like to do now is to present a supplementary hypothesis for the differential growth of the two kinds of areas to which Europeans have gone. I start out with the generalization that people who go from the West to low-income countries usually come back vividly impressed by social obstacles to growth. Their judgments are not subject to quantitative test, but the concert of these judgments obviously should be taken seriously. The usual non-economic emphasis holds that European culture, in certain defined ways, encourages economic progress; and that indigenous cultures outside of Europe in general do not. You can talk of the Hebrew-Greek-Roman civilization, the Renaissance and Reformation, democracy, social discipline, a propensity to save and invest, better technology, better health and energy from superior knowledge, sanitation, medical care, and so on; and you can variously combine these explanations of why Europeans were effective in economic activity.

8. H. B. Chenery, "Patterns of Industrial Growth," American Economic Review, vol. 50, no. 4 (September 1960), pp. 624-54.

9. Robert E. Baldwin, "Export Technology and Development from a Subsistence Level," The Economic Journal, vol. 73, no. 289 (March 1963), pp. 80-92.

There is some weakening of this hypothesis from
the fact that people have moved out of their home areas
from other places than Europe and distinguished themselves abroad. Jewish people have gone to many areas
in the world; Arabs to the East Coast of Africa; Tamils
to many parts of South Asia, East Asia, and the Pacific;
Chinese similarly to the Philippines, Indonesia, and
other parts of the world, and so on.

Now it is obviously true that the Europeans did
carry with them superior techniques and very likely
possessed superior ability to organize in economic ways.
These advantages served them well. Many of the people
who moved were also self-selected for their energy, hope-
fulness, and ambition, which clearly are highly important kinds of assets for migrants between areas, between
different countries, and between sections of countries.
Such qualities of migrants tend to disperse regional
rates of economic growth, because people move from less
attractive to more attractive areas.

Many people, however, moved out of Europe by com-
pulsion, as slaves or convicts; or they were forced out
of their homelands by personal ill-success or general
disaster. Carter Goodrich has made some special study
of this and has estimated that well over half the people
in the Colonies at the time of the Revolution had come
to the New World as slaves, convicts, or indentured servants. This weakens the personal qualities argument for
the effectiveness of immigrants in the U.S., although I
should guess that the balance is still probably favorable. There is a further argument, I suggest, for the
brilliant economic success of the newly settled as compared with the old settled areas. It is a variant of
the pioneer society hypothesis, and is the supplement I
am proposing to add to the other causes of growth.

Consider the values and objectives of people who
live in old settled parts of the world in comparison
with those who have grown up in new settled areas. In
other words, what are the sources of status and prestige
in one area as compared with the other? In every society, the people at the top of the social structure influence value systems, so far as they can, to sustain
and reinforce their own prestige. In the typical traditional agricultural society the landlords--the land owners and aristocrats to whom the people at large look up,
and who are able to influence the value system most ef-

fectively of all the social groups--have an interest in
evolving and maintaining a value system that gives them
maximum status.

This interest implies that they will not set up
"accomplishment," by any definition, as the criterion
of social merit--physical or mental energy, ability in
production or trade, or courage or skill in battle.
Only in the remote, more primitive days, when violence
was a way of life and more stable societies were only
gradually being evolved, did the criterion of "accomplishment" hold uniquely. There are the father images
of Romulus and Remus, King Arthur, and Charlemagne as
examples.

For the top social group, one shaking up of the
social heap in a millenium is quite enough. They cannot accept accomplishment and ability in general as the
criteria of social merit; neither can they point to ex-
ceptional personal merit within their own group as justification for their status, for in every social group
and generation high ability of any sort is rare.

Income, of course, can be a support for status.
Everybody wants it. The high-status people have historically obtained it through land rents, taxes, ran-
soms, robbery, regular charges to merchants passing
through, or through ceremonial or customary gifts; and
these have sustained their position. The search for a
justification for status leads to a last-ditch and, in
a sense, conclusive argument, that one deserves emi-
nence because of who he is. He doesn't have to earn it;
he has it. He has his personal right, or he is a member of a family, all of whom have status.

Given the tight hold of such a status structure,
an able and ambitious individual without initial status
can hope to achieve it--how? If the structure is holding well, only by fitting in. For example, you can
produce goods for the king or otherwise serve him, and
so share in his status. But when this kind of society
is losing its grip, then there are chinks in the sta-
tus-armor, and prestige can be obtained in some measure
outside the pattern; perhaps by becoming eminent in law
or medicine but especially by achieving success in
politics.

A traditional agrarian society with a folk memory
of conquest and predation as the normal route to ac-
quiring status, power and wealth encourages energetic

young people to seek political success as their way up.

The route of politics is a flexible one, with great advantages. In a fairly stable status structure the successful politician assimilates himself into the existing hierarchy, supplementing and supporting it. Where there is more instability, the most promising task for the ambitious politician is to pledge reform or urge revolution. His aims may turn out, in fact, once he gets into office, to involve making the best of both worlds: an optimum compromise--to assimilate with the old hierarchy to some extent while reforming or supplanting it.

In the traditional low-income areas of the world, the demonstration effect in its widest sense will continue to foment political instability. As communications continue to improve--as they have improved fantastically by historical comparison in the last 20-odd years--there will be increasing awareness of the wide gap in standard of living between the low- and high-income countries. Absolutely, and probably relatively, this gap continues to widen. In such societies, if the inevitable tensions lead to increased political turbulence rather than to increased economic effort and accomplishment, then economic advance will be slowed down.

You have, of course, a potential vicious circle. The rate of economic progress may be shifted still further toward low or negative levels, if the canons of status in these societies discourage energetic and creative activities, the sort we have spoken of earlier today: if it is no credit to you to do physical work, or to be able to solve mechanical, chemical, practical problems.

If innovatory production and trade activities, the close calculation of money gain and loss, and business preoccupations and huckstering merit contempt in society, then what will the ambitious youngster do? With complete rationality he will look for a better field of activity. He will not go into private business life, nor will he want to work for commercial or industrial organizations of the government. He will direct his energies to where they will do him the most good; this may very likely be in the political area. The maximizing calculus leads away from economic effort: the divergence between private and social marginal product is wide.

In its pure form this logic of ambition in low-income societies is illustrated in the student centers of political dissidence and intrigue in Latin American universities and, to some extent, in the student strikes and revolts in Near East and South Asian universities and schools.

With the disadvantages for growth in this kind of society, I should like to contrast the overwhelming economic advantages found in the newly settled parts of the world: North America, Australia, New Zealand and parts of South America, where the native populations were too small to submerge the newcomers in the old system, or to enable the newcomers to set up a new superior-inferior status sytems which would discourage effort.

In a pioneer environment, survival and real income depend on personal qualities of strength, wits, and courage. Since these qualities are valuable, they are the self-evident basis of status. "Who you are equals who your family is" is no longer relevant. The younger son of a distinguished European family, out in the prairies or in the Rockies, had to pull his own weight if he was to win the local respect that counted. The acceptance of personal accomplishment as the source of status was invaluable for favoring economic and other progress, lasting for some generations beyond the pioneer environment that gives rise to it.

What about post-pioneer influences on such a value system? A commercial and industrial environment tends to sustain it, since energy and (business) ingenuity have their rewards and indolence and business folly have their punishments. So there is constant shifting over the years, or a few generations, in the persons and families of the elite.

Progressive taxation and effective practical education tend to sustain such a status system. War also offers, in its way, a stimulus to growth, offsetting a considerable amount of physical destruction through the prestige given in conflict to strength, wits, and ability in the achievement of concrete results. The survival value of these qualities tends to raise their prestige in all pursuits.

In contrast, an agricultural environment tends to destroy the status-through-accomplishment system, in

that ownership rights, clung to zealously, have suf-
ficed in many places and times to support a fixed elite
group, generation after generation. The modern practice of professional property management also tends to
destroy it by facilitating the continued high incomes
and status of people who have no need to be other than
unenterprising and unimaginative. There is a modest
offset in that professional managers are chosen, presumably, for ability. This offers a small leaven of
social mobility to the class structure.

   This, then, is the argument. It does suggest that
policymakers should have conspicuously in view the non-
trade and non-investment conditions of growth, and they
should look to the feedback effect of specific economic
and other measures into the status structure. The
question left with us is how to give prestige to the
qualities and habits that are useful to economic production, and so channel the efforts of the ambitious
and able in an economic direction.

   In the unitary kind of society that is normal in
the low-income areas, class divisions are deep. They
are conspicuous; they cut through all aspects of life.
In such a unilinear society you must diminish prestige
for the upper groups if you increase it for the others.
But existing prestige holders do not willingly abdicate
their prestige. You have the problem of developing the
delicate arts of political compromise and reform, perhaps along the uncertain road suggested by Hirschman.
He says you cannot bet on successful reform, but it is
possible. Change can occur by slow degrees in the existing status and power structure; or else, in a harsh-
er gamble, there can be a drastic overthrow of the
structure in whose debris, under favorable circumstances, the ambitious and able may seek status through
economic activities. But the debris following violent
change is all too likely to advertise to the ambitious
that their best chance lies in repeating the example
previously given: of seeking success through a new political overthrow.

   An alternative, for a policymaker or for anyone
else who can influence the situation, is to attempt to
move toward a plural kind of society in which there are
many channels of activities and competition, so that an
individual can get a sense of worthwhileness, of significance, of success, in many different lines. The ordin-

ary and correct argument against deep class divisions
is the static economic argument, the bad fit between
abilities and existing opportunities. We have added to
this static argument a dynamic one: that the plural
society blurs the class interest of individuals, and so
weakens the conservative impulse to hold on to the present status pattern, and makes possible more reforms
that are requisite for economic growth.

In fact, the traditional status holders may even
not be sure, as more and more channels of competition
are developed, that they are really injured by a given
change. Their interests are complex and mixed. This
reasoning holds also for other people below the top
level in the society. They may tolerate reforms or
even welcome them on the grounds of a more stable social structure developing, or perhaps because of the
social approbation to be gained through favoring reform.

Mr. BARANSON: I feel that in one way this is a
very challenging paper. It covers the gamut of the
kind of things that concern us in development. If I
may briefly summarize the paper, as I understand it,
you are looking at the engines of growth during the
nineteenth century. You alluded to the heavy reliance
upon investment and trade during the nineteenth century
as engines of growth. Development policy people today
place a large emphasis on capital resource mobilization.

You then offered as an alternative hypothesis that
there is also an essential human ingredient built into
immigrants who brought skills and know-how with them
that is just as important as the material capital. The
hypothesis here is one of human resources development
and the particular protestant ethic or pioneer spirit
that people brought with them.

I would personally be inclined to redress the balance of importance between human and physical capital.
I would weigh somewhat differently investment and trade
in terms of their relative importance. I would place
more emphasis on the importance of trade. With respect
to investment, I think this is an interesting difference between underdeveloped areas today and underdeveloped areas in the nineteenth century. In the nineteenth century the real dearth was savings. There were
markets in the developed world and investments went out
to finance undertakings that could supply those markets.
Foreign capital provided an essential growth ingredient

in those days.

Among underdeveloped areas today, it is becoming increasingly clear that the deficiency is not savings but lack of viable investment opportunity. If domestic savings are deficient, there is a good deal of international finance capital from private and intergovernmental sources. But the banks today have a real problem in finding suitable investment projects. So the real dearth is in investment opportunity rather than in savings.

With respect to the importance of trade to development, I would offer certain qualifications. I feel that part of the business of providing viable investment opportunities is exploring more intensively and imaginatively the trading opportunities of underdeveloped areas. Much of the recent emphasis has been upon developing regional markets. To the degree that these regional arrangements do not end up in high-cost industries and monopoly situations, expanded markets are unquestionably an essential ingredient of industrialization and growth.

Ted Schultz has argued for developing market opportunities in the mass markets of industrially advanced countries. For example, Mexico now furnishes part of the vegetable and fruit market in the United States--an excellent opportunity to earn income abroad. In a sense this is going back to the classical economists' thoughts on the international division of labor; this is one kind of trade that can aid development considerably.

I myself have worked on international manufacturing and interchange systems. Any industrial complex, you will find, when it is broken down, depends upon a wide range of components and parts. Within this range there are always some elements that an economy is more ready to produce than others. For example, in Diesel engine manufacture: given the labor and managerial skills, a country like Mexico or like India is more capable of doing certain kinds of milling and lathe work than turning out the more sophisticated parts in fuel injection systems. Here again, is a trade opportunity, and I think there are many others that underdeveloped areas can fruitfully pursue.

The pioneer spirit hypothesis, I think, like the Weber and Tawney thesis on the Protestant ethic, has

its limitations as a growth theory. I think both trade
and investment patterns today have to be re-thought and
reworked. I think the emphasis should be on markets
and upon finding viable ways to engage in industrialization and trade. The concomitants of social conditions and human resources that you refer to are also
essential ingredients. I have recently been concerned
with the problem of technological transmittal and adaptation. Technology has been regarded largely as a passive growth factor, adjusting to local factor prices
and resource availabilities. I have looked upon technology as a creative element, whereby you can adjust
factor proportions and use levels of skills and resources as you find them. Technology becomes a creative element in the process of adjusting.

I think more than anything else that this is what
an approach to development needs: a sizing up of the
situation at hand. How do you develop in an underdeveloped environment, given resources as they are, and
given the stage of development? The approach that social development or a social ethic is the prerequisite
to growth may be a false start. Innovation in trade
and in industrialization patterns to adapt to emerging
conditions is what is needed. I think that is the kind
of innovation that the already industrially advanced
countries can bring in terms of know-how and insight.

Chairman HENDRY: The issue has been partially
joined, not with rejection, but at least with modification of the skepticism concerning the old pioneer spirit.

Mr. JOHNSTON: I should like to suggest a few
items concerning economic growth in newly settled areas
as contrasted with the older settled areas in the one
country I feel I am familiar with, namely Israel, where
I have been interested in a study of the political party system.

At the very beginning of the session tonight Professor Lewis's observation as to economics being a
trivial explanation of economic growth was recalled.
I have thought over the application of this observation
concerning Israel as to the matter of economic development and even what kind of society it has been, in
terms of the problem of typology. Israel is a society
indeed where a very large number of non-economic factors have been involved as to programs of economic de-

velopment. It seems to me that there is some value in
examining some of the different types of situations
that have developed in Israel, and comparisons that
might be made.

Let me just suggest some of these problems in
terms of this particular society, a society which indeed does fall into an interesting pattern of being
both a newly settled area, such as the Negev desert region, with projections for further development there,
and the older areas related to the coming of the Zionist immigrants in the late part of the nineteenth century. These include the coastal plain area and Galilee.
Even concerning the coastal plain there were indeed areas which had not been used significantly economically
for several centuries since the coming of the Turkish
occupation.

Now, non-economic factors which are associated with
development plans involve a point which was brought out
earlier today within another context, the point of defense. Concerning the location of the very small number of Kibbutzim that you have in the central and southern Negev area, these collective settlements constitute
among other things, militia centers, a factor related
to the surrounding Arab areas. This is obviously a
matter of major importance from the Israeli point of
view with economic consideration being clearly of a very
secondary nature.

The paper just delivered includes the observation
that the founders of new societies are certainly most
concerned with the maintenance of the original values.
This to me is one of the most interesting things that
has taken place within a discussion of Israeli politics
and economic development between the older generation,
who had a pioneering socialist Zionism which involved
settlement work and who find themselves being increasingly challenged by modern administrators like Moshe
Dayan and others who say: now, the original plans and
original concepts as to such things as the development
of the Kibbutzim, reforestation, location of these new
industries and various types of economic enterprises no
longer make sense. This instead is the kind of society
and the kind of economy we have. It would be better to
have the dairying industry closer to the Tel Aviv metropolitan complex rather than in the far reaches of the
Negev. A whole series of observations of this nature

are made by the newer generation of practical administrators and technicians.

These technicians and this newer generation of administrators are increasingly rejecting aspects of the
traditional Zionist ideology, including the older fun-
damentalist socialist pioneering and are moving on to
something else for which they are very much resented by
many in the older generation.

Ben-Gurion is in some respects an example of this
type of thing. He has had some very grandiose plans as
to a population of several million in the Negev, and
his own personal example has included living part of
the time in a small and not economically prosperous
Negev Kibbutz. It should be added, however, that Ben-
Gurion also associated himself on some issues with the
newer generation of modernizers and administrators.

Let me move on to other non-economic factors.
There are religious factors. For example, there has
been a controversy between the orthodox political parties and other groups in the community within the last
series of months as to the location of licensed animal
slaughtering. For example, there is the matter of
where you may have pig raising in the country, and a
law has been passed in the last year and a half on that,
which has nothing to do with economic factors but has
to do instead with a type of arrangement made within
the cabinet coalition between one of the major religious parties and Mapai, the party of Eshkol and Ben-
Gurion.

There are other non-economic factors dealing with
the question of where you place the new immigrants.
The new Oriental Jewish immigrants, to a rather considerable extent, are sent to the least desirable areas
because there is less available for them elsewhere.
There are also, I believe, factors here as to the people who are already present and their strength within
the society and their being able to influence to a considerable extent this pattern of the location of people.

There is the role of political parties, as to
their stake in development programs. I see problems
that are present here within the political system concerning the newer development areas now and certain elements of change and even of instability within the
party system that are beginning to turn up and which
deserve greater study. There is the weakening of party

discipline in newer development communities and munici-
pal difficulties have turned up which have called for
special elections in a number of these communities.
There are other problems which I think represent issues
that are present in the party system which are going to
appear increasingly in the decades ahead. These are in
important respects even more to be seen in newer areas
where older patterns of life, older patterns of the society, and the older traditions are present or lacking
in varying combinations.

    These are just some thoughts I have had and some
things I have perceived, which occurred to me in terms
of this one country.

GENERAL DISCUSSION

Savings vs. Investments

    Mr. MORGAN: We are dealing, I suppose, with mat-
ters of emphasis. The concept presented by Mr.
Baranson, that investment opportunities were abundant
in the nineteenth century and are relatively scarce now
in growing areas, is an interesting idea. I think it
rides on the back of the notion that investment opportunities are opened up by complex social and economic
development. You have to have these developments ini-
tially--which seems reasonable.

    Of course, I am sure that trade is often a thor-
oughly useful stimulus to an area, as it may well be in
Mexico. I just do not know how to comment on the Argen-
tina-Brazil case. It seems to me that it is a mixed
case, and probably one ought to look awfully hard at
the specific facts if he is going to interpret the mixed
experience of European--

    Mr. KREININ: Mixed in what sense?

    Mr. MORGAN: Mixed in the sense that sometimes na-
tive populations lived in the new areas in large numbers, and sometimes not--mixed also in Sanford Mosk's
sense: in a brilliant AER article[10] he compared Latin

    10.   Sanford A. Mosk, "Latin America versus the
United States," Papers and Proceedings of the 63rd Annual Meeting of the American Economic Association, Chicago, Illinois, December 27-30, 1950, American Economic
Review, vol. 41, no. 2 (May 1951), pp. 367-83.

America with the United States and found differences in
their growth experience which reflected differences in
people, their values and organization. In Argentina,
the large estates and haciendas are at the center of
the aristocratic tradition that Mosk emphasizes. Elsewhere in the Americas, there have been the foundations
of a different kind of economy and society, with more
potential for economic advance: small men pioneering.

It seems to me that we probably ought not to talk--
perhaps we do not any more--of a theory of growth. We
ought to talk of theories of growth; and then we ought
to ask ourselves which theory best fits a given problem,
at a given time, in a given country. We should have at
hand, as Joan Robinson has suggested, a kit of variously shaped tools when we are trying to say something
useful about growth possibilities.

I might mention in connection with Mr. Johnston's
comments on Israel that I had an opportunity of looking
at the views of Governor Horowitz of the Bank of Israel
on the problems of underdeveloped countries. I think
Horowitz is, with the best intentions, considerably
astray in his interpretation. He is immersed in banking concepts, and sees growth problems as turning centrally on the amounts of money flows. Prebisch's theory of the terms of trade is very prominent in his
mind. He sees Israel's remarkable recent success--it
has been the outstanding country in the world for rapid
growth in recent years--as turning on the volume of
capital investment matters. In addition, I suggest one
might analyze the morale factors and skills of immigrants to Israel, amd perhaps the shaking up of old
status patterns that occurred as they were resettled.

Mr. SCHWARTZ: Mr. Baranson has made the point
that in the nineteenth century the deficiency was savings. He maintained that there was a sufficient number
of opportunities for investment, whereas, in this century, the problem is not so much savings as a deficiency in "viable investments" or "bankable investments."

I think this has to be at least very strongly
qualified by the following: very much of the investment in the nineteenth century was in the area of
transportation and public utilities. There is still
tremendous opportunity for investment in transportation, and even more in some of the public utilities
such as electricity. The problem is that this area,

which was so attractive to private sources, either for direct or portfolio investment, has been regulated to death or simply taken over by governments. And the governments have not invested here for one reason or another. Either they hoped that they might be able to obtain the necessary investment goods with an International Bank loan or they decided upon some show--and I will not say marginal cost--price solution: some kind of a show low-price formula which did not leave them with the funds--or they decided they did not have the funds--from alternative sources to make additional investments. I just wonder, if you were to consider transportation and public utility investments in this light, whether you would come to the same strong conclusion about the relative lack of investment opportunities in this century compared to the last. I very seriously doubt it.

Mr. FATOUROS: Is it really true that today what is lacking is investment opportunities and not savings?

Mr. BARANSON: Yes.

Mr. FATOUROS: I think one argument was already raised, the fact that the kind of investment opportunities that existed in the nineteenth century also exist today in pure economic terms, although they do not exist in political terms. Public utilities, for instance, are either regulated extensively or taken over completely by the state in many less developed countries.

In addition to that, is it true--and this is really a question--is it true that the possibilities for profitable investment today in the developed countries, are much higher than they were, for instance, in the nineteenth century, as compared to the profit possibilities in the less developed countries?

There is, I understand, high profitability of investment in direct investments in developing countries today, but the difference is relatively small, while back in the nineteenth century the difference was greater.

Mr. BARANSON: There is a very recent article on this which I just read a couple of weeks ago. I cannot remember whether it is in the AER [American Economic Review] or whether it was in the SID [Society for International Development: International Development Review], but it is on this question, and it was very well documented, I thought.

I go by the experience of the banking community today, the World Bank and the Inter-American Development Bank, and these international banking institutions. They all say they have more money than they know what to do with.

Mr. MORGAN: But they are fussy.

Mr. BARANSON: Sure, they are fussy. They have to know what they are doing.

Mr. HOLT: Well, if you are going to be too careful about the way you spend your money, you are going to find yourself with lots of money on your hands.

Mr. KREININ: I think there is evidence that profitable opportunities for investments in underdeveloped countries are pretty good, but there is also a fairly high level of risk, coupled with the balance-of-payments constraint which makes it difficult to take earnings out of the country. When you speak of profitable opportunities in percentage terms, in terms of local currency, that is one thing. But to transfer earnings to American dollars and get the money out of the country is quite another. Coupled with this factor is the risk, either real or imagined, of expropriation and all that, that reduces the profitability of the investment.

The Frontier and Development

Mr. ANDERSON: There is a certain appropriateness in a Wisconsin professor picking up Turner's frontier theory and extending it. As nearly as my memory brings back to me the comments and criticisms of Turner, I think I would find the new version also shaky. For instance, if one were to compare, say sixteenth-century Europe and nineteenth-century Europe, or Europe and the overseas countries, I think you could ask: is there in modern Europe or in overseas areas actually more mobility between social classes? Is there more instability of fortunes? I am doubtful.

I am inclined to think that the absence of development is not due to the presence or absence of general characteristics of the society, and particularly for the countries copying Europe, but to the presence of specific cultural traits with certain clusters. I take a dim view of the whole line of reasoning of the frontier theory and related broad, sweeping conceptions of social structure--even as a sociologist. I think you had better stick to your international trade theory.

Mr. NASH: For what Mr. Holt calls settled societies, those with dense land-man ratios and complicated
social structure into which foreigners come: for societies such as these the lack of development has been
pretty well explained. Jonathan Levin's book, The Export Economies,[11] treats Burma and Peru and the development of a foreign factor economy which leads to about
30 years of expansion, but such a distorting of the factor proportions in the economy that, when the guano
runs out, or when other countries get into the rice
business, you are dead; you have no flexibility to
shift over and no skills to do anything else.

That is a case of the settled societies, where the
foreign influence led to about 30 years of development
and then stagnation; I think we have a pretty clear picture of how a foreign factor economy works to eventually
lead to a blockage of development.

What bothers me is that pioneers do not necessarily build social structures which are useful. I think I
remember a little more about the Turner hypothesis, maybe because I went to school later; it was not the pioneers, the people out west, who made America great, it
was the people staying back home in the dirty old slums,
with the old customs, with the European ethnic groups.
It was the offshoots, the nogoodnicks, that were going
out there and boozing it up out west. The land-man-
space, the pioneer ethic were not conducive to economic
growth in America. What really made it grow were the
settled traditional glass blowers from Antwerp and all
these kinds of people who had all of the rigidities and
turned out to be the people who gave America most of its
development. I think Oscar Handlin documents it very
well.

Mr. GINSBURG: I want to raise a point of caution
by looking at the colonization period in North America
and southern South America and comparing the situations
we observed there with the situations we observe today.
Let me explain.

In the first place, when the Americas were settled,

11. Jonathan V. Levin, The Export Economies: Their
Pattern of Development in Historical Perspective (Har-
vard Law School, International Program in Taxation;
Cambridge: Harvard University Press, 1960).

and I am thinking particularly now of North America and southern South America, there was a kind of "open world" system. In other words, there were possibilities in many places for frontier settlement, but in fact it did not appear everywhere. Now, of course, there is a relatively closed world insofar as colonization opportunities are concerned.

But at that time could, conceivably, settlers have gone into the Amazon? It was unsettled, heaven knows, and still is, but they did not do it. Where did they go? Where were the frontiers of settlement established in the seventeenth and eighteenth centuries? For the most part they were established only in certain types of world regions.

These regions offered sets of conditions which were amenable to treatment or modification, or which one could adjust to by means of the cultural apparatus that people brought with them. In other words, the settlers that went from Western Europe, and particularly Britain, to the east coast of North America were not moving to environments which were substantially different from those to which they were accustomed. The same kinds of technology that they employed in their native environmental settings were, for the most part, applicable to the new environment.

Later on--much later--as the frontier moved westward, these conditions did change, but initially they held true.

Also, at those particular times, certain kinds of resources could be exploited in these new environments for which markets already were in existence. For example, Britain was pretty well running out of timber for ship building. The east coast of North America was a God-given area for the British ship-building industry, and this was an important factor in the settlement of that great region.

My point is that for the most part the lands that were settled by Europeans were empty lands which were amenable to development by means of the technology available to Europeans at that time. They did not go into the tropics where there were vacant areas. They went to areas which were familiar to them and with which they were able to cope.

Now, one can ask, "Well, what about developed areas?" The fact is that there really were no already developed densely settled areas in the world that were accessible to Europeans and which presented environmental conditions to which the European technology of the time was adaptable, or which presented possibilities for exploitation in terms of markets already existing in Europe. China might have been such a case, but it was closed to Europeans.

If one looks at India, for example, even apart from all the people, it was exceedingly unlikely that European settlers would have gone there. They also could have gone to Java but they did not; and they could have gone to sparsely settled Borneo, but they did not--although these were a long way, I grant you. There were, in short, good reasons why they chose to go where they did.

I am not sure what my conclusion is, but although I do not object to the frontier hypothesis as you stated it, I would argue that it may hold better under some circumstances than in others.

Social Structure and Economic Growth

Mr. HOLT: I was very much taken by Professor Morgan's treatment here of social mobility and social status as elements that might be involved. I have done some research on pre-modern Britain, France, China, and Japan, which I think is probably very relevant to the comments he was making.

One of the interesting factors that links England and Japan as similar cases and contrasts them with France and China deals with this factor of social mobility, but it is a little bit different than the one you are suggesting. You find that in England and Japan there were very rigid legal restraints on mobility from the middle classes into the titled aristocracy. Where mobility was essentially blocked in England and Japan, it was actively encouraged by the government of ancien France and Manchu China, so that you will find, if you look at the figures, that the sale of titles ran rampant in France throughout this entire period. From 1600 to 1642, for example, about 28 per cent of the total French government revenues came from the sale of titles, and this was during the period in which the French kings were collecting about five times as much tax per capita as their English counterpart. You will find, if you examine the scholar-gentry class in China in the late eighteenth and the beginning of the nineteenth century, that it reached a point where almost 30 per cent had purchased their academic degrees rather than working up through the regular examination system.

You get a view here, that where you have societies in which the middle class, the merchant and entrepreneurial groups, are blocked by law from achieving these upper-status positions, they tend to stay on in the entrepreneurial or merchant kinds of role, whereas in France and China they purchase a title and then use what capital they have, after the purchase of a title, for the purchase of land.

Mr. GINSBURG: If I may just comment on the last remark, I do not know what the situation was in France, but I do not think your reference to China holds in the same way, because, although there was corruption as measured by the purchase of posts in the civil service of China, these posts were not inherited; in other words, no title went with them that could be passed from father to son.   Only one generation was involved and this is an important difference.

Mr. HOLT: This is one differentiation, yes.   But if you look at the gross numbers, it is an exceedingly impressive number.

Mr. KING: Mr. Holt made the point, as I understood it, that there was considerable social mobility in China, that in Manchu or nineteenth-century China there was insignificant economic growth, and he tried to connect these factors.   Yet it was a particular kind of social mobility that existed in China.   It was a kind in which a peasant, through education, through hard study, might very well become a leading official. His power remained, however, completely subject to the whim of an authoritarian state.   The social mobility that occurred in England occurred in a free society and is hardly comparable.   Historians have concluded that there was little social mobility in England (based on Cambridge University graduates, for example), yet, when the few lower-class university graduates entered society, they moved into a position of independent authority and independent action.

To turn to China again, those who bought degrees, who changed to the gentry status, did not necessarily take official positions and many of them were numbered among the few entrepreneurs that China had.

Mr. HOLT: I was talking very specifically about
mobility into the aristocracy. I was not talking about
mobility in any other place in society.

Secondly, I did not address myself to the phenomenon of downward mobility out of the aristocracy, which
I think is an additional part of the argument here.
One further comment. When I am talking about social
mobility here, I am talking about it solely in terms of
prestige and not in terms of power. What was purchased
in France and China was prestige. The intendances and
the authoritative counsellors to the King of France
were not for sale and the crucial position of the Dis-
trict Magistrate in China was not for sale.

Theory Formation

Mr. BARANSON: I hear so much of this business of
the Meiji Restoration and the Chinese societies and
all these other things, and I am delighted; I think it
is good intellectual exercise, but what in the world
does this have to do with development? Do you mean to
tell me that you are actually going to take some of
these analogies and you are going to be sort of a
Toynbee? Are you going to reverse historical challenge
and response and project it into the future to induce
social mobility? What is this all about?

Mr. HOLT: If you are talking here about what kind
of a social or political engineer I am going to be, I
am not going to be one at all. All I am concerned with
here is the analysis of a particular phenomenon of political and social development.

I find a rather interesting pattern in the contrast between the development of England and Japan on
the one hand and France and China on the other hand,
and I think it is worth looking at these particular
cases because it is very difficult to believe that the
similarities between France and China come from a prolonged period of culture contact. If, indeed, you do
find 12 or 14 different dimensions on which China and
France resemble one another and on which England and
France are different, it seems to me that you may have
your hand on data that aid in the development of a set
of hypothesis that are worth looking at in developing
areas today. That is what I am concerned with. This

information may aid in the development of a scientific
theory of development. The careful formulation of good
hypotheses is an essential part of the process of theory creation. If I find a number of patterns that prevail in societies that developed successfully, which
are in contrast to those that prevail in countries that
had great difficulty developing, I have the empirical
basis for some hypotheses. If, further, I find that
similar hypotheses could be deduced from existing theories in the social sciences, I have a good justification for spending money to test the hypotheses by examining contemporary developing countries.

Mr. BARANSON: What do you do, for example, in the
case of China, where this was, say, an 83 per cent
weighted factor that you explained as a necessary and
sufficient cause, but in the other society you do not
know if it is one, two, or eighty-five?

Mr. HOLT: I think this is the kind of a thing you
have to begin investigating. This is what is worth
finding out.

Mr. BARANSON: Well, as a tool it is useless, then,
and this is what I am concerned about. There has been
a lot of these kinds of analogies and the further we go
along the more there are of people who are attracted to
this kind of thing.

I am talking about comparisons of the Jews in
Romania to the Chinese in Manila, and things of this
sort. (Laughter.) It is interesting, it is delightful, but, considering the objectives to which we should
be devoting outselves, it is rather incredible.

Mr. HOLT: But the relevant question here is: from
whence cometh your hypotheses? Are they hunches that
come rolling out of the back of your head?

The argument is essentially as follows: One, I
find the empirical patterns and I can, from these patterns, generate a hypothesis. Two, I find a body of
theory in the social sciences from which I can also deduce the same hypothesis. This makes it worth testing
in my mind, and you find in the developing countries to
today the laboratory in which they can be tested. This
is no argument from analogy.

Mr. FATOUROS: A footnote to your argument is that,
of course, there are all kinds of problems that are
created out of such a study. For instance, in France,
and I suppose--I do not know--in China, this method of

selling prestige and keeping power was certainly used
by the governing class in order to stabilize the government. The same method was used to some extent in
England by the sale of commissions in the army. This
last was, to a great extent, a very conscious effort
not to have the kind of army that led to the creation
of a Napoleon, and this was the reason it was retained
for so long, up to the middle of the nineteenth century. How do you account, though, for the fact that the
relative rigidity of entry from the non-nobility to the
nobility in England did not lead to a lack of stability
for the government?

I think the problem with such analogies is that
you have to bring in more and more factors to explain
why the analogy does not work in another case. There
is an analogy between A and B, but when you consider
another aspect of A, say C, it does not gibe with B.

Mr. MIRACLE: I want to refer to the general priority that should be attached to a hypothesis like the
one Professor Morgan has given us. It seems to me that
as a hypothesis it has a lot of plausibility. That is,
when you talk about ability and achievement spurring
people on, driving the developing mechanism, and when
one thinks about looking at historical cases and trying
to work out the path or see if this happened. There
has been doubt expressed about whether this is the single explanation of the particular case, but I wonder if
we have a better hypothesis to explain the particular
division that he has pointed out?

It seems to me that it fits pretty well in the
countries he mentioned, and you can add one or two
more. Most of the African cases fit this business of
either having a large native population--as they do not
like to be called any more, but indigenous population--
or an imported social system in which one does not
really have to achieve very much.

This was just a plea, perhaps, for some interdisciplinary attack on how in fact achievement and a variant of this within existing underdeveloped countries
can be successfully carried out. I am thinking, for
example, that in some places there are 50 to 100 ethnic
groups within a national boundary and there are very
great variations in the amount that individuals are allowed to achieve. There are people who think they see,
in many cases, considerable differences.

When you hear that this tribe or this group are more aggressive, that they are the economic men more than certain others, that they are the ones who are getting ahead, is there not some way that we could get another check on this hypothesis, either with data that are already in but in the hands of anthropologists or sociologists and not available to economists--or by work of historians?

It is really a question of whether we could not make a fairly quick check on this from some other sources; at least it would be rather interesting to try.

Mr. NASH: Every once in a while we oversell anthropology; we teach everybody about culture and its constraints and its values and we leave out the situational role performance criteria.   Lebanon is a pretty poor country and overpopulated.   The West Indies, for example, is not overpopulated for Lebanese with the same culture.   Whenever they go there they get prosperous.

We see this phenomena in many places.   India is pretty poor for Indians, but when they go to Africa they prosper.   With the same culture, the caste system, and all the things that are supposed to be barriers back home, they do very well in their new environment. So I think culture and values are very important but, if you do not take any role performance or economic opportunities into consideration you have less than the shadow of the story.

Chairman HENDRY: In Vietnam the Chinese are considered to be the dynamic people and in Cambodia the Vietnamese have become the dynamic element in the society.

Transformation and Trade

Mr. KREININ: Whether or not trade can be a stimulant to development depends on what Kindleberger calls the ability of the economy to transform.   Most underdeveloped countries have a very limited ability to transform.   Therefore, while some trade might be a prerequisite, I do not know that trade can be the major factor in the developmental process.

It is more likely that countries will develop through import substitution than through export-led growth. The ability to transform is something which affects not only the underdeveloped economies; it also affects the developed economies, where, for one reason or another, institutional or otherwise, they either are unable to readjust themselves to changing export market conditions or their factor remunerations have come to be out of line with factor endowments.

We see that in England today, where part of the external imbalance can be traced to the inability to transform. I suppose it might be argued that the pound is overvalued, and there are a variety of other reasons, but inability to transform is one reason.

The balance of payments constraint on the development of underdeveloped countries and on the growth of developed countries--I suppose this is a difference in terminology--exists wherever you are.

It is true that there are other non-economic factors in the Israeli situation and therefore it is really not a good example for any development case. But economic constraints exist in Israel much the same as they exist elsewhere, and Israel is facing a severe balance-of-payments problem despite the huge inflow of capital.

I do not know that countries can really count on trade as the major stimulant for growth. It might be a subsidiary prerequisite, but let's take a look at the very few cases where countries have shifted, in the postwar period, from underdeveloped to developed status. We talk an awful lot about development but, let's face it, we have had 20 years of talk, and the number of countries which have actually developed can be counted on one hand.

Israel is one country that was so transformed but it is a poor example. It is an unusual case from which few general conclusions can be drawn. Japan, I suppose, is another case, and so perhaps is Mexico. When you start studying what the elements were in the engine of growth, you would like to determine why some countries developed and others did not, but it is very difficult to find examples. Take the Mexican case: would you say that Mexico experiences an export-led growth? I am no expert on Mexico, but I have a feeling that import substitution played a more important role there.

I doubt, therefore, that the developing countries have the kind of ability to transform that would make

possible export-led growth. Do not forget another
thing: without rapid transformation, countries often
get a huge deterioration in the commodity terms of
trade. What I am trying to suggest is that they lose
some of their gains from growth in technology, as a result of deterioration of their terms of trade.

I suppose with export-led growth more is lost
than with import-substitution. Although Ted Morgan
might dispute the idea that anything is lost that way,
I think there is some loss involved, and it would be
more with export-led growth.

Mr. NASH: In the case of Mexico, which I have
followed with some interest, a tremendous amount of its
economic development has come in agriculture with irrigation in the north Pacific states.

I think there is a moral to be learned from that
and the moral I learn is, don't ever mess around with
traditional agriculture. If the people are already
settled peasants, let them starve and then start somewhere else; this way you will solve your food problem--
otherwise, they are unsavable.

There are, however, great economic opportunities
in modern agriculture and Mexico has done a lot in this
area.

Sister THOMASINE: We are in a position, now, after 15 or 20 years, not only to reassess export-led
growth for this period, as Mr. Kreinin says, but also
to contrast it with the export-led growth of a century
ago.

It is pretty hard to be a country now, in my opinion, and to be forced to depend upon exports. Despite
what Mr. Lewis said, I take a dim view of the export
position of many of these countries: what could they
do even if they wanted to export? I really do not know
where they would get rid of their exports, to be frank
about it.

Mr. KING: Mr. Kreinin stated there was imperfec-
tion in trade as a weapon in the development process.
But in the nineteenth century the export economies were
more passive. When there was a boom it was regarded as
a fortuitous circumstance. There was no reason why the
rest of the economy, why the state of thinking in the
economy, or why the level of education would be at a
point where developmental advantage could be taken of
the export boom. This presumably is where the modern

study of economic development is effecting a change.

When we consider the 15-year period and say that we should have expected more development, I wonder if we shouldn't recognize that 15 years is really a very short time. When you think of the first conscious planning of the use of export earnings for investment and development purposes you can only go back about ten years in many of the former colonies--especially in Africa. Even in Malaya the first development plan began in 1955-56. Before that it was merely a continuation of a government capital-expenditure program. Perhaps we may be a little overly pessimistic in this condemnation of the failure to take advantage of the trade benefits.

Mr. SCHWARTZ: In any event, with respect to export-led growth and ability to transform, I do not know that you can deny how important export-led growth has been to so many economies and what a significant first step it certainly could continue to be.

Having said that, however, I would note that, in most cases where there was some tremendous export opportunity which was not accompanied by a significant ability to transform, little more came of it. I guess the most famous case is that of Brazil, which had a sugar boom, a rubber boom, and a coffee boom: three export booms in a century without much in the way of continuing development.

In the postwar period Ecuador did not experience a very substantial change in its level of economic development--despite a very substantial export boom.

Mr. KREININ: In what product?

Mr. SCHWARTZ: In bananas. Not too much resulted from it, and I think this was in part due to this inability to transform that you are speaking of.

I do not think, therefore, that you can deny the stimulus and potential which export situations can lead to, but I think the other is probably a necessary condition.

Mr. BARANSON: I would like to add a footnote to this business of transformation and trade. Kindleberger has some sophisticated thoughts on this subject of transformation and export and import-displacing industry.

I have done some work on industrialization in Central America. It is much more difficult to set up a paint and copper wire factory in Honduras, which is an import-displacing industry, than to provide a range of copper wire products. You ought to see how many supporting industries you need in order to get a copper wire plant started. It is much more of an undertaking than some people might imagine.

I gather from one or two remarks here that some people think that import-displacing is relatively simple and export industries are more difficult to develop. In most of the cases I have looked into, it is just the other way around. As a matter of fact, the worst choice you could make, in terms of what the economy can handle may be what they happen to import now, be it copper wire or paint. You may end up with the worst choices of industries operating at high production costs.

Mr. KREININ: Concerning the earlier point of ability to transform, we are again talking about the same thing we talked about yesterday: it depends on which industry. Certainly there are import-substitution industries which are more difficult to develop than some export industries.

This is not the kind of import-substitution under discussion, and the ability to develop industry--export industry per se--is not the sole problem of transformation. The problem of transformation involves also the diffusion of the benefits from that industry throughout the economy, and that is more difficult.

It depends, therefore, what industries you are talking about. If a Latin American country wants to develop production of electronic equipment, certainly it would be very difficult, whether for export or for local use.

I wonder whether, from your experience, you could tell us how you would characterize the Mexican growth. Would you characterize it as export-led or more import-substitution?

Mr. BARANSON: You would be hard pressed in most underdeveloped countries--even Brazil or Argentina--to find an industry that does not have to be hot-housed with a tariff. If you establish a high enough tariff level you can have any production cost base. The real thing you are talking about in transformation is the ability to carry on an industrial activity at fairly efficient costs.

In the case of Mexico, and this is part of the Prebisch argument, he argues for instant industries and he argues that the only way to get started is to hot-house them; there is no question but what this is how Mexico got started.

Mexico and Brazil both are well on their way now. I am familiar with the Diesel engine industry. A Diesel engine has 750 parts. It takes about 200 plants in this country to build one engine, that is, 200 plants to provide the 750 parts. In that range there are probably about ten parts Mexico can produce competitively because it is a particular part that uses a high amount of relatively unskilled labor. Thus they can use the kind of machines they can get without using up too much foreign exchange.

I am suggesting here that there are many more low-cost activities that should be the leading areas of industrialization, that could be developed for trade and export. This other path, which is essentially a way of artificially creating markets through tariff barriers, either in the country or through regional arrangements, is one thing on which I really felt I should take exception to Professor Lewis. This business of talking about the kind of things that they can trade with one another is vitiated by the fact that they can set up direct trade barriers. I know that today one of the big problems is that Mexico does not want to be supplied with certain parts from Brazil; she wants to get them either from Denmark or from Belgium or from the United States where she gets both the price and the quality she wants. It is only under artificially contrived conditions that you are going to get this kind of industrial trade.

Mr. MIRACLE: This very neatly touches a point that I was going to address myself to. It is really a footnote to what you called a footnote earlier, and that is, that a lot of the trade is agricultural and in many of these countries it is very highly concentrated. In fact, this is one of the characteristics of the tropical belt: its high concentration in one or two exports, and in many cases a single export crop. This then means that we do have theories rather than a theory of trade, and we have to look somewhat differently at transforming an export crop when there are few alternatives, particularly if it is an export crop that is produced by plantation methods, where it is very difficult to redistribute this capital to something else.

The Concept of Technological Breakthrough

Mr. NASH: Since we seem to be seeking sort of a magic key either in migrants or given capital or trade, I will put up a candidate. I think economic development takes place when there is some investment which is a technological breakthrough. Now, nobody knows what a technological breakthrough is until it occurs, but the search for it and the investment in it gets you over some critical hump which has a whole lot of--I wish I could use the language better--link effects, et cetera.

Mr. BARANSON: Multipliers.

Mr. NASH: --multipliers and linkages which change the character of the economy. Look at Mexico; they found two or three high payoff technological breakthroughs and invested in them and it has been going like crazy. The problem, or the dilemma, of Mexican economic development is that they always have to find the next one.

Economic development is having your society geared in such a manner that there are people always searching for and anticipating a technological breakthrough and having the investment to make it. In the twentieth century it is not hard to get the money. The problem is to find the technological breakthroughs. That is my candidate for the most influential factor in development.

Religion and Economic Development

Sister THOMASINE: As a person who has done some research on the place of religion in economic development, I would not discount it. I am thinking of Latin America. I know a little bit more about that.

Taking my own Church: I think it has proved an obstacle to economic growth in Latin America. I think a change has come now, a change in the Catholic Church, which is very fruitful. In my opinion, however, the Church in Latin America held back development; it was not the missionary in a California spirit. In Latin America economic growth was held back by the colonial

spirit of Spain and the Church. I do not think there
is any question about that. It has changed now, however.

Mr. SCHWARTZ: I want to make three summary comments. One is in relation to the church item. In
Argentina, the Chubut River Valley in Patagonia was set-
led by Welshmen in the middle of the nineteenth centu-
ry--at a time when even parts of the province of Buenos
Aires were Indian territory and dangerous for newcomers.
The settlement prospered at first, but for many years
in the twentieth century the Valley has been experienc-
ing a rather slow rate of economic growth. When asked
about the reason for this, one Argentine church official replied, "Well, they're all Welsh." (Laughter.)

There are many people in Chubut who would object
to this line of reasoning, but at any rate, it is interesting that this kind of provincialism exists everywhere. I think it is, to some extent, too strong to
think that Catholicism has different consequences for
economic growth, e.g., according to whether it comes
from Northern or Southern Europe, or that Catholicism
would necessarily lead to this kind of result. But at
any rate--

Sister THOMASINE: If you were on the inside, you
would know the difference. (Laughter.)

Foreign Factor Economy

Mr. KING: Let me just comment on the foreign factor economy. It does not seem to me that it is today
completely at variance with the idea of, or need for,
technological change. The difference between the nineteenth century and today lies in the fact that the local population of a foreign factor economy was long unconscious of the potential for change. When it did
become conscious, the foreign factor economy could be
used to further development goals--this is the difference. People are now conscious of the potential for
change and therefore they can use these export booms if
they are wise; they can use the resources they gather
during these brief periods in order to implement a beginning development plan and to achieve that first technological change.

Mr. MORGAN: The Chairman asked me whether I wanted
to say anything in conclusion and I said I probably

should, because otherwise I would be taken to feel that the argument had failed.

It seems to me that in summing up all of these comments, what we have been doing is to give out of our own individual experiences the degree of emphasis we think ought to apply to this and that cause, and this and that block to causes; in that sense there is not so much conflict as supplementation in our discussion.

SESSION V

CULTURAL CHANGE IN DEVELOPMENT

    Chairman KING: In view of the fact that the eco-
nomic solution to development is trivial or simple, we
economists have solved our own problems and we can now
turn to look into the problems of the anthropologists
in this session.

    The principal discussant this morning is Mr.
Manning Nash, whom obviously you know very well, who
has done a great deal of work in Guatemala and Burma,
was recently editor of Economic Development and Cultural Change, and is author of works too numerous to mention.

    I suggest that we move right into the discussion.

    Mr. NASH: In thinking about "Cultural Change in
Economic Development," anthropologists typically do it
through two lenses. The first lens gives a very, very
long view and the long view tells you just what sort of
change--social and cultural change--the process of development in modernization is.

    I will sketch about two minutes of the long view
and give you some of the yield from that and then move
on to the short view. If you look at humanity as a
single human career, from way up with the bird's eye,
there seem to have been three major transformations.
We call them revolutions: the Neolithic Revolution, the
Urban Revolution, and the Industrial Revolution. In
the long view, the societies which have undertaken self-
sustained, economic growth are those societies which
have invested or participated in the Industrial Revolution. Economic development then is the kind of transformation which allows you to do a very simple thing:
to take tested, scientific knowledge and apply it to
the daily life of a society in continuously new incre-
ments.

    When a society is structured to apply tested know-
ledge normally to its productive process and to a lot
of its daily life, it will get rich. What kinds of

societies are able to do this? No society is fully
adapted to do it. Look at our calendar and our measur-
ing system; we know a lot better but we do not do it.
There are cultural constraints even with respect to
those things we do know, but we know a society has to
have at least these general features: it has to have a
high tolerance for ontological uncertainty. The world
has to be pretty loose and a lot of people have to be
able to have the personalities to live with a loose
world.

It has to have a social structure in which economic performance is important in conferring real material
rewards and status. It has to have a lot of mobility,
both spatially and socially, and it has to have a political system which is not dedicated to order alone,
but to some equalitarian or redistributive economic
goals.

At least, that is the way I look at the larger
parts of the social structure and value system which
have been characteristic of those societies which are
able, continuously, to put novel scientific stuff into
their daily life.

This long view does not tell us anything about
economic development at this particular moment. If we
elaborate it and spell it out, it gives us historical
perspective so that, when we look at societies now, we
may be able to tell whether they are changing in the
direction and toward the kinds of societies which have
economic growth as part of their constitution.

Let me restate what the long view teaches you, or
has taught me, in one sentence. It has taught that
there is a sort of society which has two major characteristics: it grows economically in consequence of its
daily operation, and it has a social structure which
generates and absorbs change without disorganization.

Now, let me move to the short view. The short
view is used to look at societies now undergoing, or
attempting to undergo, the process of modernization or
economic development. When you look at societies in
the short view, you get more microscopic, and I think
you ask three kinds of researchable questions.

The first thing you want to know about any society
from the social and cultural point of view is: who is
likely to undertake a course of modernization? By
"who," I mean what social segment in the society? For

which social group is economic development a viable, an
actionable set of goals?

There are techniques for identifying these groups
in a society with some good probability. Maybe you can
point to a society and say, "Nobody. This society does
not have a segment that will undertake economic development." If so, the social and cultural anthropologist
has nothing to study there unless he is interested in
kinship, but from a social change point of view, there
is nothing. The first thing, therefore, is to identify
those people who will undertake change in the direction
of modernization.

The second question is, whom do they face? What
other segments do they face as they try to do it? This
is one of the things I argue with Hagen. He has not a
good, not a bad, but a moderate technique for identifying the groups that are likely to undertake social and
cultural change, but it never puts him in an honest-to-
goodness social structure. He never tells you whom
they face. Once you have the group, you are off and
away, and I think that is naive because you have to
deal with a social system. Whether you diagram it in
triangles as Mr. Holt did (Fig. 1, p. 91), or any other
way, there is a social structure and a culture pattern,
and any group attempting change does face all sorts of
other groups.

In the modern world, just as an aside, one of the
interesting things is that economic development takes
place against groups which have vested interests in a
kind of economic structure which never existed prior to
the Industrial Revolution. In Latin America, when a
group tries to industrialize it already faces an organized, entrenched working class. It does not create a
working class. The working class is built in and has
some vested interests in a kind of technology, in a
kind of arrangement with the government, and in a kind
of rent capture on their wages. And we could find
other things, the other organized groups, that are in
the social structure.

So you want to know: who are they and what will
they face? You also want to have some sense of the
possible outcomes of the courses they will take. This
requires you to have at least a stage theory of economic growth.

The first two parts of the short view, I think, are

very well laid out between anthropologists and sociologists. The third part, the minimal temporal length sequence, which gets you from the state of transition to modernization is blank--at least in my reading. I know of no convincing set of stages--not taking seriously Rostow's Airplane Theory of Growth; there are too many airports and too many consequences. We have no minimal set of temporally defined sequences, and I think, if we need research priorities, this is one I would suggest.

Mr. ANDERSON: What is the significance of your inserting the word "temporally" in the term "temporally defined"?

Mr. NASH: Because it is a process over time, and a cross-sectional analysis may or may not get you to length stages. If you want to know where you are going, you have to have some idea of what the process looks like.

In the remaining couple of minutes, let me say what some of the yield has been--at least in anthropology--in the study of economic development as an indicator of a modern society. I now prefer to use the term, and I think the word is better, "modernization," because the economy is only one segment of the changing society.

We have empirical generalizations on several levels, some of which have a truth value number assigned which gives you confidence, and some of which is a funded nonsense or wisdom of the business which circulates it. I will just give you a couple of them.

The first one I think of--which is pretty easy to get--is something like the less the more: the less polarized wealth is in a social stratification system, the more likely it is that a segment will appear to undertake economic development.

Mr. ANDERSON: Now, that is opposite Hagen.

Mr. NASH: Right, only this is true. (Laughter.)

Mr. ANDERSON: Since you are my colleague, of course.

Mr. NASH: There are other lower-level generalizations about the formation of dual societies.

Mr. KREININ: Why do you say this? What is your evidence?

Mr. NASH: I will document it later. I think now I would do an anecdotal defense, but I do have it

documented somewhere. If I just run through in my mind
the societies I know, and if you tell me the societies
you know, the generalization may not fit all cases but
it has a good probability number on it.

Mr. MORGAN: By "polarized," you mean concentrated?

Mr. NASH: Yes, and sort of held in, too, by social constraints.

Mr. KREININ: This is what we would say: the less
equal the income distribution or the wealth distribution? Is that what you mean?

Mr. NASH: Well, polarization is only one component in the status hierarchy. There are mechanisms of
status conferral, career, modes of recruitment, and so
forth. I do not intend to teach my colleagues anthropology and sociology, but the word is used to refer to
a whole kind of social arrangements of power, wealth,
influence, and prestige, which are parts of the institutional structure of the society as against the performance level of individuals. That is one component--
and only one component--as wealth is only one component.

Mr. KREININ: So you use it as an indication of
mobility, of class mobility?

Mr. NASH: Well, mobility is one of the aspects.
I am using it as an indicator that under conditions I
have given, it is more or less likely that a group will
begin to undertake economic development. Let us take a
polar example such as Laos. On this generalization
there are zero people in Laos ready to undertake economic development. Somebody might start it in from the
outside, but I doubt it.

There are lots of other empirical generalizations
on the formations of kinds of societies. There is a
typical pathology now, in the middle of the development
process, which results in a form of technological and
economic dualism and a multiplicity in social organization, which keeps lots of societies on dead center and
not able to move off. I think Indonesia is probably
the hearth on which this model has been built.

Finally, we get a low level yield, but probably
the most useful one for practitioners. This is the
diagnostic yield. If you ask anthropologists and sociologists what to look for in the social order, I think
they can give you a reasonable budget of things, so
that you do not have to do the mind-dizzying business

of taking everything into account.

Some way or other I have seen sort of a checklist that comes out in books like Cooperation in Change,[1] Goodenough's latest book, and Lucy Mair's New Nations.[2] They are sort of checklists of what it is that anthropologists take to be the main factors to look for, and that might save the practitioner some time.

The last word is that the minimal time span--and this is sheer opinion--of economic development is minimally a generation and probably two, because it is a process of cultural learning and resocialization and reformulation of a whole generation of people; the minimal temporal scope of the modernization process, I would guess, is about 40 years.

What good does this advice do? It saves planners, visitors and governments a lot of unnecessary anguish when they do not achieve modernization in five years.

Mr. KING: Thank you very much, Mr. Nash. We will next hear from our discussant, Mr. Daniel Wit, who has done field work in Thailand, and is the author of Labor Law and Practice in Thailand[3] and other works. He is now with Northern Illinois University. Mr. Wit.

Mr. WIT: I tend to approach this as a political scientist and so I approach it in two ways. First, I approach it intellectually: in terms of basic interest in trying to understand the interrelationship between the cultural and the political, along with the economic.

I also approach it operationally: in the sense that I am interested in problems of technical assistance and in what government can do.

Basically, I guess I have been indoctrinated to some extent by Mr. Nash's type of analysis because this makes sense to me. The question it leaves open, however, is the type of professional question with which I am most concerned, really, which is: what can government do? This gets back to our big debate of yesterday,

1. Ward Hunt Goodenough, Cooperation in Change; an Anthropological Approach to Community Development (New York: Russell Sage Foundation, 1963).

2. Lucy Philip Mair, New Nations (Chicago: University of Chicago Press, 1963).

3. Daniel Wit, Labor Law and Practice in Thailand (BLS Report No. 267) (Washington, D.C.: Bureau of Labor Statistics, 1964).

or rather, our rather lengthy discussion on the role of
the political scientist. Is there some development
strategy that can be employed, which recognizes the
necessity for taking into consideration the cultural
factors and the need for cultural change?

I personally think that cultural change is a critical factor. I would include in cultural change not
only attitudes concerning work, for example, where we
have something very tangible in terms of ethnic differences, but I would also include motivation. I have
been impressed by McClelland's efforts and other clini-
cal psychological efforts to apply the whole concept of
achievement and motivation to the field. But what,
then, can government do in this regard?

Well, I think first it has to realize the importance of culture. I have been very much impressed,
operationally, by the extent to which both indigenous
governments and sometimes American government agencies
have not been really very concerned about this point.
There is a certain pattern of assistance that we engage
in, but just what does it really mean? In part, cultural differences are ignored because they appear to be
nebulous to the operationally oriented practitioners.
They do not know how to deal with them.

As I say, I am impressed by the need for government to take cultural factors into consideration. I am
impressed also by the many occasions in which economically sound recommendations or administratively sound
ones--and I have been involved in public administration
technical assistance--are completely worthless, either
because they are ignored or because they are "handled,"
for reasons of political expediency, by the host government; the government wants the assistance or the
money, but then intentionally circumvents the recommendations because, culturally, they do not make any
sense.

If we have a government which is committed to de-
velopment--which we often do not have--but if we have
one, then it seems to me that what is required in this
day and age is a strategy which attempts to blend a
number of these factors.

I do not "buy" the notion that one must transform
the entire society before one can get on with the work
of development, because this is a morass one sinks into,
and also this becomes undirected effort to transform.

I also do not see a government as being capable, in itself, of conducting such a total revolution within any
meaningful time-frame.

I do see, however, the possibility for government
running a checklist of those cultural factors, including psychological factors, which can be counted as assets for the promotion of development, and running a
research checklist of those factors which can be noted
as obstacles and liabilities, and then building it into
the strategy for the promotion of development.

In other words, I think that one stage in the formulation of strategy for development by a government
must be the incorporation into the development plan of
what can be learned from this type of sociological and
anthropological research.

This has to be associated with the effort at scientific economic analysis which in turn, to be realistic,
must also be adjusted to the political realities and
the administrative realities of the society, apart from
the cultural realities. Again, I am searching for what
we were discussing yesterday when Mr. Blanksten put his
finger on it for me in saying, "Can we mesh in any way?"
Operationally, I think we have to mesh.

I see, therefore, government as being able to utilize this type of analysis of facilitators and obstacles
within the cultural and the social sphere, just as it
can utilize the political and administrative strengths
and weaknesses of a society and associate them with the
economics of development. I also think that it becomes
critical from the point of view of a government which is
committed to development--I am only talking about that
fairly rare bird, from my point of view--it becomes essential that it go through the effort of attempting to
identify that group within a society which has either
rebelled against or emerged from the traditional culture sufficiently to be potentially flexible and able
to provide the necessary entrepreneurial spirit. Whether one talks just about managers, of which there are
shortages, obviously, or whether one just talks about
"attitude" without necessarily pinning it down to someone like a plant manager, I think these types of people
have to be identified and have to be associated with
the strategy of implementing a comprehensive plan.

I think, here, we can get help from the psychologists, combined with the anthropologists who are con-

cerned with a given country. I recognize fully that we do not know much, for example, about mental health in many countries; it becomes very difficult, if you do not know much about mental health in some countries, to know how one promotes development in them when development requires the tapping of psychological forces and eliminating psychological obstacles. But, I think this is <u>the</u> challenge. I also think that the very fact that these demands on government are so complex, is the reason for the relative lack of success of many governments in doing much about the generation of development, apart from the matter of time-span to date, which has been very brief. I see these several types of demand upon a government which is committed to the promotion of development.

There are other things, of course, that one could "toss in" as a political scientist. "Commitment" to development by the government is obviously not enough, either. It must also have certain types of capability. I regard administrative capability as a very critical factor.

I do not necessarily "buy" some of the public administration analysis of all world civilization as a product of successful administration, but, on the other hand, I do think that the administrative capacity of a government is critical. This, too, is a cultural problem, in the sense that much technical advice for reforming administration is totally meaningless, given the specific developmental stage of a society and its culture.

Parenthetically, may I just mention a very delightful talk which was given by a Filipino to a group of American foreign aid people gathered together in Manila. In that particular talk, the speaker took to task the whole American effort in the Philippines to introduce into government such things as performance budgeting, and also to get at nepotism and corruption, on the grounds that this is dysfunctional from the Western point of view. The whole "pitch" of this Filipino with a Michigan Ph.D. and all of the other Western trappings was that this is nonsense at this particular stage in the Philippines. At this particular stage in the Philippines, he claimed, if one attempted to achieve this American objective as part of the modernization process, all that would happen would be that we would

throw the Filipino administration into chaos. Why?
Because we are dealing with a society in which people
do not trust each other, or, if they trust each other,
they trust their <u>compadre</u> only. Nepotism, he stated,
is the only way in which you can get any decentraliza-
tion at this time--which is also another administrative
objective--and so on and so forth. So, scientific modernization in administration, like scientific modernization in economics, is meaningless without the attempt to develop a modernization strategy which blends
cultural factors into it.

I am in complete sympathy with the types of insight provided by sociology and anthropology, but I
also desperately search for operational means of getting that insight out of the conference room and into
the field; this is the sort of thing I am personally
wrestling with at the moment.

GENERAL DISCUSSION

Chairman KING: I have just one or two general
comments. With respect to the estimate of the time-
span as being 40 years or two generations, the questions that come up in my mind are connected with something that you brought up, Dr. Wit, namely: now that we
are conscious of the problems of development, can this
time-span be consciously shortened--perhaps by seeking
to improve the political capabilities? Is it possible
for a ruling class or a ruling group to willingly destroy itself or transform itself into another class that
can be identified? Or can the ruling class give itself
a new interest that can be better identified with the
development process, and given this consciousness and
this possibility of transference of interest, can the
role of the civil service, which may belong to the ruling class by family ties and so forth, be given other
horizons, perhaps other experiences, so that it can
perform a role in the development process which will
somehow shorten the time-span?

Professor Nash gave us two views, a long view and
a short view. He stated general principles here which
we can discuss as such, or we can bring specific examples to bear on their relevance or irrelevance to the
development process.

Time and Signs of Change

Mr. SCHWARTZ: You were talking about economic development in a minimal period of time-span, in a generation or 40 years, and this seems to me a little bit in contrast with your stress on situational differences in other respects.

After a certain period of rapid development in some societies there is more concern, more consciousness of the need and desire for development, perhaps influenced by a relatively advanced degree of communication. In such a situation, a more curtailed time period might be all that would be necessary. But this could lead to an effort to do it in too short a period of time, which might cause a reaction against the development plans--particularly if the shortened timetable were not met. The result might be a consensus that the time necessary might be not shorter but, indeed, longer than originally estimated. In any event, I would think there would be differences from time to time, and from society to society, as to what the minimal development period would be, and that these might be as different as between ten and one hundred years. This would be the sort of thing which I would expect to hear, as a matter of fact, from the sociologists and anthropologists. Why do you seem to insist on a generation?

Mr. NASH: I had in mind, when I said that, the new nations, the societies of Africa and Asia. I think Argentina could get off center in a lot under 40 years because Argentina is in many senses a pathological modern, if I can use that term. It has a lot of the institutions and markets, the people with firms, and the labor forces, which are absent from Thailand, Burma, Cambodia, and many of the African countries. That minimal time-span has to do with the transformation of the recently independent nations, which I think form a special category by themselves.

Remember, I said that as a matter of opinion. If you pin me to the wall with some fact in opposition to it I will give up that opinion.

Mr. SERRIE: Allan Homberg's project in Vicos, Peru, caused an incredibly basic transformation in an essentially peasant population characterized by fatalism and tremendous suspicion and fear of the outside;

and everything in only ten years, not in your minimal
span of 40 years.

This, of course, was only on a village level, but
how would you deal with this kind of thing?

Mr. NASH: Well, I am not sure yet that if Cornell
University pulled out of the Vicos project it would be
a self-sustaining hacienda, and I would have to go look.

The literature of the Cornell School has not convinced me that the change is built into the social
organization and the minds and hearts of the Vicosinos
yet, and that doubt is widely shared in Peru; I do not
think we have a clear instance there which would knock
off my hypothesis. There is one other thing you must
remember: with respect to communal development, when
the time of the developers exceeds the time of the people living in the village, you have a bad investment,
and I think that is what Vicos looks like. When the
anthropological hours exceed the hours lived by the in-
digenes, it is not worth studying any more.

Mr. KREININ: It seems that you are in search of
indicators--sociological indicators--so you can look at
a country in much the same way the National Bureau
thinks it can look at the economy; identify certain
living indicators and say, "Now, the economy is going
to develop," or, "Now the economy is not going to make
it." I wonder whether this is essentially what you are
doing, and, if you are, can you give us an example?
Can you stick your neck out on this?

Mr. NASH: My crystal ball is about as cloudy as
the National Bureau's, and I leave forecasting to the
astrologers. (Laughter.) By the time I would make a
prediction it would have so many OTE's [other things
being equal] hanging around that it would not hit the
case anyway. I do not think I should try to make a
prediction now, but I think it is true that I am looking for a shorthand set, somewhere between the level of
features that Talcott Parsons, Marion Levy, and other
third-story theorists would lay out for a modern society and the bottom rung of the anthropologist who says
that you have to take everything into account, culture
trait by culture trait. What I am trying to do is become a second-story man, get off the ground a little,
but not look up and let the skylight dazzle me--with
apologies to Oliver Wendell Holmes.

Stage Theory

Mr. BLANKSTEN: I would like to comment on something Professor Nash said at the beginning of this session about the need for a viable stage theory of development.

I think it is clear that, if we do not have one,
it is not because nobody has tried--as witness the airplane theory and some other attempts. Among the various things we have attempted, the stage theory has some
special kinds of difficulty. There are problems in the
definition of stage and how you use it in theory and
so on, but the question I would like to put to you,
Manning, is this: it seems to me that of all of the
social science disciplines involved in this kind of effort, probably anthropology has had the most traumatic
brush with problems of stage theory and evolutionism
and so on. I wonder if there is anything that comes
out of this experience, in terms of a kind of an intellectual history of anthropology or however else you
want to frame it. What are the special things we have
to be careful about as we try to develop the stage
theory that you say we need? I am not asking you here
to spin out a stage theory for us, or anything like
this; but what do we need to do?

Mr. NASH: One of the things that topples the mag-
nificent edifice of evolutionary theory that anthropology has is, of course, the facts. They made mistakes,
I think, in laying out a kind of stage theory which
could not be faulted. You could select things from it.
They made the mistake of getting formal succession from
stage to stage without ever any mechanisms of transformation. They went from savagery to barbarism to civilization, and they had formal definitions, but nobody
was interested in how you went, or how you got there.
Stage theory without mechanisms is a spectral mass of
bloodless categories.

Take Rostow: he adds to our vocabulary, but not
to our knowledge. He adds propensities. I think these
are the special pitfalls in trying to construct a stage
theory.

Ontological Uncertainty

Mr. FATOUROS: I would like to ask a question

about another of the indicator requisites, and it is simply this: what is "ontological uncertainty"? I like the term, and I like its existentialist overtones. You mentioned that the military does not like it and that makes me like it all the more. So will you explain: what is it? (Laughter.)

Mr. NASH: Well, "ontological uncertainty" means that there is not a creed, or a dogma, or a set of cultural values held in an overcommitted way throughout the entire population. There is a lot of variety in the commitment to the values; lots of people in the society are loosely committed, and there are competing value systems.

Now, when I give a proposition and I give it in my own scientist guise, I am ontologically uncertain as to how it fits the world; if you give me reason to reject the hypothesis, that psychological stance and that value system, allow me to take on your new hypothesis easily.

Mr. FATOUROS: ·Would that have any relationship to the relations between cultural values, religious values, and political structure?

Mr. NASH: Surely.

Mr. FATOUROS: That is, if there is no direct relationship between the three, then you would have a higher degree of ontological uncertainty?

Mr. NASH: Possibly. The conditions for the creation of ontological uncertainty, I do not know. That is a researchable problem. How it is infused in a society--partly in the education system, partly in the family socialization, and partly in the kinds of groups competing with each other--makes for ontological uncertainty. It takes a special kind of person to live in that sort of environment.

The Guatemalan Indians, by and large, are not ontologically uncertain about the most important things in the world. If you ask in Cantel, "Where is the center of the world?" they will answer, "Here." "Why is it here?" A saint was born here and lived in a certain cave. They have a structure which is hard to get through.

Mr. FATOUROS: Are the Antioqueños ontologically uncertain?

Mr. NASH: I haven't a clue. What I know about the Antioqueños is the hearsay I read in Hagen's book.

(Laughter.)

The Case of Modernizing Oligarchies

Mr. NASH: I want to say something about the question that was asked about transforming groups. There is a kind of group called the modernizing oligarchy, which has empirically existed in starting modernization. These are the people who led the Japanese transformation, and the remnants of the princely class in contemporary Java, who are attempting to run business as modernizing oligarchies. The precise identification of the group which will take on modernization is a very, very difficult process, and it does not have any particular set of generalizable features. I think it is situationally specific, so that we are always slipping between--I am always slipping between--my levels of generalization and the diagnostic kickback for any one given society.

The linkage between my medical-like case skills in looking at poverty and constructing a general theory of health--if I can use Jack's kind of analogy here-- is about as good as such generalization and prediction are in medicine. I am a little over the break-even point, but not much.

Mr. WIT: One additional thought that comes to mind with regard to this possibility, or what happens with the modernizing oligarchy, is rooted in my concern about Thailand. In the case of Thailand, one finds a situation in which whatever significant change has occurred in society, including significant modernization, the government has had a hand in, although they also have been very relaxed about non-regulated and undirected economic change in the society. But they have been so very relaxed about it because there has not been any significant percolation; the society basically being complacent, basically being quite happy--at least as far as the masses are concerned--with something close to the "traditional." Nevertheless, the oligarchy, the civil service bureaucracy and political leadership, have played a primary role and the society, in 700 years of continuous existence in Southeast Asia, has undergone several major transformations.

Very interestingly, one faces then the question of what sort of definition of change and development a

bureaucracy provides. In that sense, Thailand is a
good case study. The definition it provides, or has
provided, is one in which economic growth, as such,
has low priority. I think this is very significant,
because development in different societies is defined,
obviously, in different ways, and a non-economic definition is sometimes the dominant definition.

In the case of Thailand, I have the feeling the
following has been true: the ruling oligarchy, which
is a bureaucratized oligarchy, has seen the necessity
for modernization, usually in response to external
stimulus (which gets us back to the discussions of environment): the threat of invasion, the necessity at
the end of the nineteenth century of playing off French
and British imperialism in order to survive. At that
time, the country needed to look modern enough to
Westerners to be allowed to retain its independence,
so the oligarchy defined their development needs. But
they did not define them in terms of economic growth,
and they did not define them in terms of drastic transformation, either of the economy or the society or the
culture. They did, and still do define them conserva-
tively in terms of the necessity to save as much of that
society which they enjoy and in which they are well embedded, as they possibly can. They create the least
number of political problems and tensions for themselves
by a very controlled economic growth which is not primarily oriented toward industrialization--or has not
been--but toward bolstering the peasantry, helping to
keep them satisfied, providing administrative services
plus some of the selected trappings of modernity which,
for reasons of cultural flexibility, they have been
pragmatically willing to incorporate. All of this suggests, then, that bureaucracies can preside over a conservative development in which, perhaps, their definition of development is not primarily economic growth,
but has to do with stability, control, and perpetuation
of the role of the elites.

Now, how can a government get away with this form
of controlled development? Well, it can get away with
it, it seems to me, only in a certain type of society.
In another type of society we may end up with the bloody
rebellion that was suggested yesterday, as the only
means of achieving a real transformation. But in a pe-
culiar situation like the Thai, they can get away with

it--although the world is now increasingly closing in.

Mr. BARANSON: There is one aspect of this that has always interested me. I was with the CED Mission, the Committee for Economic Development Mission, that went down to Central America about two years ago, and I remember that we met with some of the modernizing oligarchy that you mentioned, the Mendozas of Venezuela and the de Solas of Salvador.

The thing that struck me was that we have a predisposition for certain kinds of social change because there are kinds of people we feel we can talk to, who are our breed of man and understand what we are trying to do.

I was wondering if a group like this would have met with Lenin in 1917. I have often felt that as soon as you got 15 miles out of the capital city and you began to talk to the people, you find you are in another world, that the real thrust and pulse of social change was not in the rooms in which we were meeting and the people we were talking to.

We tended to meet with the kind of people we could talk to, and not with the social elements that might really determine the future. This is always something that has disturbed me.

I wonder if in your own experience you feel that there are groups in the country that think in some of these patterns?

Mr. NASH: Well, I have a professional bias to say yes to that. Anthropologists gravitate to the lowly hut, as we like to say, and look at the society from the peasant's point of view. We have learned to identify with and talk to the peasants, and to defend their interests. When we come to look at their modernizing elites, we find them to be very ignorant of their own peasantry, as being harmful to their peasantry. And when you come out of the village and go to the capital, you find that you are unable to seriously engage people in conversation about their own country. I think if you come as an administrator, clean from the United States and fairly ignorant of the culture and the society, you and he (elite) could exchange language in MIT-type syllables. But that has nothing to do with the development process in the country, and I think you are now in the third culture.

You start talking like university people, ex-

changing those symbols--and many of us here have had
this experience on these kinds of missions or in planning boards--with people trained in our own universities, who have the ability to play with the same kind
of modern symbols we do, but not really to design programs which will get traffic moving in Calcutta or
bridges up across the River Kwai, or whatever you really want to do, because they do not have much insight
about their peasants, either.

Guatemala is my favorite case. The Ladinos of
Guatemala--anyone who is not an Indian is called a
Ladino, and they are about half the population--the
Ladinos have about the same depth of knowledge, misin-
formation, and mythology about their Indians as most
of you have about ours--only there they are half the
population. They know what is good for the Indians and
what the Indians are like and how to run them; but of
course, they do not.

Let me give you one anecdote, and I will terminate.
The Burmese government looked around, at the advice of
the KTA mission [Knappen, Tippetts, and Abbett], and
told them that up in Maymyo it is cool, which is true,
and that there were cows, which was also true, and that
the Burmese consumed condensed milk, which was also
true. The mission then said, "You can put all these
together and get a milk factory up at Maymyo and it
will be efficient."

They built the milk factory and it has not squirt-
ed one drop of milk. Now, that is a combination of bad
advice from Americans and ignorance on the part of the
planners. If they had looked carefully at upper Burma,
which is pretty dry, they would have seen that you need
transhumance; the size of herds is very, very small and
they go from place to place, they are not fixed; they
could not stay big enough and in one place long enough
to supply a milk factory.

What the herds do supply are hundreds of Burmese
villagers who have bathtubs and who get the milk and
cook it into condensed milk. This is a local industry
done with a nifty production function which meets the
needs. You do not need a factory and never did, but
these fellows had been away from the villages so long
they had forgotten that.

Mr. BINDER: If they practiced transhumance, how
did they get the milk back to the bathtub?

Mr. NASH: It is not the same people who take care of the cows who do the cooking. They come near a village and they sell their milk to people who have bathtubs. When they move to other pastures, they sell to other people and these people cook as very much a part-time job.

Mr. KREININ: How about a bathtub factory? Would that go well there? (Laughter.)

Mr. NASH: Why not just continue to import the bathtubs?

Mr. KREININ: That is capital-intensive: a bathtub factory. When were you last in Burma?

Mr. NASH: In 1960-61. No Burman, by the way, has ever taken a bath in a bathtub.

Chairman KING: I used to hear that the coal miners in Wales put coal in the bathtubs, but this is a new story to me.

Mr. HARING: I wanted to ask about the Burmese milk factory. I was thinking of English cloth manufacture 150 years ago.

There was a dandy system for making cloth in cottages. Then we set up the factory system. Now, what would have been the difference in the anthropologist's analysis of the putting out, or cottage system, and the erection of factories which destroyed that system? What would be the difference between looking at that and looking at your Burmese milk factory?

Mr. NASH: Well, the difference is obvious. Those factories were more efficient and had some supply factors on their side and they produced cotton. In the Burmese case, they explored the demand side, using somebody else's language, and failed to take into account the technological constraints on the supply side in the scale of production.

Of course, nobody knew about these things. These are simple facts and you could have ascertained them on the ground. There is not there the size of herd, or the transhumance pattern, or the permanence which would allow an efficient, steady supply of milk to keep the factory going.

Mr. BINDER: Did they take the bathtubs with them when they went to get their milk?

Mr. NASH: No. The bathtubs were fixed in the village.

Mr. GINSBURG: Mr. Nash, with respect to the milk

factory, it seems to me that you might be deriving more mileage from it than it deserves. Robert Nathan and Associates gave bad advice, perhaps because they did not have any geographers on the staff.

Which leads me to say something else: it is so customary to point to the separation between adminis- trative elites--I made this point myself yesterday, I think--and the mass of the population, that one ought to regard the proposition with considerable suspicion.

Mr. Wit's remarks concerning the Thai situation suggests that this is not always the case anyway, that there are instances where an elite apparently under- stands well enough what is going on in the country as a whole so as to be able to keep fairly firm control.

My own bias, just to match yours, is one of great suspicion as to the peasant's conception of what is good for his country. In the first place, in many cases he does not even know what his country is. There is a tendency, quite understandable, for anthropologists who live in a particular village and come to understand quite well what its people are thinking to overestimate the relevance of what is being thought about in that microcosm to the general polity or economy of which it is a part.

Of course, there are cases which illustrate the other side of the equation. Certainly in Cambodia, the elite, however you define it--as a group or an oligar- chy or one man--apparently knows what the people want pretty much, or so it appears, and the people seem willing to be led. But if you were in a Cambodian vil- lage for a long period of time, I am not sure you would really understand the situation any better. The same probably is true in Thailand and in Malaya. I do not know the situation in Burma. In parts of India it is the same, however, though in other parts of India it might be quite different. I hate to see you mouse- trapped into assuming something to be a general truth when it might at best be only a partial truth.

Mr. NASH: I think that is a very good sobering caveat, and perhaps the way to rephrase it is to unpack the societies. I have been talking about nation states as if they were unitary; when we get to a specific case we really have to explore the way it is hinged together in the different segments, what they know about each other and how they do in fact communicate with each other. The fact that, empirically, on the ground of my generalization, elites, by and large, do not know where the technological and economic breakthroughs are for their peasantry, is not to say they do not know enough to rule their country very well or cannot enlist and mobilize the peasantry.

Let me give you another example, from which I will not get so much mileage. They have an ARDC, an Agricultural Redevelopment Commission, in Burma and it goes around to villages. They give advice--the Burmese themselves--and they show movies of McCormick reapers, tractors, chemical manures, and so forth. I asked some of them, "Why don't you get small things like the Japanese plows for rice fields? They have a whole lot of technology that you can use," and they said, "Well, I don't know about it. I know these big things and that is what we have pictures of and that is what we are instructed in."

Mr. GINSBURG: Yes, but I would like to respond with another kind of story. The Rural Industrial Development Authority in Malaya is said to be making a hash of everything it attempts to do, which may be true, but there is a farm training center up near Ipoh, full of machinery lying on the ground rusting. What sort of machinery is it? It is great big Harvester combines, which are suitable for Kansas, not for Malaya.

Mr. NASH: That was my point.

Mr. GINSBURG: But it was not the Malaysians, or RIDA for that matter, who asked for this stuff. It was given to them by the United States; and they either had to turn it down, saying, "Don't be stupid," or they had to take it, and that's what they got. They know very well what there is in Japan--no question about it. However, I do not know what generalization you can make out of that case except that it illustrates only one example of the stupidity of some American officials. Back in 1950 one American aid technician came to Java all fresh from Utah State and told the Javanese that they had to grow hybrid corn all over the place. The Indonesian officials were very polite about it. They knew they could get more calories per unit of area out of hybrid corn, but in the Javanese value system corn was pig, not human, food. The elite understood it, the peasantry understood it, everybody understood it--except our boy.

Mr. NASH: A very good point. I just want to say that I will accept your proposition that they do know.

This reminds me of an American experience in the Depression of an extension officer coming to a poor farmer; he was going to give him an education in extension services. The farmer looked at him and he said, "I already know better than I do." (Laughter.)

Mr. WHITEFORD: I want to comment on the matter of the modernizing oligarchy that Professor Nash brought out. This is really one of the crucial issues, not only in Latin America but also in many other parts of the world as well. Somebody said that what we are trying to do at this point in Latin America is to convince our own best friends that they should vote themselves out of existence. This is a very difficult kind of thing but we must recognize the matter of generational change which is taking place. This reflects the result of the filtering in of outside influences.

If you get back into a Burmese village or if you get back up into a village in the Andes, the filter factor has been very much reduced; but if you are working with metropolitan communities, even relatively small communities, you find an amazing number of the second-generation members of the oligarchy have been educated in Europe or in the United States. They come back to their communities with a very different point of view from their oligarchial predecessors--from the viewpoints of their fathers and grandfathers.

In Popayán, for example, the sons--or the grandsons actually--of the men who resisted the arrival of the railroad are bringing back all kinds of ideas from their education in the United States and other places, about new methods of raising cattle, about new means of developing land resources and so forth. These people are much more receptive now to the development of industries in their own community than their grandfathers were. Furthermore, they are also aware of the total world picture, and, increasingly, they realize that if they do not make changes, somebody else is going to make them and they are going to be left out. There is, from what I have seen in this very traditional community, a changing process in the oligarchy which, in a sense, is an attempt to save itself, although not conceived of in those terms.

A situation where this did not happen is in Uganda. Among the Bunyoro, the traditional group of leaders, was one stratum, one clan, the Bito. The Bito group, which had been the traditional rulers of the country, maintained its own traditional position, while other people were going to Europe and being educated, or going into the missionary schools and getting educated. When a bureaucracy began to develop, the educated people were not members of the Bito. The educated men were the only ones who could fill the offices, but this matter of going to missionary schools had been below the attention of the Bito, so eventually the ruling clan just "uneducated" itself out of existence as a strong factor in the society.

I do not think this is going to happen in Latin America.

Mr. WIT: A final thought on traditional oligarchies, since we have been wrestling with the problem of whether a traditional oligarchy can preside over development. It seems to me that we mentioned a number of problems of the traditional oligarchy in attempting to do so. However, one thing can help it considerably in its success in presiding over controlled development--which, in many cases, is really what American policy is angling for, since we cannot afford to destroy our friends if the replacements are obviously our enemies. One of the important facilitators, then, is the "opening up" of the oligarchy. What has struck me, going back to the Thai experience, is the fact that the motivated people--at least those that are achievement-oriented in the society--get absorbed into the oligarchy.

Thailand is a society in which there is a clear-cut elite, and it is a bureaucratized elite. The nature of the absorption of achievement-oriented people is not necessarily conducive to economic growth, because they are absorbed into the government rather than into the economy. Nonetheless, these persons do find career satisfaction and personal satisfaction. This is one of the reasons why in Thailand you do not develop leaders for peasant revolts even if the peasants are of a mind to try revolt.

Mr. KREININ: Are you talking about ruling classes that might lend themselves, or identify themselves, with development? Let's take three examples, Nkrumah,

Nasser, and Ne Win. I have no use for Nasser, you know that, but leaving emotional feelings aside, what do you think of them as possible people to associate with development?

Mr. NASH: Well, the only one I have any sense about is Ne Win. I think this military group has about as much chance of modernizing Burma as a snowball in Hades, for three clear reasons. The army colonels who run it have no accountability system and no feedback on their performance; when they ran the DSI, the defense service industries, they ran it the same way. They made decisions, and, whether they were carried out or how they affected the agencies, they never got any feedback and there is nobody to dislodge them.

Secondly, I think the army is peculiarly unfitted for maintaining conditions of ontological uncertainty. The Burmese army, and maybe all armies, when they really get out on the street, want to get the betel nut sellers out, make you pull up your socks, brush the streets; all the useless junk that armies always get involved in. They have nothing to do with development.

Thirdly, they do not have the confidence of the peasantry. At night, I am sure, the country belongs to the peasants, and in the daytime it belongs to the army. They are in power because they leave the peasants alone. They bother the people in Rangoon, and they blow up Student Union buildings. If they start to bother the peasantry in any real sense, they will be out of power.

This [drawing snail-like diagram, Fig. 2, on

Fig. 2.--Social structure and social space.

blackboard⌋ is social structure and social space. This
is my favorite shape. It is my ontological reality.
Everything distributes that way.

   In regard to cultural norms in a stable society, I
think you always have something like this ⌊indicating
central hump⌋: 80 per cent of the members in any stable society are well built-in members; they take the
culture, they live by the norms, they play their roles,
and they have the normal troubles of living, dying,
procreating and carrying it on. Ten per cent are overcommitted. They provide the upholders of the norms,
the readers of texts, the censors, everybody who be-
lieves that this stuff is graven in gold and stone.

   Ten per cent are in the 3D category: the deviants,
the defectives, and the delinquents. Part of the people who go in for social change are usually found in
this category. Somebody out in this end of the distribution has to invent and discover something that will
appeal to that large mass in the middle. As I envision
cultural change, it is in part the creative solutions
of some people in the 3D's, which then solves some of
the problems of the well built-in members. The 3D's
are deviant, defective and delinquent because they are
having excessive troubles with the same problems which
the well built-in members have as normal troubles.
Then you get a redistribution and the curve itself
moves over and you get another kind of society, and so
forth.

   Mr. KREININ: Isn't your representation on the
board there in fact backward?

   Mr. NASH: All right. We will put the head over
here ⌊indicating he would move 3D's to far right⌋ and
the tail this way ⌊indicating he would put the overcommitted at far left⌋.

   Mr. BARANSON: I just wanted to comment on something you were saying about the oligarchy. In Honduras,
I think it is well to keep in mind that the local culture will take from another world what suits it best
and will utilize it in an entirely different way from
what you had in mind.

   I remember, down in Honduras, I ran into this one
family. One son had come to the United States and
brought back an MIT education, an American wife, a
short-wave radio set to listen to the World Series, a
Thompson submachine gun, and an idea of starting a

General Motors distributorship, which he had tried to obtain for some time without success. So he and his brother finally got together and helped overthrow the government, and he got his distributorship.

We have one thing in mind and they take what fits their situation and rework it in their own way.

On the ontological viewpoint, a lot has to do, it seems to me, with who is involved in change. If they have at hand the means of using terror, if they have ways of shaking up ontological certainty, this is entirely different from gaining consensus through a democratic process. It also makes all the difference in the world whether there are social groups who are disposed to deal with ontological uncertainty and have the necessary means at hand. It makes a difference if it is a professor who is going down to teach the oncoming generation modernizing ideas, or the American government with only the CIA and economic aid to do the job.

Mr. NASH: I think that is a research problem which has not been touched, and Americans do not touch it, the substitutability between guns and ideology, or coercion and commitment.

Mr. BARANSON: Sort of a marginal rate of substitution occurs?

Mr. NASH: Yes, and we ought to figure out how much they are interchangeable, and I do not see any research on that. I think that is an American middle-class bias of a clean-scrubbed democratic kid. They do not publish. (Laughter.)

Polarization and Change

Mr. HERLIHY: You said in the long view one of the factors that is necessary for modernization is equalitarianism, and then in the short view you were also talking about polarization; I think you were talking about the same thing. I would like you to explain to me just why this is necessary for modernization.

Mr. NASH: Well, one of the sustaining energies in modernization, for the people undergoing it, is actual distribution of real goods, and the actual distribution of real goods in a performance-oriented economy tends, over time, to lead to equalization. There has to be some commitment of redistribution of what comes out of the economic development.

Mr. HERLIHY: By "commitment," do you mean actual redistribution?

Mr. NASH: Yes; part of it government-sponsored and part of it not. I think all of these governments at least seem to be engaged in what has been called the politics of equality. They all have some sort of welfare notions, and they all have some notion of distributive justice apart from economic performance.

Part of it is that a modern economy tends, more than unmodern economies, to spread shares out more equally--and I think that can be statistically documented. Modern governments tend to play the game of the politics of equality.

It has taken us a long time; it has taken us a hundred years to get around to a War on Poverty--if we get around to it.

Mr. HERLIHY: But is this a necessary condition, then, of modernization?

Mr. NASH: No. This is one of the products of modernization.

Mr. HERLIHY: In other words, it is not a necessary condition.

Mr. NASH: It is what a modern society does, that is right.

Mr. HERLIHY: I thought you were saying something different, that this was a necessary condition.

Mr. KREININ: Yes. My understanding also was that your disagreement with Higgins was on the necessary-condition kind of thing.

Mr. NASH: Yes, but then I made a polarization kind of hypothesis. The other was a characteristic. Perhaps I spoke too rapidly.

The first was a characteristic of what a modern society looks like. The other proposition was that the less polarized the elements, and the status, and the stratification system are, the more likely it is, and so forth.

Mr. KREININ: That means a pre-condition, then.

Mr. NASH: Yes.

Mr. KREININ: In all likelihood it is a pre-condition.

Mr. NASH: Well, it does not have to happen. It is a matter of probability.

Mr. HERLIHY: This was not true in Japan, was it?

Mr. KREININ: No. That is not what he is saying.

Mr. WHITEFORD: Could I introduce one or two instances which I think tend to support Mr. Nash's
generalization. I would like to describe briefly two
communities in Latin America in which I have worked and
which are quite different from each other in many respects. One is a very traditional, highly stratified,
aristocratic community, Popayán in Colombia; the other
one is a more rapidly modernizing community, Querétaro
in central Mexico, where the stratified system has
broken down to a considerable extent.

In one situation, in Popayán, where the hierarchy,
the oligarchy, has maintained its position almost completely unchallenged up until the present day, modernization is going on very slowly. Most Colombians and
the Popayanejos themselves say that no change is occurring in the city. When I went back after ten years of
absence, on my way down, in Bogotá, Cali, and other
places I asked about Popayán and they all said, "Nothing has happened in Popayán. Nothing has happened.
It's always the same. It never changes." When I got
there and spoke to the people themselves, they also
told me that nothing had happened, that everything was
exactly the same. But, after my ten years of absence,
I was aware of a considerable number of changes that
had taken place in the community; they were not major
changes but they were there.

In spite of the changes, there had been no real
dislodgement of the oligarchy. It was still there and
still in power. It seems to me that this suggests some
validity in the generalization about the polarization of
power and the polarization of wealth; as long as it continues to exist in Popayán, it will be one of the factors acting as a deterrent on modernization and change.

In the Querétaro situation, the first thing that
happened, with the revolutions in Mexico and various
other factors, was the breakdown of the old land-hold-
ing aristocracy. There are still remnants of it in the
community which enjoy social prestige, but not very
much power.

There has been emerging in the last ten or fifteen
years a new segment in the society, partly by immigra-
tion, but also from middle-class individuals who have
been getting education and who have also been alert to
the developing possibilities brought in by the arrival,
for example, of the Pan-American Highway and the neces-

sity for garages. These people have started garages,
they have procured the franchises for automobiles, and
now they have taken over the franchises for pumps and
various other things in which the remnants of the old
aristocracy have not expressed much interest. As a
result there has emerged in Querétaro a very potent
upper middle class. Many of the individuals have moved
into a position where, stratigraphically, they have to
be recognized now as a lower upper class.

In the matter of social prestige we found that
this group ranked in the community just below the remnants of the old aristocracy, but it has very much more
power, very much more wealth, and even in the time
since we were first there it was interesting to see the
accumulation of political power that some of these people had attained.

For instance, one man who came from a middle-class
family and who was a real entrepreneur managed to get
land and also franchises for Dodge and then later
Chevrolet automobiles. During a period of two or three
years he managed to pick up a number of other smaller
franchises and, at the end of our period there, was in
the process of being elected as a senator for the state.
He is very definitely on the way up so far as political
power and financial power are concerned.

Mr. HERLIHY: It seems to me that there is a fundamental difference here between Arthur Lewis's position
on the trade-union devil and equalization. We are now
saying that equalization or redistribution of income is
a necessary characteristic of a modernizing society or
economy. We have also said that trade unions are a
factor in this process of redistribution. And yet, if
I understood him correctly, Dr. Lewis says that labor
unions tend to hold back modernization.

Mr. HOLT: I would like to talk a little bit about
this. It seems to me that this is precisely the area
in which Professor Nash's stage theory comes in.

In the studies I have done there is some indication that at a pre-industrial stage it is nice to have
polarization, perhaps to a considerable degree, in the
distribution of wealth, some polarization in the distribution of prestige, and relatively little in the
distribution of power. Then as you move into the beginnings of a modernizing stage, the modernizing class
should take over power (preferably by peaceful means)

and the distribution of power should become more polarized.

You may have at the beginning, therefore a relative equality of power, as illustrated by the existence
of various veto groups which cannot initiate policies,
but which can prevent the adoption of an anti-modern-
izing policy from an old aristocratic class and then
move in at a later stage to positions of power, and
here you have a disequalization of power; you have it
concentrated in the hands of those people who are the
modernizing force.

This is the point at which you might prevent labor
unions from exercising power, whereas, at a previous
stage, you might want to have them as veto groups.
There are, therefore, definite stages and shifting in
this respect, as I look at it.

Mr. WHITEFORD: Your point about the peaceful
transition is important because in Querétaro there was
a violent overthrow at one point, of course, but since
the Diaz regime there has been a period of relatively
peaceful transition which has been brought in by
changing transportation and industrialization. People
have taken advantage of it.

In Popayán I have been very much concerned with
the difficulties involved in this peaceful transition.
In talking with young men of the middle class or lower
middle class, I find that they are very much upset
about it. They cannot see that the situation is developing in such a way that they can eventually attain
anything for themselves, so they continually talk about
the necessity of "breaking the ring." This is the
communist appeal to them. They feel extremely frustrated.

In the past, people who became frustrated were
simply drained off because they went down into the
Cauca Valley and worked in Cali, but today people want
to stay in their own community. Apparently, they have
a broader view and they would like to see changes
brought about in their own native city but they feel
frustrated because they do not see how they can break
into the structure as it is now established.

Mr. KREININ: I think the point before us is of
fundamental importance. There is, you see, an actual
conflict here between the view of the psychologist-
anthropologist and the view of the economist. I think

that the conflict Professor Nash had with Ben Higgins
can be traced back to the same thing, if I interpret
Nash correctly: talking about the requisites rather
than results. The economist would say that non-equal
distribution of income is necessary to produce savings,
whereas Professor Nash says that income has to be
equally distributed in order to produce--

Mr. SCHWARTZ: No. He did not say any such thing.

Chairman KING: Excuse me. Are you being correctly interpreted here?

Mr. NASH: No, I am not.

Mr. KREININ: No, no, no. This is what Higgins
would say.

Chairman KING: Oh.

Mr. KREININ: He would say the opposite, you see.

Chairman KING: I see.

Mr. KREININ: I am saying that what Nash says is
the opposite.

Mr. SCHWARTZ: Why says which?

Mr. KREININ: Nash says that he would like to see
income as equally distributed as possible.

Mr. NASH: No. I have fought with Higgins about
other things, but not about that.

Mr. KREININ: Well, this polarization: isn't
that how it is reflected in the income distribution?

Mr. NASH: Part of it. I just said that there is
a point of polarization in the stratification system
where there is little possibility that anybody will
undertake economic development, there will not be a
group available, and it is as simple as Mr. Whiteford
said: the group that controls the resources, recruitment, and means of mobility has a good thing going
and there is nobody else with enough power to change
that good thing, so they keep that kind of society
going.

If there were less polarization in that status
structure, then they could not keep the society running in the same way. They would have to take account
of other changes, other stimuli, so it is just that
simple a statement. I am sorry that I picked that
particular empirical generalization because I do not
love it that much. I have others.

Mr. ANDERSON: That is a bad word, "equalization."

Mr. NASH: Yes.

Mr. ANDERSON: You had better choose another one.

It throws people.

Mr. NASH: Yes.

Mr. SCHWARTZ: There is not necessarily a conflict between this--whatever you want to call it: drive toward equalization, or necessity for equalization, or correlation of equalization--and the Lewis kind of presentation of trying to hold back labor unions, among other groups, and hold down wage levels. There need not be any conflict between these two approaches because, as Lewis pointed out, there have been increasingly smaller additions to employment resulting from a given amount of investment. One of the examples he gave showed that, with a particular wage level, you could expect only a rather reduced number of laborers, whereas, at a different wage level, you might expect a much larger number. So, you are really talking about high wages for what becomes an increasingly small proportion of the population and, insofar as this is true, unionization and higher wages are not necessarily going to improve the equalization. While I do not necessarily agree completely with this point, there is not necessarily a conflict between this and the Lewis presentation.

Mr. KREININ: Could it be a matter of degree, too? That is, how much will it disturb the equilibrium? Perhaps a little higher wages is all right but too much isn't; a little would produce incentives but too much will hold back the process?

Chairman KING: This was his point. He said there was a differential, if I recall it, if we are talking about Professor Lewis.

Mr. KREININ: Yes, but the amount of the differential: could that be an explanation?

Mr. FATOUROS: Oh, yes. He did mention the fact that it could be higher up to some degree but not too much.

Mr. HOLT: Yes, but the implication of what he was saying there, it seems to me, again is lack of correlation between the income distribution and the power distribution. In order to reduce the ratio of wages to something he would consider desirable, it would seem to me that it would be necessary to clamp controls on the labor unions, and in effect to deprive them of power and, in a sense, increase the polarization of power and decrease the polarization in income. Al-

though in some general survey analysis you would get a
high correlation between power and prestige and wealth,
what is interesting is that you may maximize the opportunities for development when they are not highly cor-
related.

Chairman KING: Is it not a question of checking
the power of the unions, or a question of whether the
government which has the power merely abdicates it or
not to the unions at a particular time?

Mr. HOLT: I think it is going to be very difficult for a government to get voluntary cooperation
from the unions over a long period of time to hold wages down. Lewis himself said that in case after case
the unions put a government in power and then the government turned around and kicked it in the teeth.

Mr. BARANSON: I think on this matter of indicators, as soon as you begin to think in terms of policy
terms, the indicators you select and how you read them
take on an entirely different light. It is not only a
matter of the disciplines. Religious church groups,
who are missionaries, want to introduce a certain kind
of change: they may go in and teach the language first
because, if they are going to bring the word of God,
this is the first thing to do.

I know when the CED went into Colombia there was
a Father Salcedo [Monsignor José Salcedo] who was working on the communist influence in villages. Father
Salcedo tried to negotiate with Sears Roebuck in Colombia to provide small radios and drop them into the
villages so that Father Salcedo could broadcast to
them. The CED decided it was not the CIA, so we went
back to our modernizing oligarchies.

I also remember running into a young agronomist
in Colombia at Tibaitatá. The Rockefeller Foundation
had one of the finest agricultural experiment stations
in the world that they build outside of Bogotá. The
young agronomist who was from Minnesota had been there
four or five years.

I asked him what brought him down there and he
said he could not get facilities for experimenting with
hybrid corn anywhere in the United States as fine as
they were at Tibaitatá. He also told me that they had
a backlog of something like 20 years in innovations on
improved strains of corn, rice, and potatoes. What the
people really needed was ways to store potatoes and

other crops.

The price range in one year went from something like three to over a hundred pesos, and the real difficulty was to find ways to store potatoes so as to help stabilize prices--not to develop new strains.

What I am trying to say here is that general indicators are poor guides to policy. You must have particular reference to the kind of social instrument of change you are working with, and pick your spectrum of indicators accordingly.

Mr. NASH: That must be true. I have never affected policy anywhere in the world. Nobody has ever asked my advice in that regard.

Mr. BARANSON: You never know.

Mr. WHITEFORD: I like very much what Mr. Baranson was saying about moving into a society where you are trying to analyze the situation regarding possible change. One of the things you have to keep in mind is the kind of change you are going to try to institute. It seems to me that, in many of these areas, one of the things we should try to determine, although it might be difficult, is: what kind of changes do they want? Frequently we go in with our own pre-determined concepts of the kind of industrialization or the kind of economic reforms a country should have--from our own academic background or our own practical background--without taking the time to really investigate the situation to see how applicable our program might be or how much it might be desired by the people.

In talking with Mr. Hendry yesterday about field research, we agreed that one of the factors which is always present is the time factor. You cannot determine these things simply by doing sort of a helicopter survey, or, as Mr. Baranson says, by talking to the people in the top echelons, who speak your language, because they may be just as foreign to their own culture as you are.

I would, therefore, like to enter a continuing plea for prior, thorough investigation--research--in the areas where we are going to work in order to identify the groups with which we will have to work, and which may be the factors to institute change, as well as the groups which may oppose them; to identify the resources which may contribute to change; and also to examine the whole pattern of what is regarded as desirable by the people who are going to be affected by it.

Mr. BINDER: I have a number of notes with respect to points I want to make. Actually, these began to occur in chain reaction with the excitement over the problem of polarization and the trade unions, but I will tie them up with some things that were said later on, too.

One thing that I certainly hope we have not accepted, the one proposal that was put forward: that trade unions should be clobbered in developing societies. I do not consider it prudent.

I would suggest to Professor Nash, however, that this polarization concept, it seems to me, is best to apply to small societies, or to those having obviously a relatively simple structure. I do not know how many people there are in Laos or Cambodia or wherever it was, where you said that the number of people who were going to institute economic development or cultural change is probably zero.

Chairman KING: Two million.

Mr. BINDER: Thank you. This is about it. Of course, there are societies with two million people that are much more complicated in their structure. I think probably Lebanon is one such.

I would like to give a very brief example of a similar polarization, not of a traditional society, but what I presume would be a modern society. I will not name the place, but it is in Israel and it is a Moshav (privately owned land) and whatever cooperation goes on is on the basis of ad hoc agreements or contracts between the people who are going to cooperate. In this particular place I have in mind it was decided that industry should not be brought in, and by golly, industry was not brought in. I suppose the Mapai, the labor party, was not brought in at the same time.

These were people who certainly were not traditionals, but the great majority of the original settlers in this town were from Europe, and they had higher education, or at least the beginnings of a higher education.

This leads me to suggest what I always suggest whenever I hear Mr. Nash talking this way: that one of the areas of cultural change has to do with the high and written tradition. This has a great deal to do with the import and export of ideology, I suppose,

but it is not only the unwritten traditions of the
villager one has to be concerned with; one has to be
concerned also with the high tradition that one finds
only in the capital cities and perhaps only fully controlled by the traditional intellectuals. In the case
of the Moshav, of which I have given you an example,
these are not traditional intellectuals, but they are
intellectuals who were also involved in the mass movement.

     This high tradition and rich tradition is often
that which is not shown to the foreigner by the administrator or the person in the capital city in the country which you are going to advise. He talks to you in
these MIT symbols, but he perhaps has latched on to the
high tradition, and he may very well know that he is
not going to show it to you. But he does not share
this with the peasant, except in a very vague way, and
somehow or other you have to penetrate that rather
special tradition of the upper classes, which is indigenous and not shared with the third culture, if you
are going to bring about a change. Now, perhaps this
is what Manning means, or what Manning is getting at,
when he insists upon the importance of ontological uncertainty. That is, you somehow have to blast apart
the high tradition, and you have to get at that by
means that are not used to disturb the peasantry. That
is, you might disturb the peasantry by changing the
shape of the bathtubs in which they boil the milk, but
you are not going to get at the high tradition except
through intellectual discussion, through experience
which is tied, perhaps, to some kind of philosophical
exchange.

     The problem then, I think, is one going beyond
ontological uncertainty, because all the uncertainty
does not give the motivation to bring about change;
one has to also think about the value change.

     Somehow or other the things that are associated
with development have to be valued, and I think we do
have a problem of connecting value orientations with
this situation of ontological uncertainty. I do not
have the answer, but I think that here is a profound
problem that must concern us and it is a question of
cultural change. It is connected with development:
what kinds of value orientation are compatible with a
condition of ontological uncertainty, or what range of

ontological possibility being admitted in the culture
would be compatible with certain kinds of value orientation that are compatible with economic development?

Again, I do not have the answers but I think the
questions are worth posing.

Sister THOMASINE: With reference to some of the
remarks about trade unions, I would like to side with
Mr. Kreinin. I still think that what Mr. Lewis had in
mind, and I hope I did not misunderstand him, was not
a darkling thought of just clobbering the labor unions.
I think he was thinking--at least I gained that impression from conversations before and after that that I
had with him--of the pace of change and of the degree
and differences in change. I think that is what he
has in mind, and has very seriously in mind. It is
this reflection that has changed his own thoughts on
the subject. Whereas he may have given the more radical impression, I do not think that is what he meant.

Identifying Societal Segments

Mr. MORGAN: I was hoping to ask Mr. Nash about
the two central points I understood he was presenting
in his long-run analysis. One was to identify the
people who would undertake modernization. I should be
glad to have a comment on that. And then, whom do
these people face? I guess we have talked a little
about that, but perhaps something might be added.

Mr. NASH: How do you do that in a society? If
you go to a place, you have to get fairly saturated in
the knowledge about the country and find out what
groups have what sorts of goals--what they are aiming
at.

If I were to diagram a society--and this recalls
Professor Holt's social spaces, his round minus square
--it would be made up of all sorts of role sets, to
use our terms. What you would explore is: what kind
of resources do these people command, what span of
control do they have over other sorts of persons, and
what is it that they do in the operation of their
roles? What are their goals? Are they out to expand,
to do X, Y, or Z?

Then, from describing the society, you would find,
let us say--as in Guatemala where I once tried this--
that there are segments of the upper classes who are

modern, willing to modernize, and who have tried it and
keep trying it successfully. So, you have to identify
the groups, and determine what they face. They face
other groups in the society: the cosmopolitans, who run
the large landed estates; they face a rural gentry with
an absentee technique; they face the United Fruit Company with a foreign factor economy; they face the Indian population which is alien to them and whose problems they cannot solve.

     In this kind of competitive system, therefore,
your prediction always comes up to this: the tension between this upper literate segment of performance-oriented economic Guatemalan actors and the landholders, the
rural gentry and the Indian population is always re-
solved--not always, but most frequently--by the cuarte-
lazo [army revolt].

     When these groups start moving and the equilibrium
shifts enough, this group in the background, the army,
allies itself with one or another sector and stabilizes
the situation.   Sometimes, as in the case of Arévalo,
they held the arena open and, for a while, they allied
themselves with segments of this middle-mass and with
the Arbenzistas, to get it down to the lowest level.
But then they started to eliminate a big section of
this middle-mass because they went left, the army disaffiliated, and Arbenz went out.

     If the army had hung on, you would have had in
Guatemala what you have in Cuba; they would have transformed it and thrown out the unassimilable part of that
modernizing group. I do not know what they would have
done with the Indians, but they certainly would have
taken these people and the urban working class into the
political process. That is sort of the way you use
these diagnostic tools.

     Mr. FATOUROS: So Castro's technique of breaking
the army up, on the first opportunity available, would
be, from his point of view, very well taken.

     Mr. NASH: Yes. The thing that strikes me about
armies in underdeveloped countries is that they are very
strange animals. By and large they exist for the
slaughter of their own people and not for national defense, or whatever armies are for. I guess the Guatemalan army has fired a shot or two in anger at Salvador
and Mexico, but, by and large, their war trophies are
against other Guatemalans.

Mr. WHITEFORD: In answer to Mr. Kreinin--this is ex post facto, of course--I think it would be possible to look at Popayán and determine on the basis of a fairly simple analysis where the locus of power lay and where the locus of wealth lay; to see that, for the upper class in Popayán, there was no need for further expansion. They felt no necessity for greater wealth than they already had, they were as wealthy as they needed to be; and you would also see, if you looked closely, that there had been very definite indications of rejection of modernization. For instance, the old generation resisted the arrival of the railroad. They did not want the railroad to come into Popayán; they tried to get it to stop in Cali. They felt that it would bring in too much change and they liked it the way it was.

Nestlé's came in with the idea of--I hate to introduce milk plants again, but this is a stock-raising area and they wanted to establish a milk plant. But the people who owned the milk producers rejected the idea; they just made it so difficult even to get the place started that the company eventually gave up in disgust and went back down into the Cauca Valley to Cali.

There have been several instances of this sort of situation where the old generation not only failed to take advantage of modernization but actually rejected it. On the other hand, I think you could look at the societal structure in Querétaro and identify the rising entrepreneurs, the changing middle class, and certainly the greater spread of power and of wealth as compared to Popayán and, following what Manning has said, identify one as a situation conducive to rapid modernization and the other as a situation which would be resistant.

As far as identification is concerned, I would say, although this is not what I have been concerned with primarily, that there are certain clues, there are certain factors, which can be identified; we might eventually be able to say that some are indicators of greater potential for rapid development and others are not.

Sister THOMASINE: The subject matter discussed today which may link with our talk this afternoon was the subject matter of--I do not know whether you want to call it oligarchy, the elite, the high-thinking or what--and the filtering process that you mentioned, Mr.

Whiteford.

I think, because we are either a semi- or completely learned group, we tend sometimes to be unrealistic and a little bit without hope. It is because we
know not quite enough--but a lot. There is a great
deal of hope in this filtering process. Let me illustrate this point by referring once more to the record
of my own Church.

Fifteen years ago, looking at the future of the
Church in the continent in which I am particularly interested, that is Latin America, I would have been very
dismal. But I have seen a tremendous filtering process
there and, for those of you who want to know the inside
view, I will cover it very quickly.

If I were to tell someone who is not acquainted
with this about what happened to the Church, and had to
do it in two minutes as I am doing it now, I would say
something like this--and there are millions of other
things to be said, things you know that I do not know--
I think what went wrong in the Church in Latin America,
and by "the Church" I mean the Catholic Church, were
three things. I will list them here:

There was the paternalism with which the Catholic
Church started out because it was with the Spanish
Crown, which itself had a paternalism that militated
against leadership. It came over with the Crown, and
looked upon not only the Indian but also the Spaniard
and Creole who were born over there as being children.
We should understand this in the United States. For we
have done that. We looked upon certain people as children, as did the Church in Latin America and as did the
Spanish government also.

Second, a sort of medieval concept came with the
Church, an idea which is not wrong and which is shared
by Protestantism in its right form; namely, that every
state of life is good and therefore it is sort of fixed.
Carried to its extreme, this idea ruined, you might say,
the social outlook of the Church. Carried to its right-
ful place it has meaning, certainly, for people everywhere.

The landholding of the Church was very often acquired justly and often used well in the beginning--not
always, certainly, but often used well in a charitable
form. Yet these lands were looked upon as an elite
would look upon them, as something that was due to the

holders, something that went from Church generation to Church generation.

Then came the situation that Mr. Nash mentioned. Churchmen were put against the wall. After the nineteenth-century independence movement, the Catholic Church was put against the wall and deprived of its landholdings. When the Church came back to Latin America after this movement, it had no means of subsistence except what it could get occasionally from the wealthy groups. So it took, I really think, the infiltration of the changing Church, which you people recognize in the Council going on today, and it took communism--"for whom the bell tolls." It took that.

Now, in Latin America, remember that this is an established group. It is true that the vocations of the Church have come from the middle classes, from the educated classes and from some of the peasant people; but in Chile, as many of you know, in parts of Colombia and in the Brazilian northeast, the Church is doing remarkable things. It is divesting itself deliberately. Perhaps you can say that this is because it is the only way it can last, true; but it is a good thing, and it is doing it wisely in many countries--wisely and well.

The Chilean example, I think, is the best. Before the lands were divided, Chilean experts were brought in to tell the people how to use their lands. What I am saying is that it did not come from any university directly, but it was an infiltration of immense importance.

This movement is not to perpetuate the Catholic Church in Latin America. It is to perpetuate, I hope, the good life. That, I think, is linked to education and I hope it is, in some way, what we will talk about this afternoon.

I did not mean to make a speech, but this is something you do not have an opportunity to know. This is the inside story as well as I know it.

Chairman KING: I think this is a most interesting summary and very useful.

Cross-Disciplinary Influence

Mr. MIRACLE: It seems to me that Manning Nash has made a pretty convincing case that societies we call

underdeveloped, and that are changing, have a number
of dimensions to that change which are something other
than political or economic, as we usually have been
talking about them in this conference.

Some others, the economist Ted Schultz, for example, have recently lauded the contribution made by anthropologists and our understanding of how to transform
peasant economies. I have also heard an argument recently by Aidan Southall, who is a British anthropologist, that economists working on underdeveloped countries should at some point sit in a village a while--if
only a week or two--with the anthropologists, and maybe
the anthropologists should sit with the economists some-
where--or something like this.

Chairman KING: That is what we are doing here,
sir.

Mr. MIRACLE: My question goes to methodology.
Should all of us be sitting in a village, or can we
divide up the specializations and let the anthropologists alone go out to the villages? That is one question, and purely a question. What do I tell my graduate students? If they want to be the rising stars ten
years hence in economic development, in transforming
peasant economies, can they go along the way we have
been going in economics or had they better get into
Manning's courses at some point?

Mr. NASH: Since I do not get paid on a per capita
basis, keep them home. (Laughter.)

Sister THOMASINE: I would like to make a roundup
of comments and then perhaps one that will lead to the
afternoon's discussion. At least, I hope it will. I
have been in several meetings with Mr. Nash, and I
never can resist making a few remarks about anthropologists. One is an old joke that I recall from my undergraduate days; but before I tell it I want to say that
I think that anthropologists are changing--and for the
better. (Laughter.)

Incidentally, I should add that I feel they are
terribly necessary. The joke I recall was about the
woman who was glad she married an anthropologist because the older she got the more he loved her.
(Laughter.) Perhaps this is why I seem to like anthropologists more and more as time goes on.

Mr. KREININ: One point about anthropology and economics. You know, it is making progress. Economics--

Mr. NASH: Which?

Mr. KREININ: Anthropology.   (Laughter.)   Economics can be defined as the science in which everything is tangent to everything else.   Once you introduce marginal factors of substitution in anthropology, you have it half-way.   Now you have to find something for it to be tangent to, and you've got it made.   (Laughter.)

Mr. HENDRY: I am very much interested in this viewpoint of Mr. Nash's with respect to the idea of identifying groups responsible for change and the forces opposing them, trying to get indicators, and so on.

I would like to ask about something that has been touched on to have it made a little more explicit, and that is that many of the things which are introduced, particularly in peasant societies, just do not make much economic sense.   I have in mind the kind of example where, in East Pakistan, recommendations for fertilizer application, based on some rather questionable results at fertilizer trial-and-experiment stations, called for something like 40 pounds of nitrogen per acre, while farmers were using on the average, where they used it at all, something around ten pounds.

Well, some further experimentation, which has just recently been done, indicates that probably anything above eight pounds of nitrogen per acre is beginning to generate a negative response.   The farmers had in part begun to appreciate this by their use of it and the recommendation at this stage is something which is contrary to an essentially sound economic judgment on the part of the farmers.

In addition to looking for these kinds of things, perhaps the sort of work Mr. Miracle was talking about where the anthropologists and economists sit down together would result in recommendations within an anthropological framework and an economic framework which would make a lot more sense than what we have had up to this point.

Mr. GINSBURG: May I interject and say that the last people I would like to see make decisions about fertilizer would be anthropologists or economists, either singly or in combination.   (Laughter.)

Mr. WIT: I had a couple of fragmented thoughts earlier, one with regard to Mr. Whiteford's proper

call that we find out what "they" want to do. It
struck me as also fairly obvious that we have to keep
in mind that there are many "they's." We also have to
keep in mind some of the research which demonstrates
that all segments of peasant societies do not necessarily want development. I think, for example, of Mrs.
Nair's study, <u>Blossoms in the Dust</u>,[4] which is very enlightening in terms of the trials and tribulations of
at least Indian planners from one perspective, the
peasant perspective.

The other related thought that comes to mind from
that same volume is the diversity among the masses.
Apart from worrying about what the elites want, the
fact remains that some of the masses may want development and some may not want development.

This, then, ties in with the comment that development defined economically is not necessarily the primary objective in many of these societies; or at least
the disagreement about definitions of development and
"need" is so great that any economically rational analysis is not realistic.

Then, in terms of the comment made about the conflict between the groups who are motivated for change
and those who are not: this to me, obviously again
suggests something concerning the potential strategy
of the "committed" government, as well as the obvious
problems of the "committed" government. The potential
strategy is clearly to throw the weight of political
and administrative power behind groups which it has
identified as being committed to development.

The problems we all see immediately, too: many of
the groups resisting change, even if they are not closely associated with and propping up the government, are
nonetheless powerful enough so that, politically, they
must be accommodated. This has a lot to do with why
even well-motivated governments do not necessarily play
out the strategy successfully.

4. Kusum Nair, <u>Blossoms in the Dust: The Human
Factor in Indian Development</u> (New York: Frederick A.
Praeger, Inc., 1962).

Conclusion

Mr. NASH: If I can ask your indulgence for two
or three minutes, I would like to place in some sort of
historical perspective the evolution of economic theory
and the evolution of culture change theory to show you
why I think they have come together, and why the conversation will be a continuing one and a fruitful one.

Economists started thinking about economic development in its modern sense around the time of the Marshall Plan, and they saw the miracle achieved by pouring
ing in capital to war-devastated Europe and putting it
back on its feet. Economists are quick to learn, and
they learned from that that the engine of economic development was capital and capital accumulation. It
took about 15 years, and a lot of money down a lot of
rat holes, before somebody decided that it is not just
capital but the form and the quality of capital. They
went on then to develop education theories, technological theories, and so forth.

It took about another five years before that wore
out, and economists finally decided that they must con-
front the social and cultural systems head-on. The do-
it-yourself efforts of Rostow, Hagen, and others are
responses to the situation--and Professor Lewis's remarks, too, that the economic problems are trivial, that
the confrontation is between decisions in a social and
cultural structure. So the economists are now at the
point where they have a lot of interesting problems in
dealing with social systems and have begun to think
about them.

Anthropologists and sociologists, the other part
of the team--when it is a team--started out at a high
level of index theory. There are 15 or 16 features of
a traditional society, 15 or 16 features of a modern
society, and they get transformed--stemming from the
heritage of Max Weber, Karl Marx, and Talcott Parsons.
We made up index typologies.

That did not do too well because it was so far re-
moved from empirical reality that there were no constraints on generalization. We moved from functional
particularism to specificity diffuseness, but no one in
the world knew when that was taking place. Everything
was mixed.

They then moved on to a kind of an acculturation

theory. They saw the problem of social and cultural
change as a movement of technology in organizations,
and ideas from the developed to the less-developed
countries. But this kind of pitchforking--item by item
by item--with the new social systems, was not very satisfactory either. We are now, I think, trying to construct what I have given my version of in its rudimen-
tary form: this is a decision theory of social and cultural change, which gets us down to contact with the
economists. They know all about decisions; now we want
to think about decisions which affect the social and
cultural constitution of a society, and not only the
allocation of resources.

I think we have an area of real mutual overlap,
and we got there because we tried to stay away from
each other and found that we could not. Where that
leaves the policy man, I do not know.

Mr. HARING: Now, having gotten the decisions, you
will soon find that you need the political scientist.

Mr. NASH: Well, I think a political scientist is
a sociologist with a strange vocabulary. (Laughter.)

Chairman KING: On that note, gentlemen, we will
adjourn.

SESSION VI

PERSPECTIVES FOR COOPERATIVE RESEARCH

Chairman HARING: One word on why this Conference
has been a success, a judgment which I do not have to
belabor at all. I have heard it informally, outside
the Conference, all through the weekend. It is that,
unlike many conferences, this one did not consist of
the production of a series of scholarly papers all
typed and neat about which the author knew everything
and nobody else knew much. This has been, as we have
said, a brainstorming session, and this is the secret
of the whole thing, and a great credit to the committee
that set it up in this fashion. Everybody has said
unanimously, "I've learned an awful lot."
     Now, I want to introduce the speakers. We have
first Mr. C. Arnold Anderson, who was an educational
specialist with the World Bank and has been particularly concerned with Kenya. He has taught in Sweden. He
is now Director of the Comparative Education Center at
the University of Chicago and a member of the Sociology
Department.
     Mr. T. David Williams was educated in England and
Canada and the United States--at MIT. He has done work
in Ghana and at Harvard and is now Professor of Economics and Education at Northwestern.
     Mr. Norton S. Ginsburg is a Professor of Geography
and Associate Dean of the College at the University of
Chicago and did his work here at Chicago. He has also
been considerably active in Southeast Asia, Malaysia,
and Indonesia, as you know.
     Mr. ANDERSON: I shall proceed to talk about edu-
cation in the form of a series of dicta which would be,
so to speak, the topic sentences for paragraphs, if I
had written a paper--which I did not. Let me first indicate that I think we might consider schools, or formal education, as having principally five functions.
One is, of course, to indoctrinate children and give

them loyalties and objects of identification and self-
conceptions. The second is to prepare them to share re-
spectively in the universals, specialities, and alternatives of their culture. Third, schools perpetuate and
elaborate intellectual systems and particularly the educational system itself. Schools select and mold elites.
Finally, and least important, schools prepare individuals ready to be trained for vocations.

I would like to make next a few comments on how education plays its part in development. I think it is a
remarkable and often unnoticed fact that formal education of the kind with which we have been familiar for
many generations in the West is remarkably easy to
transfer to other societies and to get operating as a
going system. Always, of course, there will be some
new results and a lack of some old ones, but the broader
sorts of influences that one might call education rather
than schooling, which are important for development--
economic or political--are not so easy to transfer.
Therein lie many of the problems we have been talking
about.

Now, there is actually a very uncertain and ambigu-
ous correlation between formal education and economic
development. Most of the literature setting forth correlation coefficients and so on is a tissue of exaggera-
tions and half-truths. One difficulty is that we fail
to distinguish the long- from the short-run effects,
for they are quite different.

Clearly, you cannot have technological development
without skills in the population to operate that technology, and this requires training. It does not follow,
however, that a proliferation and extension of schooling of any kind will produce development. There is also the very uncertain problem of lead and lag between
economic development and formal education. Such evidence as we now have indicates that, in the short run,
it is economic development which leads and formal education which lags. This is the real proof contained in
the new Harbison-Myers book,[1] contrary to the authors'
own assertions.

I think it is also very important to keep in mind,

1. Frederick Harris Harbison and C. A. Myers, Education, Manpower and Economic Growth: Strategies of Human
Resource Development (New York: McGraw-Hill, 1964).

though we know very little about this in detail, that
the usefulness of school to a society, and the usefulness of the graduates of schools, depend upon how these
individuals are taken hold of by other agencies or institutions in the society and how these other agencies
motivate the products of schools to use what they presumably learned in the schools.

Looking at our own history, I think that we frequently do not realize that in our past the ways of
life of the populace were the stuff of economic activity and of economic change. Changes in those activities
that we now call economic development did not require
the populace to rapidly acquire a whole new civilization, which is more or less the burden that is being
put on the peoples of many countries around the world
today.

It is risky to extrapolate Western experience for,
among other reasons, the following: today education is
more demanded because it has become a political object,
regarded as good in itself. Second, the technology being developed today--being borrowed around the world--
is much more complex than that of the past. Third,
there is the fact that countries today want rapid economic development, a conception that was relatively
foreign to our ancestors. Fourth, that these countries,
in many instances, must develop both their polity and
their economy simultaneously, a task that very few
Western societies faced.

I think then, that we have to conclude that the
payoff in economic terms from a given amount of formal
education will be less in today's developing countries
than it was in our countries. Nevertheless, and this
is not really a paradox, the incremental effect--or the
distinctive effect--of education could be greater in
the new countries than it was in our society.

I am always impressed, as I go back and reread it,
with Walinsky's remarks. He points out repeatedly essentially the following: there was no important economic project in Burma which was held up, frustrated,
or seriously compromised because of the lack of trained
manpower.[2] I think this is a statement that we are

2. Louis J. Walinsky, Economic Development in
Burma, 1951-1960 (New York: The Twentieth Century
Fund, 1962).

going to find being made more and more about developing countries--which essentially is to elaborate a point that Manning Nash made at the end of his paper.

Now, some comments on the problem of balancing economic and other criteria of education. Obviously, nobody in his right mind would say that the main purpose or sole purpose of education is to produce economic development. We happen to be living in a period when people are obsessed with the manpower view of education. The payoff in conferences and discussions and consultantships and so on for one specializing in education is to relate it to economic development, but this is clearly a partial and provincial view.

One of the things I think we too often fail to ask ourselves in looking at the manpower studies is: what are the so-called needs for manpower that these studies set forth? You can read planning documents by the score, with elaborate tables often down to the individual unit, of the number of different kinds of trained manpower needed. It is almost impossible, however, to find out the criteria of need that are used.

Simultaneously, you have the fact that these countries face staggering unemployment--as Arthur Lewis was pointing out--and yet, curiously, both things are set forth by international agencies this way: "This country has great unemployment of educated people; this country needs an enormous increase in the number of educated people." That is ridiculous.

Now, there is always, in trying to assess the role of education in development, the investment problem, and investment choices are marginal. It makes no sense to say that this country would be much better off if it would spend X billion dollars, or X million pounds, or francs, or whatever on schools. It has to make choices at the margins between schools and other agencies, and the problem of conserving resources that are truly scarce is a formidable one.

Most of the people who are writing the pronouncements on manpower and education fail to face the problem of what might be accomplished in development by shifting money away from education. Parenthetically, I would be very happy if every developing country would take 10 per cent annually from now on of its education budget, and use it as a subsidy for the advertising industry, as a prod to development. That is a dictum.

I think we need to relate educational programming in an ecological framework to the ecological processes of development (political, economic, and social) which are going on. One of the most impressive things one finds in all of these countries is that there are large local differences in the readiness for education, the willingness to use it if it is made available, the willingness to make a substantial financial contribution to it. The indexes of readiness all vary enormously among the ecological areas or zones of the country, and there is a rather close correlation with the evidences of economic development when those are also put in ecological terms.

One could comment extensively on the formidable technical problem in international trade, of the international trade and skills. There has been almost nothing written on this and it is, I think, an important problem.

Now, with respect to some criteria for policy, one important dilemma we face is whether we are going to manage people's choices of jobs and schools in accordance with some manpower expert's judgment of what is good for people, or whether we are going to develop mechanisms so that the "spontaneous choices" that people make in education and vocations will be allowed to express themselves in the determination of educational policy.

I would say in very brief compass that much of the literature on educational planning which has been written is nonsense. The most formidable difficulty with the literature as it exists now is that nearly every statement is based upon the assumption that there are fixed coefficients of a demand for certain kinds of skills for certain kinds of activities in the economy. This, I think, cannot be defended; even as a non-economist, I think that such assumptions of fixed coefficients are fallacious.

There is also an over-simple idea of the correlation between the jobs that people perform and their schooling. I recommend that you look at the U.S. census, or the census of Israel, or the census of India, or any other country that has tabulated education against occupation. In no country is the correlation much more than about .5, and that's hardly gambler's odds.

There is always, in making plans, the formidable problem of balancing three criteria: efficiency, equity, and free choice. There are always compromises needed. On so-called democratic grounds, many countries will argue for equity in providing educational opportunity; but no developing country can afford to operate on the basis of equity because this would be a formula for dispersing its resources into a whole series of bottomless pits.

They must operate to a greater extent on the basis of efficient allocation of resources for schooling in relation to the use that will be made of it. This means that they must also take account of the choices that individuals would like to make, but to see that those choices are linked in with other development processes.

I would also point out that most of the literature that argues that education is the instrument of social mobility is fallacious, both with regard to developing countries and to our own society. The correlation between education and vertical social mobility is very modest.

If you have been enamored of the Soviet claims for educational planning, I suggest you read more carefully the literature which is becoming available, which is making it very clear that the Russians have, for the most part, not in fact conducted educational planning, and they are now admitting it.

Now, some comments on the problem of balance and complementarities in the educational tasks between schools and other agencies. Obviously, human resource development is not synonymous with education, and obviously education is not synonymous with schools, but, to a very large extent, societies in policy-making do think mainly of schools.

Here is a country and it has these "needs" for economic development. So you then ask: how could you tell whether the school system of this country is or is not adapted to the needs or the characteristics of the country? The literature is filled with statements that the school system must be adapted to the needs of a changing and developing society. How would you know if it were adapted? Is American education adapted to the needs of American society?

This is, I think, an essentially unanswerable ques-

tion because it is stated in far too broad terms. One
is led immediately into raising questions about the
balance between general education and technical education, on which there is not time to comment. I do
think there is beginning to emerge a consensus that the
principal task of schools, through secondary education,
is to prepare people to be ready for vocational education and that, in most countries--until they are well
developed--the setting up of specific technical schools
is a misplaced use of resources.

One can state that alternatively: in general,
technical training should be given, as nearly as possible, at the point of use. There is, of course, also
in the literature--you read it yourselves--a great
deal of talk about the importance of localizing curricula; that the countries will make more use of their
education, and that their citizens will be better educated, if they study a localized curriculum instead of
one that was originally brought to them by the British,
or the French, or the Americans.

I suggest that you look at the school books your
own children have used, and ask how much of what they
are being taught is localized to the United States--or
ever was. The great McGuffey's readers, which are supposed to have been the foundation for American society
in recent generations, in very large part were made up
of material which is not American; it is British, it is
medieval, it is Greek, it is Roman, it is fairy tales.

The concept of a localized curriculum, except in
certain obvious areas such as geography, is a concept
with little meaning. Most of the discussion which goes
on to the effect that, if we would just teach the little children in the right way, they would all like to
be good little farmers, is nonsense. We never learned
how to do it, so why should we expect Ghana to learn
how to do it?

The more fundamental point is that curricula make
very little contribution to motivation, except under
unusual circumstances. Incidentally, the work that is
coming out now on political socialization of the
Russian youth indicates very clearly that the system
did not work.

There is also a real dilemma--and this touches on
many points we have talked about--as to whether schools
shall be used to produce national consensus, or shall

schools be permitted or encouraged to relate people to
a somewhat smaller and warmer society of their own
province, or tribe, or locality?

I think the idea that somehow you pick little
Kikuyu children up in a bush, and you make Kenya citizens out of them in six or seven years--and possibly
even citizens of the United Nations--may be asking the
schools to do too much.

The general questions we have to ask on most speci-
fications for using schools for development is the following: are not people overloading the schools? We
have difficulty here in this respect, you know.

In Chicago there is a very large proportion of the
schools that operate only with a policeman inside the
building. Now, why can't we socialize our children?
We have all the resources available, but apparently we
cannot do it. How, then, should one expect these countries to use schools (which are very formal, impersonal,
and abstract mechanisms) to create a whole new human
nature?

Another task we need to face is the building of
adaptability into the educational system. I would
argue that the particular content of schools, or the
particular structure of a country, is much less important than whether or not there is flexibility so that
different parts of the society can do different things,
or different schools can do different things, and so
that individuals can manipulate the educational opportunities open to them.

I think, next, that we have to take a new look at
the question of quality. It is true that many countries will insist upon quality because they think this
is the only way they can get respectability in the eyes
of the world. They want to have an education as good
as their colonial masters had--and all of this sort of
thing. If one separates out the political issue, the
concept of quality is very dangerous for two reasons.

To give you an ad hoc illustration, the United
States built the world's technologically most advanced
and economically most dynamic society with what has
generally been regarded as the world'd worst educational system among the developed countries: a system
which had no standards and which, as yet, has no standards, which has never succeeded in producing a university degree that has any recognizable definition. Yet

we manage to operate an amazing society.

The problem of quality is a red herring. I think one can illustrate this by indicating some of the reasons why elaborate examination systems, which are so much favored in many countries, prove to be dysfunctional. First of all, I doubt that the skills tested by academic examinations are very good predictors of the kinds of skills which will make men productive in any activity. Second, examinations tend to lead to the stereotyping of schools. Teachers teach what children are going to be examined on, and children will study only what they know they are going to be examined on.

Third, the use of examinations and the related worry about quality leads to the undue prolongation of schooling, to putting too much schooling into children for the current needs of the society.

Fourth, there is the concern for academic orderliness. I suppose there is a certain kind of selectivity of people who become academics. Academic orderliness tends to be antipathetic to flexibility. The net result of concern for standards, as one finds it, for instance, in Ghana or some other parts of the world, is to diminish the elasticity of the supply of skills. Yet what a developing country needs is a very elastic supply curve for all kinds of skills.

Fifth, a school system that is built around a rigid examination system produces too narrow an elite for the demands of a changing society.

There are three principal ways, it seems to me, in which schools serve to recruit elites. You have the kind of system we had in the United States, and I suppose in essence still have: that the schools give part of the training to part of the people in an extremely diversified set of elites. Second, you have a system like nineteenth-century England, where the schools mainly polish the people who are predestined in any event to become the leaders of the society. Finally, you have what now one finds in many places in Africa and elsewhere: that the schools beyond the elementary years are available to very few people, and you cannot get into the elite unless you go through those particular schools.

You get very different results, depending upon which of these particular recruitment patterns you have, and I suspect you get very different impacts upon the development processes.

I think also, we gain--and this was implicit in
much of the discussion in these days of the conference--
by viewing elites as devices for linking the energies
of the populace to the actions which produce development. Then the questions we have to ask are: which
kinds of elites can do this for which kinds of activities, for which sub-populations, and so on. This, of
course, touches on points Manning Nash raised.

How does the system of education affect the relations of elites to each other? I was very much impressed in Kenya with the disgruntlement of the British
technically trained people with the monopoly on good
jobs held by the British arts-degree graduates. This
is one example and you can find many others. Imagine
what American society and education would be like if
Harvard and Princeton and Yale had ever had the degree
of dominance in determining educational policy that
Oxford and Cambridge had in England. Our society would
be at least different, and I suspect it would be one
that we would less like to live in. The question of
how schools affect the relations among different parts
of the elite, or different sub-elites, is, therefore,
important.

Finally, I am impressed with the fact that a very
large part of the intellectuals in many new countries
are being sterilized for policy-making, because the
party or the civil service absorbs them; and the party
and the civil service are one. There are few independent sources of decision-making or of opinion-making.
In a sense, therefore, you have to discount a large
part of the intellectual roster of many countries. It
has been sterilized for decision-making. This is an
aspect of the one-party system in some new countries
that I think one does not always give attention to.

Then, there is the question: do elites have a
chance to function so as to express the interests--in
the good old hardboiled sense of the word "interests"--
the interests that are the texture of development? Development is not an abstract set of equations. Development is activities, and these activities are related to,
expressed as, or exemplified in the hard economic interests that are the stuff of development, and the stuff
of politics. The question, then, is: in what ways can
the elites serve to express these interests, to articu-

late them, to phrase them in ways that contribute to or hold back development?

For example, a centralized press means that there can be no local elites who can use the printed word as a device for trying to tell the public, in all sorts of ways, what is expected of it if it is to contribute to, or participate in, development. One can illustrate this in many other ways. Let me describe the American town of the nineteenth century and early twentieth century--in a set of circumstances which was almost optimal for development. The spread of schooling was occurring in communities possessing an elaborate equipment of other cultural agencies--agencies that were needed as auxiliaries to schools.

For centuries Western communities generally possessed a representative of the learned clergy, who more or less effectively conveyed the powerful influences of Christianity upon aspirations and conduct. Often there were representatives of the legal and medical professions and growing numbers of teachers. There were literate businessmen and representatives of the crafts. At the end of the fifteenth century, even, practically all businessmen in London were literate. The local press was well established by the nineteenth century. There were substantial proportions of literate mothers. And always there was a thickening network of communications with the world of technology, business, and knowledge. In the United States, the presses began turning out books on the frontier as soon as settlement took place. There were many stimuli to rationality, to social consensus and to economic change. Extra-school training--apprenticeship, on-the-job experiences, and work in family enterprises--was a major part of the educational process. A large proportion of the literates acquired even that skill outside of the schools.

Now, this is the kind of community setting for development which one can find in very few parts of the world today. How many of those things can you leave out, and still get development with any kind of conceivable elaboration of mere formal education.

Mr. WILLIAMS: The relationship between what I have to say and what Professor Anderson has said may remind some of you of the dictum of Sidney Smith, that a man should never read a book before reviewing it because it always prejudices you so.

I had, in fact, jotted down a few things that I wanted to say before I saw what Professor Anderson was going to say, although there is perhaps some relationship between them. I want to deal with a few topics in each case, to suggest the development of sub-categories which might enable us to distinguish between different types of problems. The topics start off with: the effective changes in the level and amount of education, the government as entrepreneur, forms of expression of work-protest--more or less as it relates to trade unions--and, possibly, some comments on the use of the symbolic investment.

First let me say a few words about the payoff to educational expansion. Let us look first at the outputs of education.

There is the question of whether or not an undeveloped country should place its priority on high-level manpower or on a more widespread primary system. The distinction, of course, cannot be a complete one since an adequate selection of high-level manpower requires a fairly broad base of primary and secondary education, while widespread primary education requires an expansion of high-level education in teacher training and school administrators.

Newly independent countries with the most primitive levels of education are critically short of the number of administrators, bureaucrats, diplomats, schoolteachers, and so on, required for the most elementary forms of the new nation's business. Here it is evident that the amount of indigenous high-level manpower should be increased as quickly as possible, and should be given first priority within the educational system.

Some of the more advanced but still underdeveloped areas--Ghana, for example--can meet their own basic needs, and even lend experts to international agencies in other African countries. Their demand for high-level manpower is due to: one, a substantial expansion of government functions; two, the planned rapid expansion of the so-called modern sector of the economy; and three, a program of universal primary education.

In saying that these are distinct stages of development, I have used the question-begging phrase that "they can meet the basic functional requirements of independent states." I wonder whether, in this connection, political scientists can tell us anything about the minimal administrative requirements of effective independent states, and the approximate levels of competence required for various tasks. Once one is over that hump--wherever it comes--and in terms of meeting these minimal requirements, one should give more serious consideration to starting and improving primary education. Here, it seems to me, one might be able to distinguish between states, or regions of states, where there is already some demonstrated short-run growth potential, and those where it is a much more long-run speculative thing.

Let me give an example. In Ghana, there has, in the last 50 years, been a striking development of effective, small-scale entrepreneurship, and a desire for self-improvement which is manifested in the great degree of sacrifice the people are willing to undertake in order to gain an education. My impression is that in Guatemala the rural areas appear to be characterized by apathy and stagnation. I do not mean that there is no change, but not nearly the same kind of change.

It is at least possible that the payoff to elementary education will be much higher in the near future in the first than in the second case; that is, the payoff will be greatest where there has already been some sort of manifest economic change.

Given the will to entrepreneurship, basic literacy should, one supposes, greatly increase the effectiveness of the entrepreneurs; adding secondary to primary education may add very little to effective functional skills. If this is so--and it raises some other problems I will deal with in a moment--the economists and the anthropologists could do a lot to locate growth cones in the economy--those areas in which a significantly large group of people are sufficiently concerned about improving their welfare to manipulate their economic environment in as favorable a way as possible.

In Ghana the cocoa farmers migrated to better lands. They formed companies to purchase land because they got a better return this way than if they purchased individually. They commissioned the building of roads and buildings, and so on.

Now, most of these things are missed in aggregative analysis, the kind of stuff that economists usually do; and indeed, much of our knowledge about the remarkable

achievements of the cocoa farmers in Ghana is due to
many years of careful and imaginative work by one person, Miss Polly Hill. She discovered, for example,
this business of building roads and bridges, much of
which had simply gone unnoticed at the time. She found
roads and bridges which were not even on the maps, and
yet they were being used effectively for the extension
of the local market.

It is, however, possible that if the cocoa farmers
had received an education they would not have been better entrepreneurs, but not entrepreneurs at all. They
might have been junior clerks or swelled the ranks of
the urban unemployed, hanging around the cities hoping
to get jobs.

This raises the question of the effects of education on aspiration--and why. Earlier, Professor
Kreinin raised the point that education appears to induce an anti-manualist mentality.

Professor Anderson, as I recall, suggested that
anti-manualism was typically associated with low wages
for manual work, rather than with any particular lack
of education. The evidence from West Africa shows
clearly enough that there are, and have been, enormous
disparities in the returns for different occupations,
or perhaps more accurately, to occupations in different
sections of the economy. There appear to be large numbers of middle-school leavers who want to be artisans;
and in this connection a very interesting study was
done by Phillip Foster of Chicago.

Mr. ANDERSON: One should also mention a whole
series of papers that are about to appear from Nigeria
by Archibald Callaway. You ought to watch for his name
in the literature, because he has some fascinating
stuff.

Mr. WILLIAMS: Yes, I have seen some of his work.
I was referring to these middle-school leavers who
want to be artisans, but want to be artisans with the
government, where they will get an apprenticeship--
where they undergo an apprenticeship and then get a good
job. Once in a good job a man is more or less set for
life in these societies. Outside the good-job group,
the passing years simply make it less likely that he
will ever get the security he wants. What needs to be
studied here, I think, is the pattern of returns to
particular job complexes, and to other aspects of the

growing power of the urban areas.

I suspect, but cannot at this stage prove, that people in Ghana respond very sensibly--by which I mean in the way we would respond--to the incentive pattern inherent in the present labor market structure in the urban-rural disparity.

Let me perhaps give you some specific examples. If a person goes to the town and wants to become a mechanic there, he gets a job if he is fortunate. Say he gets a job with Texaco. He works for several years at Texaco and he might get a formal Apprenticeship certificate as a result, or even if he does not get a formal Apprenticeship certificate, he will at least have the say-so of the manager at Texaco: "This man has performed faithful service for four years." The chances are that he will never again have any difficulty getting a good secure job.

If, however, there happened to be, as there almost always are, many more applicants for the job at Texaco than there were openings, he has two alternatives. He can either go and get a job in a small shop somewhere, a small garage or something like that, or he can hang around hoping eventually that his turn will come, and he will get the job at Texaco.

If he goes into the small shop, he is going to earn some money, but not very much, and he is going perhaps to build up some skills; but he is not going to acquire anything formal which is going to be particularly useful to him later on. Not only that, but, because of the way in which people find jobs--which is through the Labor Exchange--if he actually has a job in a small shop, he cannot even show up at the Labor Exchange.

Now, it may strike people who have not been in these areas that what he should do is to put his name down on a list at the Labor Exchange and then, when a job comes up, they will notify him of the job--at Texaco, say.

But, quite apart from the question of minor corruption and this sort of thing, the fact is that people simply do have not addresses to which you can send a letter. I had the experience of trying to find somebody in the center of Accra. I knew the man's address and I went to the police station and asked them if they could tell me where the house was; I had a rough idea of where it was, but, even so, they could not help me. The only way I found it was by walking up and down the street until eventually I found somebody who knew the man; he took me to the house.

Therefore, if you want a job at Texaco or some place like this, you simply have to go to the Labor Exchange every day, otherwise you lose your chance. By taking a job in a small shop you are, of course, losing out on this option.

There is also the fact, which I will not draw too much on, of the enormous number of advantages to be derived from living in the city--and I am not thinking just now about high-jinks in the city rather than the rural areas. Take a young chap who wants to make some sort of a mark. Let us say, as is possible in some of these areas--certainly in Ghana--he has some sort of athletic aspirations and he thinks he can make some sort of a name for himself as a member of a football team, or as a boxer or something of this sort--and there are lots of guys who want to do this and quite properly so. If he stays in his rural area, there is simply no chance whatsoever of his ever making his mark. He must go to the city to do it.

I think that one thing we ought to try to concentrate on, therefore--if we are interested in development--is to see how it may be possible to restructure this pattern of incentives so that at least there is not a disincentive to people being employed in the cities.

It does, however, raise some difficult problems. Insistence on formal qualifications, which is part of the problem at the moment for all jobs in the modern sector, does put some check on nepotism and patronage. A man may still hire his relatives, but at least his relatives must have some qualifications, unless, of course, the qualifications themselves can be bought-- but that is another matter.

Now, if we are going to try to induce people, let us say, to work in a small shop rather than hang around the Labor Exchange waiting for an opening at Texaco, we have to find some way by which a person who has had experience in a small shop can move up to some higher level--into the good-job complex.

Questions which I think need to be answered here are whether or not psychologists and sociologists, and

possibly anthropologists, can develop adequate tests
which will distinguish, in terms of competence and re-
liability, between different groups of experienced,
though not qualified, applicants (that is, not qualified in the formal sense).

Another question: can the administrative experts
and sociologists tell us anything about the effects on
the present rigidly hierarchical administrative structure if people could, in fact, be promoted from outside
the structure?

There are several other things I would like to say
about education and its effects, but I want to move on
and make a few other comments.

One person discussed the possibility that government should have a significant role as investor, and
as economic innovator, because there are no entrepreneurs in a society. This is a familiar argument. It
is contained, for example, in Ben Higgins' book on economic development.[3]

Now, do we mean, when we say that there are no entrepreneurs: A, that there are no people in the society with the complex motives and capabilities required
for successful business activity? Or do we mean: B,
that there are such people, but that the social-econom-
ic system denies them access to positions of power?

If we mean the former, there that are just no people of this kind in the society, then government investment will not help. It will merely mean that public
money will be spent on very risky projects.

If we mean the second, that there are people but
that in the existing system they are denied access to
positions of power, then we have to decide: A, how we
can locate the people with the appropriate talent; B,
how we can give these people, rather than political
hacks, access to business power; and C, how, after
having given them this access, we can insulate them
from constant political pressure.

Can the political scientists suggest institutional
requirements or possibilities for the establishment of
more or less autonomous investment agencies of public
enterprises in the developing economy?

3. Benjamin Howard Higgins, Economic Development:
Principles, Problems and Policies (New York: Norton,
1959).

Russia, I think, is not a good example. In Russia,
when the Bolsheviks came to power, there were already
big enterprises; there already was an established scientific and engineering elite. There was a highly disciplined party with a respect for managerial competence,
and even with all this, Stalin came close to wrecking
it.

A related problem, related to this question of
government investment and the government role in underdeveloped areas, concerns the requirements for effective large-scale organization. It is another thing frequently said--by Higgins among others--that, for many
reasons apart from the entrepreneurial one, the government can and should play a much larger role in these
areas than it should in the more developed areas.

How is one, however, in a large enterprise to develop the working rules and standardized objectives
which will enable effective delegation of authority?
You not only have lack of experience on the part of people in running large organizations, but you also have
virtually no experience of what the standard patterns
of behavior in a modern society are going to be like in
these societies.

Let us take one question, industrial relations.
If we are trying to work out some pattern--for example,
the way in which industrial relations should operate in
a large American firm--and we are doing this in order
to delegate authority to a personnel manager to undertake certain decisions, we have the advantage of experience over a long period of time with the way workers
operate in the American social environment in an industrial situation. There is an enormous number of peo-
ple--scholars, businessmen, trade unionists, journal-
ists, and so on--who have been writing about and examining these problems for a long period of time. There is,
I think, a reasonably good and reliable set of expectations about the way in which people will behave (in our
society).

If, however, you are trying to work out what should
be the policy of a personnel manager in a large firm,
in a new industrial complex in West Africa, you simply
do not know what the appropriate patterns of incentives
are, or how people are going to respond to certain situations.

It seems to me, therefore, that, while it would,

in fact, be a relatively simple matter to nationalize General Motors, or I.C.I. [Imperial Chemical Industries, Ltd.] in Britain; the effects of such nationalization would be just marginal. Output might go up 5 per cent or down 5 per cent--and I am not saying that this is not important--but it would be essentially a rather trivial kind of thing in terms of any overall output levels. You would simply tell people to behave in very much the same way they are behaving now.

It seems to me that it is immeasurably more diffi- cult to develop the same kind of patterns in an under- developed area.

The third point I want to deal with relates to trade unions. Here I think we have to ask ourselves: how is worker protest expressed when there are no inde- pendent forms of worker organizations? The problem I am concerned with here is whether trade unions stimu- late worker dissatisfaction or whether they channel it in a partciular direction.

Sometimes, clearly, they stimulate it; but we must ask what happens generally over the long haul if you do not have an effective trade union organization. I have in mind here, for example, the Italian experience from 1900 to 1914. There was no encouragement for sta- ble national unions. There were, nevertheless, local unions which had developed one way or the other. It seems quite possible that stable and effective national trade unions may have favored a much more orderly set of industrial relations than actually occurred. What one had was wave after wave of general strikes, in various cities and regions, which reflected a blend of frustration and, I suggest, disorganization--rather than organization.

Here I am curious as to whether sociologists and political scientists can tell us anything about the ig- nition points of dissatisfaction. When does dissatis- faction reach a point where, in the absence of some way to canalize it, it will express itself in a kind of Luddite machine-smashing and sporadic outbursts of vio- lence?

I think we want to ask, too: to what extent is a politically controlled trade union able to direct the energies of workers toward goals which are consistent with the government's plans? Here we need to know a lot more about grass-level operations, although this

may, for a variety of reasons be impossible to learn.
The Ghana trade unions, for example, may be much more
effective, from the workers' point of view, at local-
level bargaining than are the independent, but small,
poor, fragmented Nigerian trade unions.

I think we need to explore here the question of
whether or not workers will, or under what circumstances
they will, voluntarily accept lower wages--lower in the
sense that they are lower than they could get by acting
in a certain way--if these lower wages are compensated
for in other ways, for example, in job tenure, sever-
ance pay, adequate grievance procedures, and so on.

To what extent can politically oriented trade unions encourage productivity improvements? To what extent can they, within the framework of the national
plan, negotiate trade-outs between higher wages, in
which the government is giving up something on the one
hand, and greater effort or improved efficiency on the
other hand? This involves the institutional structure,
the political balance of power, and the allocation of
resources, and I think it is something about which political scientists, economists, and sociologists, all
might have something useful to say.

I now come to my fourth point, and I will deal
very briefly with this. In dealing with the question
of the building of monuments, I think we could distinguish between different types of monuments. I will
just briefly run through some distinctions.

The first I will call monuments for the masses. I
have in mind the kind of thing that is represented by
the Freedom Arch in Accra--the Freedom Arch is in a
great big square where people can watch national demon-
strations and this sort of thing.

I think this is something which does have, very
probably, a payoff. That is, the people can come there,
they can see it, and it means something to them; it
stimulates them, it gives them a feeling, you know,
that they are not working for nothing, and when the government calls upon them to make a sacrifice they can
see that, and they say, "Well, that is one of the
things we are making sacrifices for." It means something to them; whereas, if you said to them--let's say
that the cost of the Freedom Arch, if you spent it some
other way, might have made a difference in the rise of
national income of one-fourth of 1 per cent a year--

now, you can go and say to the workers, "Look, chaps, if you will really dig in we can raise your national income by one-fourth of 1 per cent per year more than we are raising it now." This does not mean anything to anybody, but the Freedom Arch does mean something, I think.

On the other hand, there is another type of this sort of expenditure--I am talking about Ghana, now-- such as the Ghana airways. It seems to me that the main thrust of this type is to influence the leaders of other countries in Africa. It is part of the Ghanian drive for a leadership position in the Pan-African movement. I doubt that there is any economic payoff at all, and I do not think that the regime expects to have a payoff. It is something that is costing quite a lot, but it is directed toward a political objective quite apart from economic growth.

Related to this are certain types of expenditures which attempt to tighten the ties with certain other countries. For example, when I was in Ghana there were some beginnings of an attempt to develop a direct tele-communication system between Accra and Conakry in Guinea and Bamako. At one level it seemed rather cra-zy. I lived nine miles outside of Accra, and every time the rains came the telephone system broke down be-tween where I lived and Accra. You might think they should, perhaps, be spending more time getting the telephones working over this nine-mile distance instead of worrying about whether they are going to establish a system over the 2,000 miles between there and Bamako.

Another type of monument-building is designed to improve the image for foreign investors. This might have a payoff. I mean, sometimes building roads, maybe even building certain kinds of fancier towers, gives the notion that this is a thriving kind of country, where people would like to invest. This might have an economic payoff.

Finally--although there was not too much of this in Ghana, you find it, I am told, in many other coun-tries--is the type where there is a significant diver-sion of expenditures toward large buildings whose prime, if not sole, function is to provide comfort for the rulers. This clearly has no economic payoff.

Mr. GINSBURG: I am grateful to both Mr. Anderson and Mr. Williams for giving me an opportunity to say something I wanted to say anyway.

Mr. Anderson spoke of ecological zones as something we ought to be concerned with, and Mr. Williams spoke of high growth potentials. I am not sure what either one of these things are, but they suggest a direction in which I would like to see our discussion move.

Nobody has mentioned geography heretofore but me, and I will mention it again. Geographers are concerned with the world ecosystem and how it operates; and within that ecosystem are a number of freely and arbitrarily given units which themselves form lesser ecosystems. We call these units "states."

We accept them as given--not naively, but for convenience--with the understanding that if we knew enough about how they operate, we might be able to determine the extent to which their "giveness" is appropriate or inappropriate--as the case may be. Then, if we become concerned with policy-making, we can make recommendations with respect to the location of boundaries and the exclusion or inclusion of areas.

The ecosystem notion has at least two major dimensions--it is a duodimensional concept--and both of these are relevant to what we are interested in here.

The more traditional dimension is one that is more strictly ecological in the common-sense notion of the term. It concerns natural resources as they relate to a particular society; as they are perceived by people in that society, because people with different cultures view their resource endowments in quite different ways; and as they are defined, utilized, managed, and even created within particular cultures. The relationships between natural conditions and the ways in which men make use of them, and transform them if need be, or depart from them, are of major interest. We are also concerned--and this relates to some of our previous discussions--with the possibilities for change in resource utilization patterns, both spatial and otherwise.

Parenthetically, perhaps you do not realize how little we know about some of the things one ordinarily accepts as well understood, with regard to this particular subject. For example, we know virtually nothing about the soils of the tropics, and most of the underdeveloped world, however, defined, is tropical. We know almost nothing--and this was referred to earlier this morning--about the relationship of fertilizers to

tropical soils. Our agronomic and engineering experts
are not expert in these particular directions. Of all
the major crops in the world--and this is not irrelevant, particularly to the Asian situation--we know
least about paddy. Relatively little is known about
rice as compared with wheat, corn, and almost any other
major grain. In fact, the talk about transferring
Japanese paddy cultivation to India is particularly
naive and does not take into account the fact that the
varieties of paddy which were bred by the Japanese, and
which played an important role in Japanese agricultural
expansion, were all short-growing varieties adapted to
the short-season growing conditions in Northern Honshu
and Hokkaido. This experience is of little value in
South and Southeast Asia. But I digress.

The second dimension of the ecosystem notion is
spatial. At the outset of my course on China, I describe China as a gigantic spatial system and the function of the course is to analyze it. Analyze it into
what? Analyze it into sub-systems; that is, spatial
sub-systems, which may be described as regions. I do
not know whether or not Mr. Anderson would call these
regions "ecological zones," but then I do not pretend
to know what an "ecological zone" is.

Now, I realize that one can carry too far this
notion of "systems analysis" which, along with the concept of "culture," has been one of the major frauds
perpetrated on American social science; but it is a
useful idea, nevertheless, just as culture is useful
in proper context.

When we are talking about a spatial system, we
are talking about an areal entity that has certain
characteristics. It has size and shape and internal
and external accessibility. It is characterized by
the distribution of resources of all kinds; and by
these I mean, not only those of natural origin, but
those of cultural origin. It has specific distribu-
tions of population, and it has, above all, a transportation network, or better, a system of circulation,
reference to which is found deeply embedded in the geo-
graphical literature. So, too, are found references
to problems of centripetal and centrifugal forces in
polities and economies, to the problem of fragmentation
and the problem of developing measures of integration.
Thus, geographers are accustomed to ask: how well in-

tegrated is a given state? How well integrated is
Thailand as compared with Indonesia? What does this
comparison tell us, if anything, about the problems and
potentials of these two spatial systems for economic
development? Linked with these questions is the general proposition which I think most of us will accept:
that all planning decisions require locational decisions. Thus, we return to the points made by Mr.
Anderson and Mr. Williams in different context and
terminology: that we ought to be able to identify
those areas within a given spatial system that have the
most promise for development.

Here there are numerous opportunities for interdisciplinary cooperation, particularly, it seems to me,
with economists; but not only with them, since the opportunities spread all the way along the social science
spectrum. For example, the nature of the political administrative hierarchy as distributed in space is something that should be of great interest to the political
scientist; but, alas, the literature does not bear this
out.

One may also question the extent to which it is
valuable and desirable in the education of the inhabi-
tants of the so-called underdeveloped areas to bring
the people to an awareness of the world about them.
Few of them are possessed of the kind of world view
that we assume they ought to have if they are to direct
their energies toward some kind of social and economic
change.

We have experimented in the teaching of geography
at lower levels with using the immediate environmental
situation of a student to introduce him to some of
these ideas; and we introduce him to the notion of scale
as well. For example, let's take the general proposition that every town or settlement has a hinterland.
This is good sound common sense to us, but it does not
do any good at all to present the student in, say,
Kuala Lumpur with the example of London to begin with.
It is even less effective to use London in the case of
students in a kampong somewhere in northeastern Malaya.

It is much better to start them out with the kampong itself and enlarge the scale of view to the nearest town, go from the nearest town to whatever is the
largest city in Malaya, thence to the largest city in
Southeast Asia, and ultimately to London, thereby

creating a kind of world view based on size-functional hierarchies.

Similarly, we can reverse scales and proceed from larger to smaller units. I have been a consultant to the Calcutta Metropolitan Planning Commission for several years. One of the major problems there has been to identify, within the Calcutta Metropolitan Area, those areas which will lend themselves to certain kinds of remedial action--if you like, "planning areas" within the metropolis. Though practical, this is a difficult problem which has major theoretical concomitants.

GENERAL DISCUSSION

Mr. WHITEFORD: I would like to ask Professor Anderson what he thinks the function of expatriate industry is in a training sense? How much of a contribution can expatriate industries in these various developing countries make to the whole educational process?

Mr. ANDERSON: Let me start out by pointing out first something which is more familiar to you than it is to me, and that is that in a large part of the world, sometimes called "colonial world," the principal source of training for non-agricultural skills has been the public service: posts, telegraphs, roads, public works, agriculture, railroads, and so on. Then, as other industries have come in, different countries have followed different policies.

Some firms, for whatever reasons, have developed very good training programs and, perhaps because they were early in the field, were able to cash in on them. As the network of industries becomes more complicated, clearly there have to be devices developed so that a firm which invests heavily in training does not lose its employees quickly to other firms.

This is leading to experiments in different countries. I think Brazil has been an innovator in ways of pooling the costs of these programs, through tax levies and rebates, so that firms will participate in providing effective training but will not suffer if there is mobility of employees.

It seems to me that there is no reason why a very large part of the training for the skills below the university level cannot be provided by firms. I think

there are enough experiments around the world that can
be generalized. Now, this does involve, as a prerequisite, that you have a fiscal office or tax system,
or whatever, in the country which can perform the necessary coordination work so that the incentives for the
firms are real ones, and not just outright impositions;
but it seems to me that a very large part of the training can be so done and is being done in many countries.

Mr. MORGAN: I would like to ask Professor Anderson
to give his evidence that the political indoctrination
of Russian youngsters has not been successful.

Mr. ANDERSON: There I fall back on my colleagues
who have been doing research extensively on and in
Russia. There is a paper by Azrael of the Chicago staff
in the forthcoming volume on education and political development shortly to be published by Princeton University Press (edited by James Coleman).[4] He has a very
long and detailed analysis of materials which he col-
lected in Russia, in which I think he has demonstrated
what we suspect from other kinds of evidence: that the
specific indoctrination above and beyond the kind of
thing that comes from A, living in a closed society,
and B, absorbing the general climate of opinion around
you--the more specific, tangible, and copper-riveted
indoctrination seems not to have been successful in the
Soviet Union. The evidence for this is mounting.

Mr. MORGAN: You are blocking out the simple fact
of ignorance. In other words, if I live in a world in
which I hear nothing within a certain range--

Mr. ANDERSON: Yes, I am blocking that out. I
used the word "indoctrination," not "control." Obviously, you can control access to information and this will
affect people's attitudes, but I mean specific indoctrination seems not to have had much take.

Mr. MORGAN: You are not throwing the baby out with
the bath? In other words, keep me ignorant of three-
quarters of the facts, and of course, I won't--

Mr. ANDERSON: Well, if you keep people ignorant,
then you have a random factor, so to speak, and it is
perfectly clear that there have been random elements.
You also have, insofar as the communications blockade

4.   James Smoot Coleman (ed.), Education and Political Development (Princeton, N.J.: Princeton University
Press, 1965).

breaks down, as it began to do, first, in the war as the armies met each other, and second in the postwar period--then you began to get spreading spirals of change going on. There clearly seems to have been more change in the areas accessible to contact.

Now, there are other factors. For instance, in the Georgian universities the students seem to be more recalcitrant--but they always have been. Leningrad students seem to be more recalcitrant, but Leningrad people in general pride themselves on being international. Some of this attitude or self-conception seems to have persisted right through the whole period since the revolution. So you get all sorts of cross-currents plus the simple fact that, as pressures began to let up a little since the death of Stalin, you had such things as the museums beginning to let people see the fabulous collections of nineteenth-century French paintings. When these began to become available, this was one of the things that undermined the Soviet conception of what good painting was. Once you lift the lid there are all sorts of spontaneous processes; but sheer indoctrination seems to have been of limited effect.

Chairman HARING: We are coming to the end of this Conference. I know I speak for everyone when I say we are extremely grateful to the sponsors of the Conference. It has been a long but most fruitful session and we are very grateful to all of you. Thank you very much.

APPENDICES

MIDWEST RESEARCH CONFERENCE
ON
EDUCATIONAL RESEARCH AND
A REAPPRAISAL OF ECONOMIC DEVELOPMENT

October 30 - November 1, 1964

Friday   Library of
Registration   Conferees   International
9:30 a.m. to   are invited to   Relations
5:30 p.m.   browse in the   660 N. Wabash

Luncheon   Honoring   Rosary College
12:30 p.m.   W. Arthur Lewis   River Forest
                  Professor of Economics and
                    International Affairs
                Woodrow Wilson School of Public
                  and International Affairs
                    Princeton University

                  Welcome to the Conference
                      Sister Thomasine

Dinner   Introductions   The Kungsholm
6:00 p.m.   and   100 E. Ontario
                    Informal Discussion

First Session   Unemployment in   The Kungsholm
7:30 p.m. to   Developing Areas
9:30 p.m.

          Conference Chairman - George I. Blanksten
              Keynote address - W. Arthur Lewis

Saturday
Second Session   Underdeveloped   Library of
10:00 a.m. to   Countries in the   International
12:00 noon   World Economy   Relations

              Chairman - Leonard Binder
          Discussion Leader - Karl de Schweinitz, Jr.
                  Discussant - Andrew H. Whiteford
                  Discussant - Raymond L. Randall

| Luncheon | Informal Discussion | The Arts Club |
| 12:30 p.m. | | 109 E. Ontario |

Third Session	The International	Library of
2:30 p.m. to	Politics and Diplomacy	International
4:30 p.m.	of Development	Relations

Chairman - George I. Blanksten
Discussion Leader - Robert T. Holt
Discussant - A. A. Fatouros
Discussant - Mordechai E. Kreinin

| Dinner | Informal Discussion | Chez Paul |
| 6:00 p.m. | | 660 N. Rush |

Fourth Session	Economic Growth in	Library of
7:30 p.m. to	Newly Settled Areas	International
9:30 p.m.	as Contrasted with	Relations
	Old Settled Areas	

Chairman - James B. Hendry
Discussion Leader - Theodore Morgan
Discussant - Scott D. Johnston
Discussant - Jack Baranson

Sunday
Fifth Session	Cultural Change	Library of
10:30 a.m. to	in Development	International
12:30 p.m.		Relations

Chairman - Frank H. H. King
Discussion Leader - Manning Nash
Discussant - Daniel Wit
Discussant - Edward E. Werner

| Luncheon | Informal Discussion | Normandy House |
| 12:45 p.m. | | 744 N. Rush |

Sixth Session	Perspectives for	Normandy House
1:30 p.m. to	Cooperative Research	
3:00 p.m.		

Chairman - Philip S. Haring
Discussion Leader - C. Arnold Anderson
Discussant - T. David Williams
Discussant - Norton S. Ginsburg

BIOGRAPHICAL NOTES ON PARTICIPANTS

C. ARNOLD ANDERSON
     Director, Comparative Education Center, and Profes-
sor of Education and of Sociology, University of
Chicago; Education Specialist on World Bank mission to
Kenya; Fulbright Professor at Uppsala, Sweden; co-edi-
tor with Mary Jean Bowman of Education and Economic Development.

ROBERT P. ARMSTRONG
     Instructor in Economics Department, Lake Forest
College; in Liberia 1961-62 as Research Associate,
Northwestern University Economic Survey of Liberia;
travel in twelve countries in the Middle East and Far
East to study practices, problems, and prospects concerning economic development, 1962-63; author of chap-
ters in Economic Survey of Liberia, Northwestern University; associate author of Puerto Rican Shipping and
the U.S. Maritime Laws: An Economic Appraisal, the
Transportation Center, Northwestern University.

JACK BARANSON
     Research Associate, International Development Re-
search Center, Indiana University; research staff member, Committee for Economic Development; Research Associate, Brookings Institution; participant in an economic development mission to Latin America; author of various studies and articles on industrialization and economic development in Latin America and other underdeveloped areas.

LEONARD BINDER
     Associate Professor of Political Science, Univer-
sity of Chicago; research on comparative politics, par-
ticularly in developing nations and on Near Eastern and
Middle Eastern politics and Islamic culture; author of
Religion and Politics in Pakistan, Iran: Political De-
velopment in a Changing Society, and several articles;
Biennial Midwest Research Conference on Underdeveloped
Areas, Advisory Committee 1964, participant 1962, 1964.

GEORGE I. BLANKSTEN

Professor and Chairman, Department of Political
Science, Northwestern University; Governing Board, Library of International Relations, since 1959; with U.S.
Coordinator of Inter-American Affairs, 1942-44; Political Analyst, U.S. Department of State, 1944-46; research and field experience in Latin American countries,
1950-59; author of books and articles on Latin American
culture and politics, including Argentina and Chile,
U.S. Role in Latin America, and Peron's Argentina; Biennial Midwest Research Conference on Underdeveloped
Areas, Advisory Committee 1959, 1962, 1964, participant
1959, 1962, 1964.

KARL DE SCHWEINITZ

Professor of Economics, Northwestern University;
in Japan 1963-64 to study economic development and political change; author of Industrialization and Democracy; Biennial Midwest Research Conference on Underdeveloped Areas, Advisory Committee 1962, participant
1962, 1964.

A. A. FATOUROS

Assistant Professor, School of Law, Indiana Uni-
versity; Lecturer and Assistant Professor, Faculty of
Law, University of Western Ontario, 1960-63; visiting
Assistant Professor, Law School, University of Chicago,
1963-64; author of Government Guarantees to Foreign
Investors and articles in legal and political science
journals, and co-author with R. N. Kelson of Canada's
Overseas Aid.

WESLEY R. FISHEL

Professor of Political Science, Michigan State
University; consultant on governmental reorganization,
South Vietnam, 1954-55; Chief of the M.S.U. Vietnam Advisory Group in Public Administration and Public Safety,
1956-58; Guggenheim Fellow in Vietnam, 1962; editor and
co-author of Problems of Freedom: South Vietnam Since
Independence; Biennial Midwest Research Conference on
Underdeveloped Areas, Advisory Committee 1964, participant 1959.

NORTON SYDNEY GINSBURG

Professor of Geography, University of Chicago, and

Associate Dean of The College; Governing Board, Library
of International Relations since 1959; member, United
Nations Technical Mission to Japan on Metropolitan Planning,1961-62; Consultant to Calcutta Metropolitan Planning Organization,1962-63; author of <u>Atlas of Economic</u>
<u>Development</u>, co-author of <u>Malaya</u> and <u>The Pattern of Asia</u>
and numerous other books and articles; Biennial Midwest
Research Conference on Underdeveloped Areas, Advisory
Committee 1959,1962,1964, participant 1959, 1964.

PHILIP S. HARING
    Associate Professor of Political Science, Knox Col-
lege, Galesburg, Illinois; field: Political Theory, Comparative Government, Economic Theory; Governing Board,
Library of International Relations 1958-63; Biennial
Midwest Research Conference on Underdeveloped Areas,
participant 1959, 1962, 1964.

PHILIP M. HAUSER
    Chairman of the Department of Sociology, and Direc-
tor of the Population Research and Training Center,
University of Chicago; Governing Board, Library of International Relations since 1955, Trustee 1959-1963, Chairman 1959-61; United States representative to the Population Commission of the United Nations; United Nations
Statistical Advisor to the Governments of Burma and
Thailand; General Rapporteur of UN/UNESCO Seminars on
urbanization in Asia and Latin America; author of <u>Popu-</u>
<u>lation Perspectives</u>, <u>The Study of Population</u>, and other
books, contributor to leading sociological journals;
Biennial Midwest Research Conference on Underdeveloped
Areas, Advisory Committee 1959, 1962, 1964, participant
1959, 1962.

JAMES B. HENDRY
    Director, Economic and Agricultural Development In-
stitute, and Associate Professor, Department of Economics and Agricultural Economics, Michigan State University; Economist with Michigan State Viet Nam Advisory
Group, 1957-59; member, Harvard University Pakistan Advisory Group, 1962-64; author of <u>The Small World of</u>
<u>Khanh Hau</u> and <u>The Work Force in Saigon</u>.

H. MURRAY HERLIHY
    Professor and Chairman, Department of Economics,

Lake Forest College; industrial and labor relations
specialist; co-author of Issues in Railroad Retirement.

ROBERT T. HOLT
Professor of Political Science, University of
Minnesota; Research Assistant, Center of International
Studies, Princeton University, 1951-52; Research Assis-
tant, ONR Project, Research in Cohesive and Disruptive
Tendencies in Coalition Type Groups, University of
Minnesota, 1952; author of various articles on psycho-
logical and political aspects of foreign affairs; co-
author of Strategic Psychological Operations and Ameri-
can Foreign Policy; author of The Political Basis of
Economic Growth: An Explanation in Comparative Political Analysis and others.

BERT F. HOSELITZ
Professor of Economics and Director of the Re-
search Center in Economic Development and Cultural
Change, University of Chicago; expert in Industrial
Economy with the United Nations Technical Mission to
El Salvador; specialist in Metropolitan Planning with
Ford Foundation project with the Ministry of Health and
Local Government of India; author and editor of many
books including Theories of Economic Growth, Sociologi-
cal Aspects of Economic Growth, A Reader's Guide to the
Social Sciences (ed.), and numerous articles in professional journals; Biennial Midwest Research Conference
on Underdeveloped Areas, Advisory Committee 1959, 1962,
1964, participant 1959, 1962.

SCOTT D. JOHNSTON
Professor and Head of Department of Political Sci-
ence, Hamline University; Director, Falk Foundation
Program in Politics; Coordinator, four-college Far East
Area Study Program; Faculty Representative, Washington
Semester Program; research in North Africa and the Mid-
dle East; author of various articles.

FRANK HENRY HAVILAND KING
Associate Professor in Economics and member of
Committee for East Asian Studies, University of Kansas;
Acting Director, Center for East Asian Studies; author
of The New Malayan Nation, The Monetary System of Hong
Kong, and numerous articles and other books on money

and finance in the Far East.

MORDECHAI E. KREININ
    Professor of Economics, Michigan State University;
Editorial Collaborator, Journal of the American Statistical Association; Consultant to Council on Foreign Relations; author of Israel and Africa, a Study in Technical Cooperation and numerous articles in professional
journals and collections.

W. ARTHUR LEWIS
    Professor of Economics and International Affairs,
Princeton University; Professor of Political Economy,
University of Manchester, 1948-58; member U.N. Group of
Experts on Underdeveloped Countries, 1951; member Colo-
nial Development Corporation, 1951-53; consultant to
U.N. Economic Commission for Asia and the Far East,
1952; Consultant to Gold Coast Government, 1953; consultant to Government of West Nigeria, 1955; Economic
Advisor to Prime Minister of Ghana, 1957-58; Principal
and Vice-Chancellor, University College in the West
Indies, 1959-62; articles in technical, economic, and
law journals; author of Industrial Development in the
Caribbean, the Principles of Economic Planning, Theory
of Economic Growth, co-author of U.N. Report, Measures
for the Economic Development of Underdeveloped Countries, and other books and articles.

MARVIN P. MIRACLE
    Assistant Professor of Agricultural Economics, Uni-
versity of Wisconsin; Research Associate, Food Research
Institute, Stanford University, 1961-62; research experience in Belgian Congo, British East Africa, Northern
Rhodesia, and other developing areas, principally in
Africa; author of articles in professional journals and
collections on African agricultural problems.

THEODORE MORGAN
    Professor of Economics, University of Wisconsin;
Consultant, Council of Economic Advisors; Deputy-Gover-
nor, Central Bank of Ceylon, 1952-53; Chairman, Wisconsin-Ford Foundation Project, Gadjah Mada University,
Jogjakarta, Indonesia, 1959-60; consultant to International Bank for Reconstruction and Development as member
of Mission to Kenya, 1961-62; co-author of The Economic

Development of Kenya and Readings in Economic Develop-
ment, and author of other books and numerous articles;
Biennial Midwest Research Conference on Underdeveloped
Areas, participant 1962, 1964.

MANNING NASH
Associate Professor of Anthropology, Graduate
School of Business, University of Chicago; Editor,
Economic Development and Cultural Change since 1958;
research in Mexico and Burma; author of Machine Age
Maya, and numerous articles; Biennial Midwest Research
Conference on Underdeveloped Areas, participant 1959,
1964.

RAYMOND L. RANDALL
Acting Director, Institute of Public Administra-
tion and Associate Professor of Government, Indiana
University; formerly Chief of Party, Indiana-Indonesian
Contract, Djakarta, Indonesia; Ford Visiting Professor
of Public Administration, University of the Philip-
pines; Advisor to the Philippine Government on the
Philippine Executive Academy; Executive Development
Advisor to the Government of Thailand; author of bro-
chures and articles on executive development for
Nation's Business, and other publications.

ELOISE ReQUA
Director, Library of International Relations; or-
ganized World Trade Reference Library for International
House, New Orleans 1946; co-author with Jane Statham of
The Developing Nations 1965; Biennial Midwest Research
Conference on Underdeveloped Areas, Advisory Committee
ex officio 1959, 1962, 1964.

HUGH H. SCHWARTZ
Acting Assistant Professor of Economics, the University of Kansas; Organization of American States research fellowship in Argentina, 1960-62; author of
articles on Argentina.

HENDRICK SERRIE
Instructor in Anthropology, Beloit College; Project Associate, developing use of solar cookers in
Oaxaca, Mexico, 1961-62; directed two films in Mexico,
1962-63; taught English at University of Aleppo, Syria,

1963-64.

JANE STATHAM
Library of International Relations, Associate Director; co-author with Eloise ReQua of The Developing Nations, 1965; Editor, World in Focus 1945-51; Editor, International Information Service since 1963; Biennial Midwest Research Conference on Underdeveloped Areas, Advisory Committee ex-officio 1959, 1962, 1964.

SISTER THOMASINE
Professor and Chairman of the Department of Economics, Rosary College; research in the Middle East, Central and South America; Executive Council, Catholic Economic Association 1957-58, 1964-66; author of various pamphlets and articles, including "A Reappraisal of the Economic Record of Venezuela, 1939-1959," in Journal of Inter-American Studies; Biennial Midwest Research Conference on Underdeveloped Areas, Advisory Committee 1964, participant 1959, 1962, 1964.

CHARLES PRESTON WARREN
Instructor in Anthropology, University of Illinois, Chicago Undergraduate Division; Fulbright Award, Research Scholar, anthropological research in the Philippine Islands; author of The Batak of Palawan: A Culture in Transition and numerous articles and papers; Biennial Midwest Research Conference on Underdeveloped Areas, participant 1962, 1964.

EDWARD E. WERNER
Associate Professor of Commerce and Director, Center for Developing Nations, University of Wisconsin; Professor and Chairman, University of Wisconsin-Ford Foundation Project at Gadjah Mada University in Jogjakarta, Indonesia, 1960-63; author of numerous articles and monographs including Some Aspects of Promotional Activities in Newly Developing Countries and Advertising in Indonesia.

ANDREW H. WHITEFORD
Professor of Anthropology and Director, Logan Museum of Anthropology, Beloit College; community research in Popayán, Colombia, 1949-52 and 1962; urban survey of Central Mexico, 1956; study of culture change

in Málaga, Spain, 1961; editor of <u>Teaching Anthropology</u> and author of <u>Two Cities of Latin America</u> and numerous articles; Biennial Midwest Research Conference on Underdeveloped Areas, Advisory Committee 1964, participant 1959, 1964.

T. DAVID WILLIAMS

Lecturer in Economics, Northwestern University; Research Associate, Center for Studies in Development and Education, Harvard University, 1962-64; Lecturer in Economics, University of Ghana, 1961-62.

DANIEL WIT

Professor of Political Science, Northern Illinois University; Public Administration Advisor to Government of Thailand and Visiting Professor, Institute of Public Administration, Bangkok, 1956-58; Director of International Studies, Governmental Affairs Institute, Washington, D.C., 1959-61; Peace Corps Lecturer for Malaya and the Philippines training programs, 1961; contract research on Thailand for U.S. Department of Labor, 1963-64; author of numerous monographs and articles.

SELECTED BIBLIOGRAPHICAL REFERENCES ON
ECONOMIC DEVELOPMENT

The following references have been selected as
representative of the major contributions to recent
literature on theories of economic growth and development. The two bibliographies listed--Hazlewood and
ReQua--provide annotated guides to numerous other
sources on economic, political, and sociological problems of development as well as on specific geographic
areas.

Bauer, P. T., and B. S. Yamey. The Economics of Under-
    developed Countries (Cambridge Economic Handbooks).
    Digswell Place, England: James Nisbet and Company;
    Cambridge, England: Cambridge University Press, 1957.

Brookings Institution. Development of the Emerging
    Countries: An Agenda for Research. Washington, D.C.:
    The Institution, 1962.

Enke, Stephen. Economics for Development. Englewood
    Cliffs, N.J.: Prentice-Hall, 1963.

Gerschenkron, Alexander. Economic Backwardness in
    Historical Perspective: A Book of Essays. Cambridge,
    Mass.: The Belknap Press of Harvard University Press,
    1962.

Ginsburg, Norton S. Atlas of Economic Development (Uni-
    versity of Chicago, Department of Geography, Research
    Paper No. 68). Chicago: University of Chicago Press,
    1961.

Harbison, Frederick H. Education, Manpower, and Eco-
    nomic Growth: Strategies of Human Resource Develop-
    ment. New York: McGraw-Hill, 1964.

Hazlewood, Arthur, comp. The Economics of 'Under-Devel-
    oped'Areas: An Annotated Reading List of Books, Ar-
    ticles, and Official Publications. (2d enl. ed.)

London: Oxford University Press for the Institute of Colonial Studies, 1962.

Higgins, Benjamin. Economic Development: Principles, Problems, and Policies. New York: W. W. Norton, 1959.

Hirschman, Albert O. The Strategy of Economic Development (Yale Studies in Economics: 10). New Haven, Conn.: Yale University Press, 1959.

Hoselitz, Bert F., ed. The Progress of Underdeveloped Areas. Chicago: University of Chicago Press, 1952.

Leibenstein, Harvey. Economic Backwardness and Economic Growth: Studies in the Theory of Economic Development. New York: John Wiley & Sons; London: Chapman & Hall, 1957.

Levin, Jonathan V. The Export Economies: Their Pattern of Development in Historical Perspective (Harvard Law School, International Program in Taxation). Cambridge, Mass.: Harvard University Press, 1960.

Lewis, W. Arthur. The Theory of Economic Growth. Homewood, Ill.: Richard D. Irwin, 1955.

McClelland, David C. The Achieving Society. Princeton, N.J.: D. Van Nostrand, 1961.

Meier, Gerald M. International Trade and Development. New York and Evanston: Harper and Row, 1963.

Millikan, Max F., and Donald L. M. Blackmer, eds. The Emerging Nations: Their Growth and United States Policy. Boston and Toronto: Little, Brown, for the Center for International Studies, Massachusetts Institute of Technology, 1961.

Myrdal, Gunnar. Economic Theory and Under-Developed Regions. London: Gerald Duckworth, 1957.

Nurske, Ragnar. Problems of Capital Formation in Underdeveloped Countries. New York: Oxford University Press, 1953.

ReQua, Eloise G., and Jane Statham. The Developing Na-
    tions: A Guide to Information Sources Concerning
    Their Economic, Political, Technical and Social
    Problems. Detroit, Mich.: Gale Research Company,
    1965.

Rostow, W. W., ed. The Economics of Take-Off into Sus-
    tained Growth; Proceedings of a Conference Held by
    the International Economic Association. New York:
    St. Martin's Press, Inc., 1963.

------. The Stages of Economic Growth: A Non-Communist
    Manifesto. Cambridge, England: Cambridge Univer-
    sity Press, 1963.

Singer, Hans W. International Development: Growth and
    Change. New York: McGraw-Hill, 1964.

United Nations. Department of Economic Affairs. Meas-
    ures for the Economic Development of Under-Developed
    Countries: Report by a Group of Experts Appointed
    by the Secretary-General of the United Nations.
    (United Nations document E/1986, St/ECA/10.) New
    York: United Nations, 1951. (Sales No.: 1951.II.B.
    2.)

United Nations. Department of Economic and Social Af-
    fairs. Processes and Problems of Industrialization
    in Under-Developed Countries. (United Nations docu-
    ment E/2670, St/ECA/29.) New York: United Nations,
    1955. (Sales No.: 1955.II.B.1.)

------. A Study of Industrial Growth. (United Nations
    document ST/ECA/74.) New York: United Nations,
    1963. (Sales No.: 63.II.B.2.)

United Nations Conference on the Application of Science
    and Technology for the Benefit of the Less Developed
    Areas, Geneva, February 1963. Science and Technol-
    ogy for Development, 8 vols. (United Nations docu-
    ment E/Conf. 39/1, Vols. I-VIII.) New York: United
    Nations, 1963. (Sales Nos.: 63.I.21-28.)

United Nations Conference on Trade and Development,
    Geneva, March 23-June 16, 1964. Proceedings, 8 vols.

(United Nations document E/Conf.46/141 Vols. I-VIII.),
New York: United Nations, 1964.   (Sales Nos.: 64.II.
B.11-18.)